FAMILIES

WHAT MAKES THEM WORK

UPDATED EDITION

DAVID H. OLSON
HAMILTON I. McCUBBIN
HOWARD L. BARNES   MARLA J. MUXEN
ANDREA S. LARSEN   MARC A. WILSON

FOREWORD BY REUBEN HILL

SAGE PUBLICATIONS
The International Professional Publishers
Newbury Park   London   New Delhi

Copyright 1989 by Sage Publications, Inc.

For information address:

SAGE Publications, Inc.
2455 Teller Road
Newbury Park, California 91320

SAGE Publications Ltd.
6 Bonhill Street
London EC2A 4PU
United Kingdom

SAGE Publications India Pvt. Ltd.
M-32 Market
Greater Kailash I
New Delhi 110 048 India

Printed in the United States of America

Library of Congress Cataloging-in-Publication Data

Olson, David H. L.
    Families, what makes them work.

    Updated ed. of: Families, what makes them work.
c1983.
    1. Family—United States—Psychological aspects—Case
studies. 2. Family—Testing. 3. Circumplex Model of
Marital and Family Systems. 4. Life cycle, Human.
I. Hamilton I. McCubbin and Associates. II. Families,
what makes them work. III. Title.
HQ536.F335   1989   306.85'0973   89-24231
ISBN 0-8039-2011-3
ISBN 0-8039-2854-8 (pbk.)

SECOND PRINTING, 1991 **UPDATED EDITION, 1989**
ORIGINAL EDITION FIRST PUBLISHED IN 1983

Contents

Preface to the Updated Edition   2

Foreword by Reuben Hill   7

Acknowledgments   11

     I   Purposes and Overview   13

     II   Families Across the Life Cycle   21

     III   Description of the Study   35

     IV   Circumplex Model of Families   47

     V   Marital and Family Types   81

     VI   Marital and Family Strengths   93

     VII   Family Stress and Change   111

     VIII   Family Coping Strategies   135

     IX   Personal Health Behaviors   163

     X   Marital and Family Satisfaction   171

     XI   Predicting Family Types   187

     XII   Predicting High- and Low-Stress Families   203

     XIII   Families with Adolescents   219

     XIV   Summary and Conclusions   233

Appendices

     A   Background Characteristics of Families (ENRICH)   241

     B   Research Scales and Reliability   245

     C   Correlations of Research Scales   267

     D   Data Collection Procedures   269

     E   Couple and Family Scores   271

     F   Comparison of High- and Low-Stress Families   281

     G   Stress Items Across the Family Life Cycle   285

References   293

About the Authors   311

PREFACE TO THE UPDATED EDITION

Since the publication of this study of 1,000 families in 1983, the development of family theory and the use of family research methods has mushroomed. This book has, in part, been one of the factors contributing to the growing interest and expansion of the family field. I am both honored and pleased to write this Preface to the Updated Edition. It is gratifying to see that this book, which has already been called by some a classic, is being reprinted.

It has been gratifying to see that many of the theoretical ideas and research methods used in this study are now being used in other studies of families. In fact, we now have documented more than 600 studies that are using the Circumplex Model and/or family research methods that were developed in this major study.

The major focus of the study was to provide normative data regarding nonclinical families across the life cycle. This is still the largest cross-sectional study of nonclinical families in the United States. The focus is a life-cycle perspective that includes young couples without children, couples that have young children, families with adolescents and, lastly, families that have launched their children. Although the sample was not a random sample nationally, it was a stratified random sample across the life cycle. It included both urban and rural families with a range of incomes and educational levels.

Another major focus was to identify why some families coped successfully across the life cycle while others failed to cope with life stressors and problems. The results clearly found differences in coping styles among families; and the significance of the marital dyad was consistently demonstrated. The normative data regarding stressors and successful and unsuccessful coping strategies continues to be a major contribution of this book.

This book, however, is not without limitations. It is truly a cross-sectional study and not a longitudinal one where families are followed across the life cycle. This study also focuses primarily on white and Protestant families and does not focus on problem families. Also, the study included traditional nuclear families and not blended or single-parent families.

Studies that have attempted to replicate these findings with other ethnic groups and different types of family structures have often found high levels of consistency, but also some new discoveries. For example, studies that have focused on the strengths of blended families and families of different ethnic composition have found them to have many strengths that are characteristic of traditional white families, but also some new strengths.

This is truly one of the few comprehensive studies that considers the family at all levels, both conceptually and empirically. Conceptually, the study was grounded in family theory using both the Circumplex Model of Marital and Family Systems developed by David Olson and colleagues and the Double ABC-X Model developed by McCubbin and colleagues. This later model was built on the ABC-X Model developed by the late Reuben Hill.

The sample also included multiple family members with couples (both husband and wife) across all stages of the life cycle and adolescents at the adolescent stage. This enabled us to have two to three members of a family reporting on how they perceived the family system.

The research methods in the study were also specifically developed so they could be used for studying families and they included many instruments that are now increasingly used in family research. These included Family Adaptability and Cohesion Evaluation Scales (FACES), Family Inventory of Life Events (FILE), and Family Coping Styles (F-COPES). Other scales developed specifically for this study included the comprehensive assessment of marital dynamics (ENRICH) and a new scale on Family Satisfaction.

In terms of the data analysis, a range of couple and family scores were developed and used to evaluate and test the various theoretical hypotheses. The results were conceptualized and reported at the couple and family level, which fed back into the development of family theory. In summary, there are still few examples of true family studies that meet the multiple criteria of using family concepts, a family sample, family methods, family analysis, and summarizing the results at the family level.

Theoretically, this study provided data to more fully test and develop both the Circumplex Model and the Double ABC-X Model (now called the FAAR Model). While the study provided further evidence for the support of both of these theoretical models, it also raised some important ideas which has helped to expand and further develop the models.

Specifically, in regard to the Circumplex Model, this study was the first to identify that there is a *linear* relationship for both cohesion and adaptability in nonclinical families. This finding has now been replicated in more than 20 additional studies by other family researchers, which clearly have established the stability of this finding. The studies that tested the Circumplex Model have typically used the self-report instrument called FACES II, which was originally developed for use in this study. Since that time, FACES III has been developed and improved in several ways over FACES II.

In regard to the Double ABC-X Model, McCubbin and associates have now developed the FAAR Model and expanded it to include a more comprehensive understanding of the pile up of events and the post-adjustment process. Some important additional work has been done in regard to the stress instrument (FILE) in that two types of items were identified in the original instrument: *events* and *strains*. While events are concrete items that either happened or not, strains represented under-lying tensions that often are accumulative over time. Recent research has demonstrated that strains are a more powerful predictor than events. Hence, strains are increasingly being used to measure stress rather than combining them with events.

Another important outcome of the study was to identify family coping strategies that were useful to families across the life cycle. The instrument used for this study was F-COPES. One of the important contributions of this study was that it clearly identified some important findings regarding stress and coping across the life cycle. More specifically, it clearly demonstrated that the adolescent stage for families was both the most stressful and the one lowest in both marital and family satisfaction. The study also clearly demonstrated what coping resources were most useful at each stage of the life cycle. Many of these findings have been supported by other studies done at particular stages of the life cycle. In general, most of the findings from this study have been replicated by other researchers using different samples but often the same instruments.

Empirically, this study has made several important contributions to the family field in general. One of the most useful contributions has been the range of self-report methods that are both reliable and valid. In addition, these instruments are multidimensional in that they tap family stress, coping, Circumplex dimensions, and adaptation. Another advantage of these instruments is that data is provided from multiple members. This study was one of the most comprehensive to clearly identify the low correlation between family members. Family members' perceptions typically only correlate from .25 to .50, which means that the common variance among members ranges from only 5 to 25 percent. This raises a real dilemma for family researchers and means that couple and family scores must be used in order to capture the complexity and richness of the family system.

The stage of the family life cycle proved to be a critical variable in most of the analyses. While some findings did hold up across stages, there were enough important differences across them that future researchers should take stage into account in their study and analysis.

This work has contributed in more significant ways than we had imagined when the study was initially proposed and launched. In many ways, it has provided national normative data on a large sample of nonclinical families. It clearly has identified the different stressors and coping strategies that these families use across the life cycle. In addition, it has advanced the theoretical developments of both the Circumplex Model and the FAAR Model, in addition to proposing new ideas and hypotheses. Empirically, it has provided a range of self-report instruments that continue to be used extensively in the family field. These instruments have, in turn, generated interest in family research because of their availability, reliability, and validity.

In many ways, this study is truly a model family research project since it carries the theme of family from the theoretical conception, to the subject selection, to the research methods, to the data analysis, and to the results which are then fed back into the theoretical models. Based on our experience with this project, it is most fitting to close this Preface with the words of Winston Churchill, who said, "This is not the end. It is not even the beginning of the end. Let us hope it is the end of the beginning."

—*David H. Olson*

FOREWORD

David Olson and his colleagues have made a major contribution in bringing this study of more than one thousand families to term. Drawn from every region of the country, although favoring the middle West, the families are also from every educational, occupational, and income level of society. In effect, they are drawn from every walk of life. The story told, therefore, is one of great variety in life experiences, in stressful events encountered, in successes and defeats, but also in persevering, for all of these families are still intact. There are no fractured homes, no clinically shored-up family units, no families with institutionalized members. There is range and variety in makeup and structure, but all of these families have in common the fact that they have survived years of marriage (and most years of parenthood) without breaking.

The mission of the authors of this study has been to discover not only how well these families have managed their lives but what explains their relative success and failure. The research team has gone beyond description, which would be a worthy contribution in its own right. After all, how much do we know about American families as a whole beyond what the census and vital statistics reveal: birthrates, death rates, marriage rates, divorce rates, age at marriage, and so on. Our leading indicators of family health provide meager enough information that we would certainly benefit from a dispassionate chronicle of the types of crises and exigencies that have beset a national sample of families. We are therefore doubly indebted to have also a careful analysis of the multivariate explanations of marital and family satisfaction to confirm or disconfirm the dozens of studies based on small local samples.

The senior authors, Olson and McCubbin, are seasoned researchers and theorists who have separately made distinctive contributions to our understanding of family phenomena. Olson is distinguished for his research on the complexities and types of marital power and for the several tests and measurements he has standardized, of which three elusive concepts of marital conflict (IMC) and family adaptability and cohesion (FACES) have achieved international visibility. McCubbin is most widely recognized for his research and reviews of family stress, coping, and adaptation and for the instruments developed for measuring these multidimensional constructs: the Family Inventory of Life Events and Changes (FILE) and Family Coping Strategies (F-COPES). Their prior activities in these separate realms have been used to their best advantage in joining forces in this national study to increase the number of dimensions of family behavior that can be authoritatively measured and analyzed. The results encompass more of the significant issues of family performance than any other study to date.

The detailed findings of the volume are too numerous to preview effectively in this Foreword. I have selected one thematic discovery among several that begs for further comment and explication; namely that the performance of families varies in an unexpected and puzzling way across the several stages of the family life span.

Common sense might have suggested that families would begin in the early months of marriage fumbling and incompetent but open to improvement, learning from experience to cope with the problems of the vocations of marriage and parenthood over time. The picture would be like physical growth in developing children, with spurts of improvement followed by plateaus of consolidation followed by further spurts of growth; always upward in improved performance, leveling off only in the later years of the marriage as the health and energy of members waned. In support of such a picture are the observations that couples are constantly facing new problems, introduced by their growing children, and by the changing expectations of the community with which they are less prepared to cope in the beginning years than later when they have built problem-solving repertoires and have developed confidence in their competence to perform in their many roles as spouses and parents. Children, too, become less dependent and more competent to assume helping roles as they mature, which should facilitate intergenerational communication and consensus building as the family moves from the early years of childbearing into the collegial years of living with adolescents and young adults. Why shouldn't the record of family performance in a national sample of essentially healthy families be one of just such incremental mastery over their several careers?

Dozens of local studies with small samples have failed to support these commonsense expectations of improvement over time, especially in the contrasts between couples before and after the arrival of children when net decrements in marital satisfactions were uniformly recorded. Other studies found decrements continued into the period of life with adolescents, changing direction only when these children as young adults left home. Would a large national sample of ordinary families not correct the disquieting findings of the smaller studies?

Olson and his colleagues administered a wide battery of tests of family performance to families located within each of seven stages of the life cycle to discover only a few parameters on which there was improvement overtime: namely, increased church participation, increase in income level, occupational advancement (a mixed picture), increase in utilizing outside supports and passive coping strategies when encountering stressful events, and a move away from egalitarian toward more centralized decision-making preferences.

On a host of other indicators of family achievement the picture is disconcertingly one of steady decline from the childless stage through the years of childbearing and middle parenthood before leveling off and recovering in the postparental period after the children have married and established homes of their own. The surviving couples are now not only grandparents but have reduced the complexity of demands on their time and energy and seem to have experienced a renewal of satisfaction with marriage and family life. Examination of the charts in this study shows this regressive pattern of disenchantment and increasing discontent while rearing children followed by recovery when parental tasks are over for a wide range of achievements: decreasing marital and family satisfaction scores (as well as a higher percentage contemplating separation and divorce), decreasing scores on family cohesion and adaptability (not as marked), decreasing adequacy of marital communication (as perceived by wife), and use of active coping patterns to deal with stressful events.

It is clear from this study that families in the country as a whole are not immunized from trouble over the life span and appear to fight a losing battle against increasing stressors during the active years of childbearing and childrearing. The miracle is that so many survive with higher appreciation of their marriages and their quality of life in the postparental phase of grandparenthood and retirement. Adaptation to stress rather than freedom from problems is the key finding to account for survival into the later years.

What reservations should be brought to bear in advancing these findings as evidence of regressive development among relatively normal families over their life cycle?

The authors remind us that it would be necessary to follow the same families over almost fifty years to confirm that the patterns described above reflect actual developmental changes by families over the life span. The families in each of these stages represent a cross-sectional sample rather than a longitudinal sample. It is therefore difficult to disentangle what is developmental (due to developmental stage) and what is due to the peculiar times and timing in which the families in these stages began their marriages (due to the marital duration cohort they belong to). Each set of families located in a specific stage in this study began marriage in a different period of historical time, entered parenthood and reared their children under distinctive circumstances.

Note that the childless couples in Stage 1 are about the age of some of the children the couples in Stage 6 have just launched into homes of their own. The retired couples in Stage 7 could be grandparents of the school-age children of the couples in Stage 3. Indeed at least four generations are represented in this national sample, among the families we have distributed in the seven stages of the family life cycle.

What correction should now be made in family development theory that implies increasing growth in competence in families over the life span to fit the contrary empirical findings of parabolic declines in performance over much of the life span? What family development theory has not adequately assessed to date are the mounting levels of stress experienced in the middle years, which put to the test and find inadequate the coping repertoires of families. We return to the theme sounded by Olson and McCubbin that adaptative strategies which combine in an optimum mix family adaptability and cohesion is the key account for survival through the beleaguered middle years into the less stressful postparental period.

In closing this Foreword I wish to commend the research team of Olson and McCubbin for securing data on the three perspectives of husband-father, wife-mother, and adolescent son or daughter. This triangulation should permit analyses at the level of the family as the behaving unit which should go beyond the findings presented in this first volume. I look forward to the impact of this groundbreaking study in the years to come.

—*Reuben Hill*
University of Minnesota

ACKNOWLEDGMENTS

This study would have not been possible without the encouragement of Charles W. Dull who initially proposed the idea of studying "normal" families across the family life cycle. He suggested that by learning how normal families seemed to cope successfully with stress and changes, we could identify their strengths as a couple and family.

He hoped that the findings of this study would help guide and direct the development of preventative programs for couples and families. Because of his support, we were able to obtain funding for this study. Two members of his staff, Chris Linn and Marge Schiebel, were particularly helpful in facilitating the data collection process from across the United States. We also wish to thank the 150 individuals who actually collected the data from these 1200 families.

There are a number of people who carried a heavy load on this project. Due to the size of this study, a group of secretaries worked endless hours on research reports and numerous drafts of this book. We wish to thank Louise Hansen and other secretaries who worked on various parts of this project, including Susan Rains-Johnson and Dorothea Berggren. Sara Wright helped provide drafts on parts of this study. Three undergraduate assistants who were very helpful in the data collection and data preparation process were Chaichan Chiraprut, Julia Geist, and Sue Michaud. We appreciated the editorial assistance of Catherine Davidson on earlier reports, and Todd McCubbin, who assisted by typing various materials.

A special thanks goes to Gloria Lawrence, who typed numerous drafts and this final manuscript. Not only did she work diligently and efficiently to meet our tight deadlines, but she always was extremely helpful and cooperative. The high-quality graphics work by Kristine Kohn is greatly appreciated.

We wish to thank Richard Sauer, Director of the Agricultural Experiment Station at the University of Minnesota, for his continuing support of family research. This study was funded in part through his office (Minn. #52-032). We also wish to thank Dean Keith McFarland and Vice President Bill Hueg, who have provided the type of research environment that facilitates family research.

11

For permission to reprint previously published material, we would like to thank the following: For Table 6.3, David Fournier, "Summary of Problem Areas," from his dissertation, VALIDATION OF PREPARE. Table 7.2 is an adaption of table 8-5 on page 179 from MARRIAGE AND FAMILY DEVELOPMENT. Fifth Edition. by Evelyn Millis Devall. Copyright © 1957, 1962, 1967, 1971, 1977, by J. B. Lippincott. Reprinted by permission of Harper & Row, Publishers, Inc. Table 7.1 is adapted from p. 25 of Erik H. Erikson, ADULTHOOD (New York: W. W. Norton, 1966). Reprinted by permission of W. W. Norton. Excerpts from THE PROPHET, by Kahlil Gibran, by permission of Alfred A. Knopf, Inc. Copyright 1923 by Kahlil Gibran and renewed 1951 by Administrators C.T.A. of Kahlil Gibran Estate, and Mary G. Gibran. Table 7.3 is reprinted from Klaus F. Riegel, "Adult Life Crises: A Dialectic Interpretation of Development," p. 10 in *Life Span Developmental Psychology,* Nancy Datan and Leon H. Ginsberg, eds. (New York: Academic, 1975). Copyright 1975 by Academic Press. Reprinted by permission of publisher and author. The "Togetherness Prayer," from MY NEEDS, YOUR NEEDS, OUR NEEDS, by Jerry Gillies (Bergenfield, NJ: New American Library, 1974). Reprinted by permission of Doubleday & Co.

Last, but not least, we wish to thank the 1200 families who took time to participate and complete our lengthy questionnaires. It was their cooperation that ultimately made this study possible.

In closing, our sincere thanks goes to this tremendous group of individuals who worked together as an efficient and productive team throughout the two years of this project. They have made this entire process an enjoyable one and they each have had an important impact on this final book.

D. H. Olson
H. I. McCubbin
H. Barnes
A. Larsen
M. Muxen
M. Wilson

chapter

I

Purposes and Overview

THIS STUDY IS AIMED AT capturing the complexity of marriage and family systems across the life cycle. To help guide and direct this search, we have relied on recent theoretical and methodological developments in the family field.

This project also builds on the theoretical and methodological foundation provided by the pioneering and expansive work of Reuben Hill. Hill's classic work on *Families Under Stress* (1949) demonstrated the conceptual value of family integration (cohesion) and adaptability in understanding family stress. In the process, he also revealed the significance of the concept of family stress and created a model (ABC-X) to describe it. His extensive work in creating the family development framework (Hill & Rodgers, 1964) also led to an emphasis on the importance of considering family life stages. In addition, Hill conducted a study of *Family Development in Three Generations* (1970), and he described alternative methods of studying the family across the life cycle (Hill, 1964).

Theoretically, we have relied heavily on the Circumplex Model of Marital and Family Systems (Olson, Russell, & Sprenkle, 1979, 1980, 1983). This model focuses on three salient dimensions of family dynamics — adaptability, cohesion, and communication. The model also enables us to classify families into types; the primary ones are Balanced, Mid-Range, and Extreme.

In addition, we have been guided by advances in family stress theory, particularly the Double ABC-X Model (McCubbin & Patterson, 1982, 1983). This model focuses on three aspects of family life (stressors and strains, family coping, and family resources) that determine how well the family will adjust to normal transitions and changes.

Methodologically, we have attempted to reveal rather than conceal the complexity of the family by obtaining the perspectives of both a husband and wife across all stages of the life cycle. At the Adolescent and Launching stages, an adolescent also presented his or her perspective on the family. Considerable work was done to develop valid and reliable research methods that would enable us to assess some of the intricacies of marital and family life.

Once the data were collected, the analysis used both individual and a variety of couple and family scores. Data analysis was facilitated by advances in computer programs and statistical techniques. These computer programs not only enabled research analysis to be done more effectively and efficiently, but it also made possible the move from a purely descriptive level to the level of prediction. The predictive analyses of family types and family stress levels are presented later (Chapters XI and XII).

Family Systems Across the Life Cycle

Family systems at seven stages of the family life cycle were systematically studied on five major theoretical dimensions: *family types, family resources, family stress and changes, family coping,* and *family satisfaction* (see Figure 1.1).

Family types are derived from the Circumplex Model, according to which families are classified into Balanced, Mid-Range, and Extreme types. *Family resources* include both marital and family strengths. Family strengths include family pride and accord, parent-adolescent communication, and congregational activities. Marital strengths include eleven important content areas in marriage, such as communication, conflict resolution, sexual relationship, family and friends, and role relationship. *Family stress and change* provides a more in-depth picture of the specific stresses and strains that each family member experiences at each stage of the family life cycle. *Family coping* focuses on the internal family resources and external support systems that families use in coping with their everyday issues. Personal health practices are considered as one way of coping on an individual level. Included as external resources are the programs and services that family members use in the community. *Family and marital satisfaction* focuses on how well these other processes work for family members. Satisfaction with the marriage, family life, and overall quality of life are each independently and collectively seen as important outcomes to consider for each family member.

These five dimensions provide the theoretical base for this study; the major linking dimension is family types based on the Circumplex Model. However, all of these dimensions can independently be related

Types of Families	Family Resources	Family Stress and Changes	Family Coping	Family Satisfaction
Balanced	Family Strengths	Family Life Events	Family Coping Strategies	Family Satisfaction
Mid-Range	Marital Strengths	Stresses and Strains	Programs and Services Used	Marital Satisfaction
Extreme				

Figure 1.1 Theoretical Overview of Study

to each other to provide a more comprehensive picture of these marriage and family systems.

In order to gain a more panoramic perspective on family life across the life cycle, each of these dimensions is explored in considerable detail in separate chapters. Data will be provided on how couples and families differ on these characteristics across the life cycle. The descriptions provided by the husband, wife, and adolescent family members will also be compared and contrasted. Because of the differences in reports between family members, this information clearly demonstrates some of the complexity of family life. It also makes the data analysis more challenging and complicated.

More specifically, this study focuses on answering the following questions:

(1) How do the family types (Balanced, Mid-Range, Extreme) vary across the family life cycle? (Chapter V)

(2) What levels of marital and family strengths do families have across the family life cycle? (Chapter VI)

(3) What types of stress do husbands, wives, and adolescents encounter at various stages of the family life cycle? (Chapter VII)

(4) What methods of coping do family members use to deal with stress at various stages of the family life cycle? (Chapter VIII)

(5) In coping with stress, what types of programs and support services do family members actually use and what kinds would they like to have available? (Chapter VIII)

(6) What are the personal health practices of various family members across the family life cycle? (Chapter IX)

(7) What are the levels of marital and family satisfaction for various family members across the family life cycle? (Chapter X)

(8) What are the characteristics of couples and families that are high in family satisfaction compared to those that are low? (Chapter X)

(9) What are the characteristics (background and family) that distinguish Balanced from Extreme families at the various stages of the family life cycle? (Chapter XI)

(10) How well do Balanced versus Extreme families function at the various stages of the family life cycle? (Chapter XI)

(11) What are the characteristics (background and family) that distinguish high-stress from low-stress families at each stage of the family life cycle? (Chapter XII)

(12) In terms of families with adolescents, how do Balanced families function differently from Extreme families and how do families high in stress differ from those low in stress at this stage? (Chapter XIII)

Circumplex Model of Marital and Family Systems

The Circumplex Model provides the basic foundation and underlying theme for this entire book. The model was developed by David Olson, Candyce Russell, and Douglas Sprenkle (1979, 1980, 1983) to integrate the seemingly diverse theoretical and therapeutic concepts used to describe families. The two central dimensions in the model are *family cohesion* and *family adaptability.* A third dimension is *family communication,* which is considered to be a facilitating dimension in that it enables couples and families to move on the cohesions and adaptability dimensions.

The Circumplex Model provides a framework for describing *types* of couples and families. There are four levels of cohesion and four levels of adaptability and putting them together forms sixteen cells or types of families (see Figure 1.2). Once couples or families have been placed into one of the sixteen types, it becomes possible to reduce the sixteen types to three more global types: Balanced, Mid-Range, and Extreme. *Balanced families* are those that fall into the two central cells of both cohesion and adaptability. *Mid-range families* are those that fall into one of the extreme cells on one dimension and a central cell on the other dimension. *Extreme families* are those that fall into an extreme cell on both dimensions.

Hypotheses derived from the Circumplex Model provide a unifying theoretical direction for this study. Specific hypotheses link the dimen-

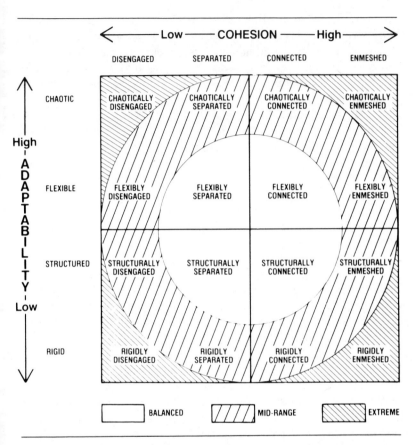

Figure 1.2 Circumplex Model: Sixteen Types of Marital and Family Systems

sions indicated in Figure 1.1. First, Balanced families will have greater *resources* (marital and family strengths) across the family life cycle. Second, because of these resources, Balanced families will be less vulnerable to *stress* and will deal more effectively with it. Third, Balanced families will also use various *coping strategies* to deal with the stressor events. Lastly, Balanced families will generally have higher levels of marital and family *satisfaction*.

Normative Study of Family Development

Although considerable work has been done describing individual development, few studies have focused on the family as it develops over time. Theorists like Erik Erikson (1959) have described the stages of development for individuals across the life cycle. Daniel Levinson (1978) focused on the adult stages of development in his book *The Seasons of a Man's Life*. Levinson's book provided the framework for Gail Sheehy's book *Passages* (1976), which made the life cycle a more popular topic.

Family development has, however, seldom been studied in a systematic and large-scale manner. The pioneering work of Reuben Hill on family development has been used for descriptive purposes, but little is known about family process within each of the major stages. Consequently, there is a lack of descriptive information about normative processes in families at different stages of the family life cycle.

Family therapists have increasingly become aware of the importance of the family development perspective. Several of the pioneers in family therapy have clearly emphasized the importance of considering the "family of origin" in the process of therapy. However, much of their work with families and most of the research with problem families has focused on what these families were lacking. There has, therefore, been little discussion of what strengths and resources characterize families that seem to be functioning well enough to not seek treatment.

In contrast to previous research, the purpose of this project is to provide information that will describe "normal" families, to indicate the types of stress they encounter and their styles of coping with it and to identify the programs and resources these families utilize and need. The focus of the study is primarily on *family development,* in that it will look at families at various stages of the family life cycle from early marriage through retirement.

Family Strengths in Normal Families

Unfortunately, most of the problems individuals have either begin or end up in the family. As a result, families today are encountering endless challenges and frustrations that both threathen their current structures and strain their available resources. To complicate their problems, society only gives lip service to the importance of families and comes to their rescue only when they are under intense stress and are unable to cope effectively. Only recently have there been conferences and books focusing specifically on family strengths (Stinnett, Cheser, DeFrain, & Knaub, 1980, 1981). Recently Walsh (1982) has edited an excellent book that describes *Normal Family Processes* from a variety of theoretical and therapeutic perspectives.

Most studies of families have focused on those that have difficulty coping with a variety of issues such as drug abuse, spouse abuse, sexual abuse, and a range of emotional and physical problems. "Normal" families have primarily been used as control groups and have not been the focus of research in their own right. As a result, we know a great deal about the characteristics of problem families and can only assume that normal families are simply lacking those characteristics. What we do not know are the positive aspects of families that help them cope and deal effectively with stress over the life cycle.

In contrast to other studies, this one focuses on the strengths and attributes that help families deal more effectively with stresses and strains. The first part of this book will focus on a description of what is normative for families at various stages of the family life cycle. This includes how family types differ, what families have as strengths, the kinds of stress they encounter, how they cope with stress, and how satisfied they are with their marriage, family and quality of life.

Moving from the descriptive level to making predictions, analysis was done to distinguish those families encountering high levels of stress from those that have less stress (see Chapter XII). After isolating the variables that separate these two groups, a predictive analysis was done to identify high-stress families' most critical resources and those resources that isolate low-stress families from the problems encountered by those wth high stress. These buffering variables are marital and family strengths.

Another predictive analysis of family strengths deals with comparing Balanced and Extreme family types based on the Circumplex Model (see Chapter II). Balanced and Extreme family types are compared in terms of their resources, stress levels, coping strategies, and levels of satisfaction at the various stages of the family life cycle. At different stages, some types of families seem to function more effectively in that they have more positive family resources (marital and family strengths), lower stress levels, higher levels of coping, and greater marital and family satisfaction. The families with these characteristics can be considered to function more adequately.

In summary, family strengths characteristic of "normal" families at various stages of the family life cycle are identified and described. Second, family strengths used by families who encounter less stress are described. These strengths can be seen as buffering these families from stress or as resources that help them cope more effectively with the stress they do encounter at various stages. Third, the specific family strengths that seem to help families function more effectively at each stage of the life cycle are identified. Using this information on family strengths, it becomes possible to develop preventive programs so that families can build and develop their own strengths.

chapter
II

Families Across the Life Cycle

Stages of the Family Life Cycle

One of the primary goals of this study is to describe normal family processes at various stages of the family life cycle. Therefore, descriptions of the specific stages of the family life cycle were needed before families were recruited and also when data were analyzed.

Acting upon the belief that the developmental needs of families changed as children are born, mature, and leave their homes, we turned to the classic work of Hill and Rodgers (1964). Their work was particularly valuable in exploring the nature of family development at different stages of the life cycle. Using this developmental framework, stage divisions were initially located by focusing on the ages of children in the family and on corresponding changes that the family encounters as children mature. The following criteria were created to help establish specific stages of the family life cycle:

(1) *Age of the oldest child.* Because families were seen as likely to have more than one child, and since this child would be the first catalyst introducing demands for family changes, developmental needs were felt to be largely determined by the age of the oldest child.

(2) *Amount of transition or change required in response to changing developmental needs of the family members.* Families in greatest transition were seen as families whose children had reached social milestones, such as the age for entering school, the age of puberty, the age for leaving home, or retirement of a parent.

(3) *Changes in family goal orientation and direction.* Families occupied with conceiving and nurturing young children were seen as being oriented toward markedly different goals than were those concerned with educating and integrating children into the community or engaged in launching children into more mature social roles outside the family.

Using these criteria, the following seven stages were used throughout the study.

Stage 1: Young Couples Without Children

Couples in this stage are concerned with formulating and negotiating individual and couple goals and mutually acceptable lifestyles. However, these families had not encountered the needs and demands of young children.

Stage 2: Childbearing Families and Families with Children in the Preschool Years

Families in this stage are similar in that the children spend most of their waking hours in the home and the family is oriented toward their growth and nurturance. Parents are primary sources of information and control, and the family is seen as child centered.

Stage 3: Families with School-Age Children

During this stage, the family is seen as being focused on the education and socialization of children. The oldest child in a family at this stage is between six and twelve years of age.

Stage 4: Families with Adolescents in the Home

Families in this stage are concerned with preparing their teenager to be launched from the home. Considerable demands are placed on the family due to the challenges of dealing with adolescents in the home.

Stage 5: Launching Families

During this stage, adolescents are beginning to leave home to establish identities and roles outside the family unit. Parental roles and rules are changing, and the family is occupied with successfully launching its children.

Stage 6: Empty Nest Families

Families at this stage are defined by the absence of children in the home. Parents still hold some former roles, but the family is largely oriented toward couple needs and establishing more differentiated relationships with children and grandchildren.

Stage 7: Families in Retirement

Families in this stage have largely completed the raising and supervising of children. They have completed major career contributions and are occupied with couple maintenance as well as relationships with extended family and friends.

TABLE 2.1   Families Across the Life Cycle

Stages of the Family Life Cycle		Couples	Adolescents	Total Individuals
Stage 1	Young Couples Without Children	121	n/a	242
Stage 2	Families with Pre-Schoolers (ages 0 to 5)	148	n/a	296
Stage 3	Families with School Age Children (ages 6 to 12)	129	n/a	258
Stage 4	Families with Adoles-cents (ages 13 to 18)	261	350	872
Stage 5	Launching Families (adolescent, age 19 or older)	191	62	444
Stage 6	Empty Nest Families (all children gone)	144	n/a	288
Stage 7	Families in Retirement (male over 65)	146	n/a	292
	Total	1,140	412	2,692

n/a = not applicable.

Description of Total Sample

A total of 2692 individuals from 31 states responded to the survey. The sample consisted of 1140 couples (2280 adults) and 412 adolescents, 206 males and 206 females. The final number of couples and families at the various stages of the family life cycle are summarized in Table 2.1. The goal was to obtain at least 100 couples and families at each stage of the life cycle, with about 200 families at the adolescent stage. Not only was that goal achieved, but data were obtained from husbands and wives at all stages and from one adolescent family member at the adolescent stage. (For more details on the data collection procedure, see Appendix D.)

The families were located in 31 states. The specific number and percentage of families from each state are indicated on the map of the United States in Figure 2.1. The heaviest concentration of families came from the midwestern states of Minnesota, Wisconsin, Iowa, Illinois, Michigan, Indiana, Ohio, Nebraska, and Kansas; the western states of California, Colorado, and Washington; the eastern states of Pennsylvania and Virginia; and the southern state of Texas. In total, they represent a rather diverse geographic distribution of American families.

TABLE 2.2   Quality of Life: Comparison of 1000 Families and Gallup Poll

	1000 Family Study[a]	Gallup Poll[b]
Family?/Family Life?	77	79
Marriage?/Marriage?	77	78
Children?/Relations with your Children?	72	81
Current housing arrangement?/Housing?	69	69
Own health?/Health?	59	70
Principal occupation (job)?/Job?	58	64
Household responsibilities?/Housework?	56	54

a. "How satisfied are you with your . . ." (in percentages).

b. "Considering everything, how satisfied are you with your . . ." (in percentages).

NOTE: 1000 Family Study question appears first; Gallup question follows.

COMPARISON OF 1000 FAMILIES AND THE GALLUP POLL

A national survey of satisfaction with quality of life was conducted by the Gallup organization at about the same time as these data were collected. These two surveys asked some of the same questions, so it is possible to compare the responses on these parallel items. Table 2.2 presents the seven most comparable items from the two studies.

The responses to this study were gathered during the summer and fall of 1981, with most of the data collected before December 20, 1981. The Gallup poll data were collected December 11-14, 1981 and the results were published in the Minneapolis Tribune on January 17, 1982. The Gallup study is based on personal interviews with 1483 adults. This study of 1000 couples and families included about 2200 adults.

The percentages in Table 2.2 indicate those persons who were highly satisfied with each particular area. Specifically, the percentages in this study represent those adults who responded with either of the two most satisfied categories on the five-point response scale. The Gallup poll percentages indicate those responding in the three most satisfied categories on a ten-point scale.

The results of these two independent surveys are very similar, indeed, almost identical on some issues. This similarity of results suggests that although this study included a more select group composed of families, in many ways it is comparable to the broader-based group of adults (married and unmarried) surveyed in the Gallup poll. The similarity of the two national surveys also increases the external validity of the present study and the relevance of the findings to other families in this country.

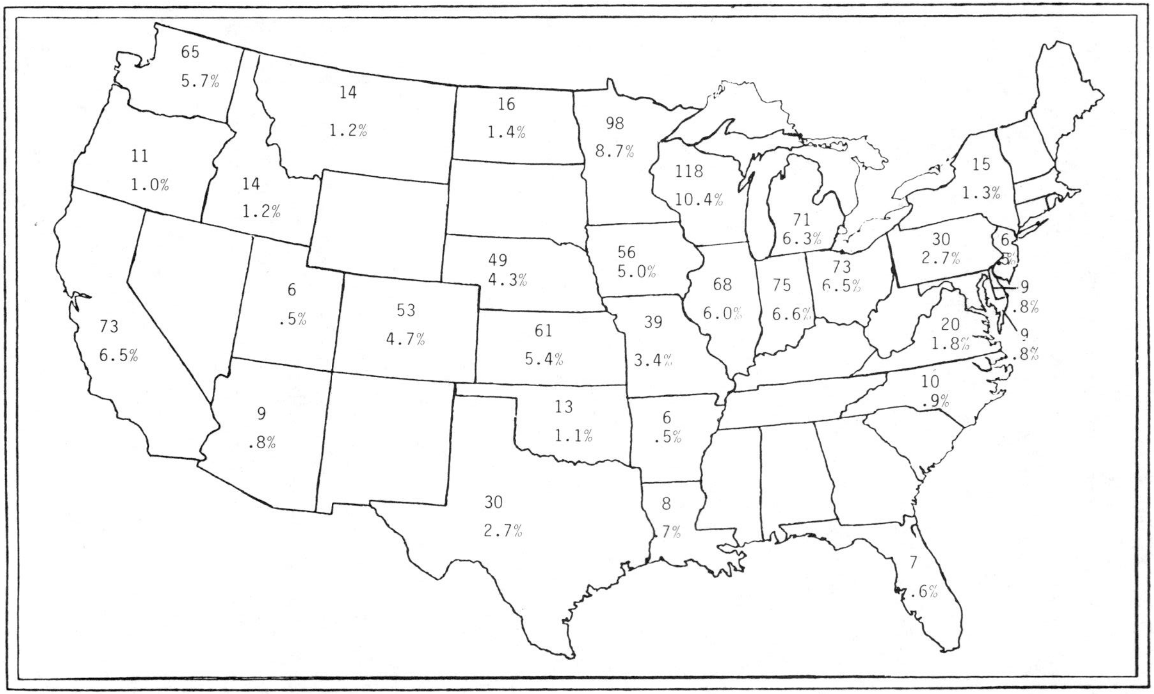

Figure 2.1 Geographic Distribution of Families

FAMILY COMPOSITION

There was an average of three children per family in this study. This number was slightly lower for families in the Childbearing and School-Age Children stages (Stages 2 and 3), where the average was only two children, and higher for families at the Launching stage (Stage 5), where the average was four children. While the smaller average number of children per family in younger families may be due to plans to limit their family size, it could be that these families have not yet finished having children and that their family size might increase.

Quite predictably, the mean age of children at each stage increased along with the age of the parenting couple and the stage of the family life cycle. Children's ages ranged from less than 1 year in Stage 2 (Childbearing)·to over 40 years at Stage 7 (Retirement). Figure 2.2 demonstrates the distribution of numbers of children in the family and the number of children still living in the parental home at each stage. The cross-sectional nature of this study is also illustrated by Figure 2.2. The number of children still in the home begins to drop markedly at Stages 4 and 5 (Families with Adolescents and Launching Families).

The fairly isolated nuclear family living in one household was not as common as might be expected. While the majority (60 percent) reported that only immediate family members lived in their household, over one-third (36 percent) listed an extended family member or nonrelative also living with the family.

Ages of family members in the study ranged from 12 to 85 years. As expected, the mean age of males and females gradually increased across the stages; males were consistently about two years older than females in respective stages. Husbands' ages ranged from 20 to 85 with a mean of 46; wives were 19 to 84 years old with a mean age of 43. The youngest adolescents were 12, while the oldest were 20, with a mean age of 16 years.

Family income for these families as reported by the husband is indicated in Table 2.3. Over one-third of the families fell in the $20,000-$29,999 income range. Slightly more than 5 percent of the sample reported an income of more than $50,000, and less than 2 percent reported no income or income less than $5,000. In general, they would probably be best described as representing the middle and upper-middle class of our society. (For more details on all the background information on these families, see Appendix A.)

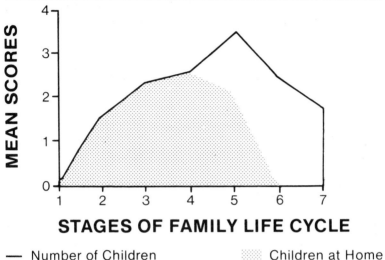

STAGES OF FAMILY LIFE CYCLE

— Number of Children   Children at Home

Figure 2.2 Number of Children at Home and Away

OCCUPATIONS AND EMPLOYMENT

About 40 percent of the males worked at white-collar jobs, and the remaining were in the building trades or were factory workers. While about 40 percent of the wives were homemakers, about 25 percent were professional workers and about 20 percent were in sales and clerical positions. For a more detailed breakdown, see Table 2.4.

The majority of males were employed full time, while about one-third of the wives worked full time. Some males (12 percent) were employed both full and part time, while fewer (6 percent) of the wives followed this pattern.

Levels of full-time employment fluctuated very little for husbands in the survey until the Retirement stage. Although 68 percent of the wives in Stage 1 (Couples Without Children) held full-time jobs, this figure dropped to 20 percent with the advent of children (Stage 2, Childbearing). About one-third of the mothers in the Adolescent stage (Stage 4) reported being fully employed outside the home; 39 percent of the

TABLE 2.3   Family Income[a]

Annual Income (in dollars)	Frequency	Percentage
no income	3	.3
1-4,999	12	1.0
5,000-9,999	14	3.8
10,000-14,999	125	10.9
15,000-19,999	185	16.1
20,000-29,999	395	34.3
30,000-39,999	240	20.8
40,000-49,999	83	7.2
50,000-74,999	53	4.6
75,000 or more	12	1.0
TOTAL	1122	100.0

a. Tabulated from husband reports.

TABLE 2.4   Occupations

	Males		Females	
	Frequency	Percentage	Frequency	Percentage
Professional, Doctor, Lawyer, Executive	132	12	7	1
Manager, Teacher, Nurse, Other Professional	332	30	269	24
Skilled and Building Trades	173	15	8	1
Sales, Technician, Clerical	132	12	202	18
Laborer, Factory Worker, Waitress	101	9	35	3
General Service Employee	34	1	29	2
Student	2	1	1	1
Unemployed	12	1	3	1
Homemaker	5	1	474	42
No Response	201	18	96	9
	1124	100	1124	100

mothers in Launching Families (Stage 5) and 36 percent of the mothers in Empty Nest Families (Stage 6) were employed full time.

Fluctuations in the current economy and family responses to economic needs were reflected in the number of people who reported holding a part-time job in addition to full-time employment. Highest figures for husbands in this category appeared at Stages 2 and 5 (Childbearing and Launching Families), with 18 percent of the husbands in both stages reporting dual employment. While most wives in Stage 1 were fully employed, about one-third of the wives held part-time jobs while raising children.

EDUCATION

Families across the family life cycle appeared to value education, with slightly more than 15 percent of those surveyed having less than a high school education. Families at the Empty Nest and Retirement stages (Stages 6 and 7) had somewhat lower levels of education than younger families. During the first three stages of the family life cycle, educational levels were fairly even for husbands and wives. However, at the later stages fewer wives had advanced degrees than did husbands.

While about one-fourth of the males (23 percent) and one-third of the females (33 percent) did not continue past high school, about one-fourth (28 percent) of the males and females had some college or technical school. While about 14 percent of the males and females had completed college, about 20 percent of the males and 10 percent of the females had some graduate or professional education.

The adolescents ranged in age from grades six through high school with only a few (12 percent) already in college or technical school. The specific breakdown for the adolescents' education was the following: sixth and seventh grade, 23 percent; eighth and ninth grade, 24 percent; tenth and eleventh, 33 percent; high school graduates, 21 percent.

RESIDENCE AND MOBILITY

While 13 percent of the sample currently live on a farm, another 14 percent live in a rural area. About 27 percent live in small towns, 21 percent live in small cities, and 24 percent live in large cities. About a third of the sample (33 percent), grew up on a farm or in a rural area, while about half (46 percent) grew up in a city of 25,000 people or more.

Younger families tended to be much more mobile than other families, with those in Stages 1 and 2 reporting an average of nearly four moves during the last ten years. It is not known, however, whether these moves occurred before or after the couple's marriage; younger adults might be expected to have been more mobile as single workers, which could account for the high frequency of moves reported. Families at other stages reported fairly stationary residences, with an average of one move during the last ten years. The most frequently listed reason for moving was job related (33 percent), with a change in quality of life a close second (29 percent).

RELIGIOUS PREFERENCE

Nearly all of the families surveyed were Lutheran church members (husbands, 92 percent; wives, 94 percent; adolescents, 88 percent).

While this characteristic is common among those surveyed, it should be noted that other characteristics were more heterogeneous. As mentioned earlier and as will be discussed in more detail in a later section, similarities between respondents to a recent Gallup poll and people in this study indicated that this uniformity in religious preference may not be a biasing factor.

Descriptions of Families at Various Stages of the Family Life Cycle

This section provides a brief summary of the major background characteristics of the couples and families at each stage of the family life cycle. The information included for each stage includes characteristics such as husband and wife ages, years married, number of children, area of residence, amount of education, occupation, amount of employment and income, and marital satisfaction. (For more detailed information on all of the major background characteristics, see Appendix A.)

STAGE 1: YOUNG MARRIED COUPLES WITHOUT CHILDREN

There were 121 couples at this stage. These couples had been married an average of 3.8 years (range = 6 months to 12 years) and had no children. Although none of the couples had children, most (46 percent) hoped to have two children. The average age for husbands was 27.6 years (range = 20 to 41), and wives' average age was 25 years (range = 19 to 36). Most of these couples (50 percent) lived in metropolitan areas with more than 25,000 people. Many of the couples reported fairly high mobility with an average of four moves during the last ten years. Many of the husbands (38 percent) and wives (32 percent) had at least four years of college, while 57 percent of the husbands and 32 percent of the wives had either finished high school or received some college or technical training.

Most of the husbands (85 percent) and wives (68 percent) worked full time. Nearly 10 percent of both husbands and wives held part-time jobs in addition to being employed full time. Many of the males (40 percent) and females (47 percent) were in professional occupations. Only 8 percent of the females reported employment as homemakers, while 26 percent of the females were employed in sales, technical, or clerical work. Most of the remainder of the husbands were employed as skilled tradesmen, salesmen, technicians, and laborers (14, 10, and 10 percent, respectively). Average annual income was $20,000 to $29,999.

Marital satisfaction among the couples in this stage was very high. Approximately 40 percent of both husbands and wives said they were "very satisfied," and nearly that many projected high marital satisfaction for their spouses. Only 10 percent had ever considered separation or divorce. As with most couples in the survey, couples in this stage had parents who were still married and living together.

STAGE 2: FAMILIES WITH PRESCHOOLERS

There were 148 families with preschool children in the study; the average age of the oldest child was 3 years. The average age for husbands in this stage was 30.5 years (range = 22 to 54), and wives' average age was 29 years (range = 21 to 48).

Most of the couples (26 percent) at this stage lived in towns with 2,500 to 25,000 people. They had moved an average of four times during the last ten years. Nearly all of both the husbands and wives in this group had finished high school, with about a third (35 percent) reporting four years of college education and about a quarter (27 percent) having graduate or professional training.

As with Stage 1, the average annual income for a family in this stage was between $20,000 and $29,999. While fewer of the females in this stage were employed full time (19 percent), about one-third (35 percent) reported part-time employment. While almost half of the males (47 percent) had white-collar positions, almost half of the wives (45 percent) reported homemaking as their principal occupation, and about one-third (32 percent) of the females were professionally employed.

Marital satisfaction for couples in Stage 2 was also reported to be quite high, and they also thought their spouses were rather happy with the marriage. However, about one-fifth (21 percent) of the couples reported considering divorce or separation at some point in their marriage.

STAGE 3: FAMILIES WITH SCHOOL-AGE CHILDREN

There were 129 families with school-age children in the study. These couples had been married an average of 11 years and had an average number of 2 children; mean age of the oldest child was 9 years. As in previous stages, average ages for husbands and wives were relatively close (35 and 33, respectively) with comparative ranges (27 to 50 years for males, 27 to 44 for females). Most of these couples lived in towns with populations between 2,500 and 25,000. They reported having moved an average of three times during the last ten years.

Half of the husbands and wives had some college or technical training (27 percent) or four years of college (23 percent). Husbands with graduate or professional training did outnumber wives at this stage (26 percent and 12 percent, respectively). The average annual income was between $20,000 and $29,000 for Stage 3 families. Again, most of the men (87 percent) were employed full time, and a third (35 percent) of the women reported part-time employment. Again, almost half of the men (47 percent) had white-collar jobs; half of the wives (49 percent) reported homemaking as their principal occupation.

About one-fifth (19 percent) of the couples indicated that they had ever considered divorce or separation. Reports of marital satisfaction showed slightly more differences between husbands and wives than did those of couples in earlier stages. The rates of marital satisfaction for both partners were down somewhat but were still rather high.

STAGE 4: FAMILIES WITH ADOLESCENTS IN THE HOME

Families with adolescents living in the home characterized Stage 4; there were 261 families in this category. Couples in this stage had been married an average of 19 years (range = 15 to 39 years). The average age of husbands was 43 (range = 31 to 57) and of wives was 40 years (range = 31 to 57). Families in this stage had an average of 3 children, and the average age of the oldest child was 16.

Most of the families (25 percent) in this stage lived in a metropolitan area with more than 100,000 people; although fairly equal numbers were distributed among large towns (18 percent), small cities (14 percent), rural areas (14 percent), and farms (13 percent).

The average annual income was between $20,000 and $29,000, with the most frequent occupation for males being professional. One-third (35 percent) of the females reported homemaking as their primary occupation, with other professions following second (22 percent). About 80 percent of the husbands were employed full time, while 30 percent of the wives worked full time; 10 percent of the husbands and 8 percent of the wives had both full-time and part-time jobs. All but 3 percent of the males and 2 percent of the females had at least a high school diploma, with one-third (32 percent) of the males and one-fifth (19 percent) of the females reporting four years or more of college.

Divorce or separation had been considered at some point in the past for 17 percent of the females in this group and 15 percent of the males. Marital satisfaction was generally slightly lower for those in Stage 4 than for those in earlier stages for both husbands and wives.

STAGE 5: LAUNCHING FAMILIES

Families who had begun to launch adolescents into independent living constituted Stage 5; 191 families were placed in this stage. Most couples had been married 25 years (range = 2 to 48); the average ages were 49 years for males and 46 years for females (ranges = 37 to 63 and 32 to 61, respectively). Most families in this group had 4 children, and the average age of the oldest child was 23 years.

As with many of the other stages, most families lived in cities with more than 25,000 people. Average annual income for families in this stage was slightly higher than it was for other stages, $30,000 to $39,999. Professional positions (36 percent) were the most frequently reported occupations for males, with females reporting homemaking as the most common occupation (36 percent). In Stage 5, 88 percent of the men were employed full time. Surprisingly, 18 percent of the males reported working a combination of full-time and part-time jobs; only in Stage 2 did a similar percentage of husbands report multiple jobs. Although far fewer wives than husbands had education beyond some college or technical training, 29 percent of the males had at least four years of college or some professional education.

As with all other stages of the family life cycle, except for Stage 1, wives in this stage reported a slightly higher incidence of contemplating separation or divorce (18 percent for the wives, 16 percent for the husbands). Husbands also tended to report slightly higher marital satisfaction than wives.

STAGE 6: EMPTY NEST FAMILIES

Families who no longer had any children living in the household made up Stage 6; there were 144 families in this stage. Couples in this stage were married an average of 34 years (range = 2 to 64 years). The average age for husbands was 58 years (range = 39 to 67) and for wives it was 56 years (range = 31 to 64). Again, most families had 3 children and the average age for the oldest was 32.

While one-fourth (25 percent) of these families lived in cities with 25,000 to 100,000 people, about 16 percent lived in towns or on farms. The average income level for families in this stage was $30,000 to $39,999, with professional occupations and homemaking the most common occupations for husbands and wives, respectively. Although

13 percent of the husbands reported no employment, 67 percent reported full-time employment. Wives were most frequently either fully employed or not employed at all (36 percent each).

Far fewer of both spouses in families at this stage reported ever having considered divorce or separation (4 percent of the husbands, 9 percent of the wives). Marital satisfaction rose again at this stage for both husbands and wives.

STAGE 7: FAMILIES IN RETIREMENT

There were 146 families who reported being in retirement. These couples had been married an average of 42 years (range = 35 to 61). The average age of husbands in this stage was 71 (range = 62 to 85); and the average age for wives was 68 (range = 56 to 84). Families in this stage had an average of 3 children and the age of the oldest child was 41.

Except for a few families in small towns (6 percent of the couples in this stage), family residences were fairly evenly distributed among large and small cities, large towns, rural nonfarm areas, and farms. Some 49 percent of the males and 55 percent of the females had a high school diploma as well as further education of some kind.

Even though the families considered themselves retired, 20 percent of the males and 4 percent of the females were still employed full time; the majority of the men were in skilled or building trades, while most women were homemakers. This was the only stage to show an income drop; the average income for families in this stage was between $10,000 and $14,999.

Fewer couples at this stage reported ever considering divorce or separation than at any other stage (3 percent of the wives and none of the husbands). Marital satisfaction was relatively high for both husbands and wives.

chapter
III
Description of the Study

Cross-Sectional Study of Intact Families

There are two important characteristics of this study that merit special attention. First, this is a study of intact families who in conventional terms might be described as "normal," "typical," "nonclinical," or "ordinary." Second, this is a cross-sectional rather than a longitudinal study — groups of families were studied at several points in the family life cycle. Because of these characteristics, one should *not* make generalizations to all families or to how families change over time. The findings of this study represent *snapshots of intact families* as they were at *one point in time* rather than describe change in families across the family life cycle.

One purpose of the study is to examine the nature of families in which married partners with or without children are living together as a single unit in a common household. Therefore, conclusions drawn from the study can only be applied to similar kinds of families.

As with any randomly selected group, the subjects in this study represented a broad spectrum of the characteristics, experiences, and problems of intact families. No attempt was made to screen out families with particular problems from the study. However, it is assumed that families with serious problems such as delinquency, chronic stress (e.g., handicapping conditions), chemical dependency, or child abuse generally did not participate. As one indication that this is not a study of a clinical population, only 7.9 percent of the adults in this study reported having been to individual, marriage, or family counseling, and only 2.9 percent reported spending more than 10 hours in counseling. In other words, this is a study of the characteristics and dynamics of what might be described as ordinary families.

A major factor by which potential subjects were screened was membership in an intact family. Although this study includes some reconstituted families and some previously divorced adults, members of other family forms such as single-parent families, divorced couples, or unmarried cohabiting couples did not participate. The temptation to apply these findings to such alternate family forms should be avoided.

Another important idea to remember about this study is its cross-sectional design. This study focuses on families at different points or stages of the family life cycle. It is assumed that families do change as they move through the family life-cycle stages. However, the only way to determine precisely how a given group of families changes is to study the same group of subjects over a period of many years. Given the 45- to 50-year span of the average family life cycle, such a longitudinal study would require repeated waves of data collection from the same subjects. Such an effort was beyond the scope of this study. (For more details on the data collection procedures, see Appendix D.)

While a longitudinal design would allow more precise interpretation of the *changes* that occur from one stage to another, that design shares an important limitation with cross-sectional studies. That is, history is assumed to play an important yet undeterminable role in both types of research. Families and their individual members are affected by their personal histories as well as by the broader historical context of the period through which they have lived. Families are affected by such things as illness of members, job layoffs, and transitions as members enter and leave the family, as well as by the historical circumstances of their time such as inflation, unemployment, and changes in laws and policies and in society's values.

While the cross-sectional approach does not allow for an assessment of *changes* from stage to stage, it does provide the opportunity to examine *differences* between families at various stages of the family life cycle. What remains open to question with this approach is which differences are due to family life-cycle stage differences and which are due to the social-historical context within which each group of subjects or age cohort has lived. Thus it is impossible to assess with certainty which dissimilarities are developmental differences and which are due to the varying ages, maturity levels, or historical contexts of the people studied.

An example of the role historical context can play in interpreting findings can be illustrated by couples' scores on egalitarian roles. While some of the couples at the early stages of the life cycle reported an egalitarian relationship, very few couples at the later stages reported such a relationship. If social-historical contexts were ignored, this disparity might be interpreted as indicating that length of marriage is inversely related to egalitarian role structure. However, considering the social-historical contexts for young versus older couples provides a different perspective. Concerns about egalitarian roles in marriage are a fairly recent phenomenon. At the time when many of the older couples in this study negotiated their relationships, traditional role structures were the norm, and concerns about equality within the marital relationship were less socially acceptable. Thus the difference between the younger and older couples in this aspect of their relationships more likely reflects historical rather than family stage differences.

Research Methods

The objectives described in Chapter I required the identification and description of the five major theoretical variables: *types of families, family resources, family stress and changes, family coping strategies,* and *marital and family satisfaction.* These variables were selected to provide a comprehensive picture of normative processes in intact families.

Twelve major research scales were compiled for this study, and nine of the instruments were specifically developed or revised for use in this study (see Figure 3.1). Five of the scales were previously developed by the research teams working with David Olson (FACES II and ENRICH scales) or Hamilton McCubbin (FILE, A-FILE, and F-COPES). Four other scales were specifically developed for this project. These were Family Satisfaction, Parent-Adolescent Communication, Family Strengths, and Quality of Life. All of these scales underwent extensive pretesting and refinement to establish their reliability and validity.

The three scales that were not changed were those developed by other authors. These were selected because of their relevance to this study, and they had each been previously used in one or more large studies. These scales measured marital satisfaction (the short form of the Locke-Wallace Marital Adjustment Scale; Locke and Wallace, 1959), personal health behaviors (Personal Health Practices Scale; Belloc and Breslow, 1972), and congregational activities (Congregational Activities Scale; Strommen, Brekke, Underwager, & Johnson, 1972).

The nine other scales are presented in Appendix B, but a more complete description on the development and final instruments is contained in the monograph *Family Inventories* (Olson, Fournier, & Druckman, 1982). This monograph also describes the reliability (inter-

Types of Families
- Family Adaptability and Cohesion Evaluation Scales (FACES II)*
  — Family cohesion
  — Family adaptability

Family Resources
- Family Strengths*
  — Family pride
  — Family accord
- Parent-Adolescent Communication*
  — Open family communication
  — Problems in family communication
- Marital Strengths (ENRICH)
  — Conventionality
  — Personality issues
  — Marital communication
  — Conflict resolution
  — Financial management
  — Leisure activities
  — Sexual relationship
  — Children and marriage
  — Family and friends
  — Egalitarian roles
  — Religious orientation
- Congregational Activities*

Family Stress and Change
- Family Life Events and Change (FILE)
  — Intrafamily
  — Marital
  — Pregnancy and childbearing
  — Finance and business
  — Work
  — Illness and family care
  — Losses
  — Transitions
  — Legal
- Adolescent-Family Stress (A-FILE)*
  — Transitions
  — Sexuality
  — Losses
  — Responsibility and strains
  — Substance use
  — Legal conflict

Family Coping Strategies
- Family Coping (F-COPES)*
  — Reframing

Figure 3.1   Research Methods and Theoretical Dimensions

— Passive appraisal
— Acquiring social support
— Mobilizing to acquire/accept help
— Seeking spiritual support
• Personal Health Practices*

Marital and Family Satisfaction
• Marital Satisfaction (ENRICH)
• Marital Satisfaction (Locke-Wallace)
• Family Satisfaction*
• Quality of Life*

*Adolescents completed these scales only.

Figure 3.1   Continued

nal consistency and test/retest), validity, scoring procedures, and norms for these scales. The following is a brief description of these nine scales.

TYPES OF FAMILIES

Family Adaptability and Cohesion Evaluation Scales (FACES II)

FACES II was used in this study to assess the type of family (Balanced, Mid-Range, or Extreme) on the Circumplex Model (see Chapter III for a more complete description of the model). This self-report instrument enables an individual to describe his or her family on the dimensions of family adaptability and cohesion.

FAMILY RESOURCES

Family Strengths

Two dimensions of family strength include family pride and family accord. *Family pride* focuses on the positive aspects of respect, trust, and loyalty within the family. It also includes the characteristics of optimism and shared values within the family. *Family accord* is concerned with the family's sense of competency, especially in dealing with conflict.

Parent-Adolescent Communication

Positive and negative aspects of communication — both content and process issues — between parents and adolescent children are assessed by this scale. It is composed of two subscales: *Open family communication* focuses on the freedom of the flow of factual and emotional information, and *problems in family communication* focuses on more destructive patterns and avoidance tactics.

Marital Strengths

ENRICH was the major scale used for measuring marital strengths in this study. This inventory can also serve as a diagnostic tool for married couples seeking marriage counseling and marriage enrichment. The total instrument contains eleven content categories and one scale that measures tendency to report conventional or socially desirable attitudes.

All twelve scales were used in the study.

- *Conventionality* measures an individual's tendency to answer questions conventionally or in a socially desirable direction.

- *Marital satisfaction* is a global measure of satisfaction and compatability with the ten aspects of the marital relationship that follow.

- *Personality issues* assesses an individual's perception of, and satisfaction with, his or her partner's personality, behavior, and habits.

- *Marital communication* focuses on whether an individual feels understood and is able to easily share feelings with his or her partner.

- *Conflict resolution* assesses an individual's perception of conflict in the marital relationship and the ways conflicts are resolved.

- *Financial management* focuses on attitudes and concerns about the ways in which economic issues are managed within the couple's relationship.

- *Leisure activities* assesses each individual's preferences and satisfaction with sharing similar interests, spending time together, and enjoying separate activities.

- *Sexual relationship* measures individual feelings and concerns about the couple's affectional and sexual relationship.

- *Children and marriage* focuses on each individual's attitudes and feelings about his or her role in child rearing and agreement on disciplining and values for children.

- *Family and friends* measures feelings and concerns about relationships with parents, relatives, in-laws, and friends.

- *Egalitarian roles* assesses individual behaviors and beliefs toward sharing marital and family roles and decision-making and household responsibilities.

- *Religious orientation* measures individual attitudes and concerns about agreement on religious beliefs and practices.

Congregational Activities

This scale assesses the level of participation and involvement in the church and church-related activities. Individuals scoring high on this scale tended to be very involved in their congregation.

FAMILY STRESS AND CHANGE

Family Inventory of Life Events (FILE)

This self-report instrument is designed to record the normative and nonnormative life events and changes experienced by the family unit. For the most part, changes that occurred in the year prior to the completion of the instrument are emphasized, although some events (such as chronic conditions or the loss of a family member) that happened earlier in the family history are included. Items in this instrument are organized into nine conceptual dimensions: *intrafamily* strains, *marital* strains, *pregnancy and childbearing* strains, *finance and business* strains, *work-family transitions* and strains, *illness and family care* strains, *losses, transitions* "in and out," and *legal* strains.

Adolescent Family Inventory of Life Events (A-FILE)

This scale provides an index of an adolescent's vulnerability as a result of the build-up of family life events and changes. Items in this scale relate to six conceptual dimensions: *transitions, sexuality, losses, responsibilities and strains, substance use,* and *legal conflict.*

FAMILY COPING STRATEGIES

Family Coping (F-COPES)

This instrument was created to identify attitudinal and behavioral strategies used by families in response to problems or difficulties. The instrument is composed of two subscales that tap internal as well as external family strategies and resources. The internal coping strategies include *reframing* and *passive appraisal.* Reframing deals with family members' belief that they can solve their own problems. Passive appraisal reflects a more inactive "wait-and-see" attitude.

The external strategies include *acquiring social support, mobilizing to accept help,* and *seeking spiritual support.* Acquiring social support relates to seeking support from friends, neighbors, and relatives. Mobilizing the family to accept help from professionals and community agencies is another coping style. Seeking spiritual support involves relying on the church, minister, and faith in God.

PERSONAL HEALTH BEHAVIORS

Belloc and Breslow (1972) developed a list of seven personal health behaviors which they used in a national survey. Because these seven items were found to be predictive of longevity and were descriptively interesting, this scale was used in this study.

MARITAL AND FAMILY SATISFACTION

Marital Satisfaction (ENRICH and Locke-Wallace)

Marital satisfaction was measured by two scales — the Locke-Wallace scale and a scale from the ENRICH inventory. The Locke-Wallace (short form) scale has been used extensively in past research and focuses on several important aspects of marriage. The ENRICH marital happiness scale assessed satisfaction on the ten other content areas in the ENRICH inventory.

Family Satisfaction

This scale was designed to assess each member's satisfaction with the family as a whole. Items were derived from the areas covered by the Circumplex Model.

Quality of Life

This instrument measures an individual's sense of well-being or life satisfaction. Two forms of this instrument were used in the study, one for adults and one for adolescent family members. The adolescent version contained items relating to the following domains: family life, friends, extended family, home, education, time, religion, financial well-being, neighborhood and community, health, and impact of mass media. The adult version included two additional domains: marriage and employment.

Data on Families

In order to provide some perspective on the magnitude of this study and amount of data that was processed, an analysis was done of the total amount of information on these families.

There are a total of 507 items in the fourteen adult scales and 295 items in the nine adolescent scales. Since there are 1140 couples (2280 adults) with partial or complete data and 412 adolescents, the total sample size is 2692 individuals. Multiplying the number of items for the adults and adolescents by the number of items that they each completed gives a total number of data.

The total amount of data for adults is over 1 million (1,155,960) items and 121,540 for the adolescents, making a grand total of 1,277,500 data bits in this study. Because of the size of this data set, it was very important that the data be well organized. In order to organize and store this data set on the computer, a master SPSS file system was built and pretested before the actual data were entered into the system.

The data were prepared for analysis as follows. First, each questionnaire was carefully checked before it was submitted for computer scanning or keypunching. Once the data were put on the computer tape and verified, frequency runs were made for each scale in order to further clean the raw data. This process of checking the data, putting it on tape, veryifying, and rechecking took four people three to four months to accomplish.

Once the data were cleaned and verified, they were then entered into the master SPSS data file. Preliminary analysis, including item analysis, alpha reliability, correlational analysis, and factor analysis — was then performed. (A summary of these analyses is reported for each scale in the *Family Inventories* manual.)

COUPLE AND FAMILY SCORES

One of the unique aspects of this study is that couple and family scores were developed for each of the major variables. There are a variety of reasons why it was considered critical that these scores be developed (Olson, 1981). First of all, this is a study of marriage and family life, and it was, therefore, considered essential to have scores that would describe a couple or family *as a unit*. This overcomes one of the major limitations of most studies in the family field, which rarely use couple and family scores.

One of the reasons that these scores are not used in many family studies is because researchers usually collect data from only one family member (Olson & Cromwell, 1975). In this study, we insisted that the data be collected from both the husband and wife at all stages of the family life cycle. At the adolescent stage, we also included one adolescent family member.

Another major reason for developing couple and family scores relates to the fact that family members often have differing perceptions of their family. There are numerous studies indicating a lack of agreement between husbands and wives and between parents and adolescents (see Olson & Cromwell, 1975). Marital and family therapists are continually confronted with the divergent perceptions of family members. In this study, fathers, mothers, and adolescents had low levels of agreement on most variables. These results will be described later in this section.

Because couple and family scores have so rarely been used in past studies, we developed a variety of different methods for obtaining these scores. In addition, the various types of couple and family scores were compared to determine their relative agreement and how well they work empirically.

The analysis that follows emphasizes couple and family scores, but some analysis is also done at the individual level (father, mother, and adolescent). Across all seven stages of the family life cycle, couple scores are used because data were obtained from both husbands and wives. At the two stages containing adolescents, Stages 4 and 5, family scores are emphasized.

AGREEMENT BETWEEN FAMILY MEMBERS

To determine the amount of agreement between family members in this study, analysis was done across family members on the major research scales. Table 3.1 summarizes the intrafamily correlations between husbands, wives, and adolescents on the major variables.

In general, the level of husband and wife agreement was rather low, ranging from correlations of .16 to .62 across all the major scales. The highest correlation (.62) reflects shared beliefs about Congregational Activities, and the lowest (.16) is an assessment of the family's ability to reframe problems in a positive light (Family Coping). The average correlation on the Marital Strengths (ENRICH) scales and Family Inventory of Life Events (FILE) was .42, but it dropped to a low of .20 for the total Family Coping scale.

As might be expected, the agreement (correlation) between parents and their adolescent children is even lower than that between parents. This may be explained somewhat by the developmental process. Adolescents may view their families differently because they are struggling to assert their own independence.

The amount of agreement between father and adolescents ranged from a low correlation coefficient of .05 on one of the Family Coping subscales (mobilizing in order to acquire and accept help) to a high of .46 on Family Cohesion. The agreement between mother and son was also low but had a smaller range. The agreement was lowest on the F-COPES scale of mobilizing to acquire help (.12) and highest on

TABLE 3.1 Agreement Between Family Members (correlations)

	Husband-Wife	Husband-Adolescent	Wife-Adolescent
FACES II			
Family Cohesion	.46	.46	.39
Family Adaptability	.32	.31	.21
Family Strengths (Total)	.40	.39	.34
Family Pride	.31	.37	.28
Family Accord	.36	.25	.23
Parent-Adolescent Communication	.30	.32	.34
Marital Strengths (ENRICH)			
Conventionality	.53	—	—
Personality issues	.37	—	—
Communication	.37	—	—
Conflict resolution	.37	—	—
Financial management	.42	—	—
Leisure activities	.30	—	—
Sexual relationship	.50	—	—
Children and marriage	.44	—	—
Family and friends	.33	—	—
Egalitarian roles	.44	—	—
Religious orientation	.56	—	—
(Average = .42)			
Congregational Activities	.62	.45	.39
Family Inventory of Life Events (Total)	.42	.29*	.35*
Family Coping (Total)	.20	.12	.14
Reframing	.16	.12	.16
Acquiring social support	.26	.15	.16
Seeking spiritual support	.31	.27	.27
Mobilizing to acquire/ accept help	.25	.05	.12
Passive appraisal	.26	.10	.14
Personal Health Behaviors	.34	.11	.20
Marital Satisfaction (ENRICH)	.45	—	—
Marital Satisfaction (Locke-Wallace)	.48	—	—
Family Satisfaction	.35	.31	.29
Quality of Life	.35	.28*	.22*

*Analysis of comparable items from the parent and adolescent scales.

Family Cohesion (.39) and Congregational Activities (.39). Overall, the low correlations certainly underscore the point that individual members have very discrepant perceptions about the families they live in.

These findings support Jesse Bernard's (1962) contention that within a marriage there exists a "his" or "hers" marriage. These data suggest that children also have different perceptions of their families. Given these discrepant perceptions, the methodological problems for computing couple and family scores are considerable.

Our objective was to develop couple and family scores that would not entirely mask these individual differences within a marriage or family relationship. The decision was made to compute couple and family scores in a variety of ways. The rationale for developing couple and family scores were:

(1) Couple and family scores might reveal more of the complexity of marital and family dynamics.

(2) Conceptually, it makes sense to compute couple and family scores that describe the marriage and family as a unit.

(3) Empirically, using these methods against each other might provide a more comprehensive picture of the marital and family system.

A variety of scoring procedures were developed to produce *couple scores* for various instruments used in this national survey: couple mean scores, maximized couple scores, couple discrepancy scores, positive couple agreement scores, and couple distance scores. (Calculation and interpretation of these scores are described in Appendix F.) Family scores are also used in this study and are discussed in greater detail in Chapter XII.

chapter
IV

Circumplex Model of Families

IN THE LAST DECADE, a plethora of concepts have emerged describing marital and family dynamics. Many of these terms originated in the field of family therapy. While many of these concepts appear unrelated, most attempt to describe a circumscribed domain of marital and family interaction. General systems theory (von Bertalanffy, 1968; Buckley, 1967) provides the central underlying base of many of these formulations. However, little attempt has been made to integrate these concepts conceptually or to place them within a systematic model.

The purpose of this chapter is to describe three aspects of marital and family behavior (cohesion, adaptability, and communication) that appear as underlying dimensions for the myriad concepts in the family field. These three dimensions have emerged from an inductive method based on factor analysis. Family cohesion and family adaptability can be organized into the Circumplex Model, which identifies sixteen types of marital and family systems. The ultimate purpose of the Circumplex Model is to facilitate bridging the gaps that often exist among theorists, researchers, and practitioners (Olson, 1976).

Family Cohesion, Adaptability (Change), and Communication

Family cohesion, adaptability, and communication are three dimensions of family behavior that emerge from a conceptual clustering of over fifty concepts developed to describe marital and family dynamics. While some of these concepts have been used for decades (e.g., power and roles), many of the concepts have been developed by individuals observing problem families from a general systems perspective (e.g., pseudomutuality, double binds).

After reviewing the conceptual definitions of many of these concepts, it became apparent that despite the creative terminology, the terms were conceptually similar and dealt with closely related family processes. One family process had to do with the degree to which an individual was separated from or connected to his or her family system and was called *family cohesion*. The second dimension was *family adaptability,* which focused on the extent to which the family system was flexible and able to change. The third dimension focused on *family communication* between various members.

FAMILY COHESION

Family cohesion is defined as *the emotional bonding that family members have toward one another.* Within the Circumplex Model, some of the specific concepts or variables that can be used to diagnose and measure the family cohesion dimensions are: *emotional bonding, boundaries, coalitions, time, space, friends, decision making,* and *interests* and *recreation.* There are four levels of cohesion (see Figure 4.1), ranging from *disengaged* (very low) to *separated* (low to moderate) to *connected* (moderate to high) to *enmeshed* (very high).

It is hypothesized that the central levels of cohesion (separated and connected) are most viable for family functioning. The extremes (disengaged or enmeshed) are generally seen as problematic. Many couples and families who come for treatment often fall into one of these extremes. When cohesion levels are high (enmeshed systems), there is overidentification so that loyalty to and consensus within the family prevent individuation of family members. At the other extremes (disengaged systems), high levels of autonomy are encouraged and family members "do their own thing," with limited attachment or commitment to their family. It is the central area (separated and connected) of the model where individuals are able to experience and balance being independent from and connected to their family.

FAMILY ADAPTABILITY

Family adaptability is defined as *the ability of a marital or family system to change its power structure, role relationships, and relationship rules* in response to situational and developmental stress. In order to describe, measure, and diagnose couples on this dimension, a variety of concepts have been taken from several social science disciplines, with heavy reliance on family sociology. These concerns include: *family power* (assertiveness, control, discipline), *negotiation styles, role relationships* and *relationship rules.* The four levels of adaptability (see Figure 4.1) range from *rigid* (very low) to *structured* (low to moderate) to *flexible* (moderate to high) to *chaotic* (very high).

As with cohesion, it it hypothesized that central levels of adaptability (structured and flexible) are more conducive to marital and family functioning, while the extremes (rigid and chaotic) are the most problematic for families as they move through the family life cycle.

Basically, adaptability focuses on the ability of the marital and family system to *change*. Much of the early application of systems theory to families emphasized the rigidity of the family and its tendency to maintain the status quo (Haley, 1959, 1962, 1963). "Morphostasis" was the term used to describe the pattern of rigidity to change, and "morphogenesis" was the potential to develop and grow as a system. Until the work of such theorists as Speer (1970) and Wertheim (1973, 1975), the importance of the potential for change received minimal attention. These authors helped to clarify the fact that systems need both stability and change and that it is the ability to change when appropriate that distinguishes functional couples and families from others.

FAMILY COMMUNICATION

This is the third dimension in the Circumplex Model, and it is considered to be a *facilitating dimension*. Communication is considered critical to movement on the other two dimensions. Because it is a facilitating dimension, communication is not included graphically in the model.

Positive communication skills (i.e., empathy, reflective listening, supportive comments) enable couples and families to share with each other their changing needs and preferences as they relate to cohesion and adaptability. Negative communication skills (i.e., double messages, double binds, criticism) minimize the ability of a couple or family members to share their feelings and, thereby, restrict their movement on these dimensions.

Brief Review of Theoretical Models of Family Systems

This review will describe theoretical models that have focused independently on variables related to the cohesion, adaptability, and communication dimensions. Most of these models have been developed in the last five years by individuals with a systems perspective of the family. The value and importance of these three dimensions is evidenced by the fact that these theorists and therapists concluded independently that

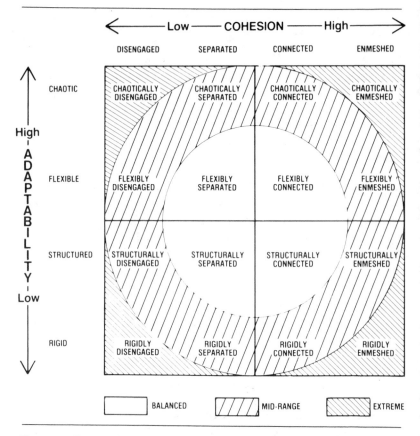

Figure 4.1 Circumplex Model: Sixteen Types of Marital and Family Systems

the variables they selected were critical for understanding and treating marital and family systems.

Table 4.1 summarizes the work of seven theorists who have worked on describing marital and family systems. Most of the recent theorizing about family dynamics and intervention has been strongly influenced by general systems theory as described by von Bertalanffy (1968) and applied to the family by Jackson (1957), Haley (1959, 1962, 1963), Speer (1970), Hill (1971), and Wertheim (1973, 1975). The current work has focused on describing both clinical and nonclinical families (Beavers, 1977; Kantor & Lehr, 1975; Lewis, Beavers, Gossert, & Philips, 1976) or has been concerned with clinical intervention (Benjamin, 1974, 1977; Constantine, 1977; Epstein, Bishop, & Levin, 1978). The early work of the psychologist Timothy Leary (1957) and Talcott Parsons and R. F. Bales (1955) was influenced less by the systems perspective, although Parsons's work had a strong systems orientation relating the family to other social systems.

Brief Description of the Circumplex Model

Figure 4.1 illustrates the two dimensions and the four levels of each dimension. The four levels of cohesion are (from low to high): *disengaged, separated, connected, enmeshed*. The four levels of adaptability are (from low to high): *rigid, structured, flexible, chaotic*. In selecting the adjectives for each level, an attempt was made to avoid the traditional diagnostic labels.

Combining the dimensions enables one to identify and describe sixteen distinct types of marital and family systems. Although it is assumed that it is possible to identify conceptually, measure empirically, and observe clinically all sixteen types, it is also assumed that some of the types occur more frequently than others. As with any circumplex model, the more central types are the most common, but it is hypothesized that couples and families having problems fall more frequently into the extreme types.

Once the types were identified and located within the model, it became clear that there were three basic groups of types. One group had scores at the two central levels on both dimensions (four balanced types); another group was extreme on both dimensions (four extreme types); and the third group was extreme on only one dimension (eight mid-range types).

Family Cohesion

The fact that at least forty concepts relate to this dimension indicates the significance of cohesion as a unifying dimension (see Table 4.1). At least six different social science fields have used this concept in some way — even though their conceptual and operational definitions are quite varied. This cross-disciplinary use of the concept also attests to its relevance and generality.

TABLE 4.1 Theoretical Models of Family Systems Utilizing Concepts Related to Cohesion, Adaptability, and Communication Dimensions

Researcher(s)	Cohesion	Adaptability	Communication	Others
Benjamin (1974 & 1977)	• Affiliation	• Interdependence		
Epstein, Bishop, & Levin (1978)	• Affective Involvement	• Behavior Control • Problem Solving • Roles	• Communication • Affective Responsiveness	
French & Guidera (1974)		• Capacity to Change • Power		• Anxiety • Role as Symptom Carrier
Kantor & Lehr (1974)	• Affect Dimension	• Power Dimension		• Meaning Dimension
Leary (1957); Constantine (1977)	• Affection-Hostility	• Dominance-Submission		
Lewis et al. (1976); Beavers (1977)	• Closeness • Autonomy • Coalitions	• Power • Negotiation	• Affect	
Parsons & Bales (1955)	• Expressive Role	• Instrumental Role		• Mythology

NOTE: See References for bibliographic information.

CONCEPTUAL DEFINITION AND SIGNIFICANCE
OF FAMILY COHESION

The definition of family cohesion used in this model has two components, both relating to the *emotional bonding* members have with one another. At the extreme of high family cohesion, *enmeshment,* there is overidentification with the family that results in extreme bonding and limited individual autonomy. The low extreme, *disengagement,* is characterized by low bonding in the family. It is hypothesized that a balanced degree of family cohesion is the most conducive to effective family functioning and to optimum individual development.

These three points on the continuum can be represented conceptually by three different poems.

Family Separateness
(Extreme)

> I do my thing, and you do your thing
> I am not in this world to live up to your
>   expectations
> And you are not in this world to live up to
>   mine
> You are you and I am I
> And if by chance we meet, it's beautiful
> If not, it can't be helped.
> — *Fritz Perls*

Family Connectedness
(Extreme)

> We do our thing together
> I am here to meet all your needs and
>   expectations
> And you are here to meet mine
> We had to meet, and it was beautiful
> I can't imagine it turning out any other way.
> — *Jerry Gillies*

A Separate-Connectedness
(Balanced)

> Sing and dance together and be joyous,
>   but let each one of you be alone

Even as the strings of a lute are alone
   though they quiver with the same music
And stand together yet not too near together;
For the pillars of the temple stand apart,
And the oak tree and the cypress grow
   not in each other's shadow
But let there be spaces in your togetherness
And let the winds of the heavens dance
   between you.

—*Kahlil Gibran*

Some specific variables that can be used to assess the degree of family cohesion are: *emotional bonding, boundaries, coalitions, time, space, friends, decision making,* and *interests and recreation.* It is hypothesized that when the levels of cohesion are balanced, there will be a more functional balance of the issues identified and the family will deal more effectively with situational stress and developmental change. Because of differences in cultural norms, it is possible for some families to operate at these extremes without problems. However, these extreme patterns are more problematic in the long run for most families who are acculturated to the norms in this society.

The significance of the cohesion dimension in our culture is attested to by the large number of terms from several different disciplines that refer to cohesion or to a concept relating to one extreme of this dimension. Psychiatrists, family therapists, family sociologists, small-group theorists, group therapists, social psychologists, and anthropologists have all utilized the cohesion dimension in their work.

Psychiatric Definitions

With a few exceptions (i.e., Olson, 1979; Hess & Handel, 1959; Rosenblatt et al., 1979), all of the recent terms describing family cohesion have been developed by psychiatrists specializing in family therapy. Most of the terms describe the two extremes of the cohesion dimension, with less attention given to the middle range, owing in large part no doubt to the fact that these extremes are more representative of the kinds of families seen by the psychiatrists who developed many of these concepts. The clinician's concern with extremely high family cohesion is also expressed in a recent report by the Group for the Advancement of Psychiatry (GAP) on the *Treatment of Families in Conflict* (1970), which reported that a primary goal of 87 percent of family therapists (N = 290) was to improve the autonomy and individuation of family members.

It is no historical accident that most of these recent concepts were developed by psychiatrists working with clinic families, within a general systems orientation, primarily describing families of schizophrenics. While the originators of these concepts shared a common interest in family-oriented treatment and a focus on families of schizophrenics, they each developed their own terminology — even when the professionals were working in the same town or even in the same building. For example, the extreme of family togetherness was described by Wynne et al. (1958) as "pseudomutuality," by Bowen (1960) as "undifferentiated family ego mass," by Stierlin (1974) as "binding," and by Reiss (1971a) as "consensus-sensitive families." All of these psychiatrists worked in the same Adult Psychiatry Branch of NIMH during the same 10-year period. Murray Bowen and Lyman Wynne first worked there together; Helm Stierlin and David Reiss later worked at NIMH while Lyman Wynne was director; and they each became acting directors after Wynne left the branch.

Wynne et al. (1958) were among the first to note that some families, particularly those with a schizophrenic, have a predominant concern with fitting together at the expense of developing personal identities, a process they called *pseudomutuality.*

> In pseudo-mutuality the subjective tension aroused by divergence or independence of expectations, including the open affirmation of a sense of personal identity, is experienced as not merely disruption of that particular transaction but as possibly demolishing the entire relation. (p. 207)

Stierlin (1974) clarified the struggle to balance separateness and togetherness in families by identifying two opposing forces: High family cohesion can be viewed as *centripetal force* pulling family members toward one another into an intellectual and emotional "oneness." This cohesiveness is contrasted with the *centrifugal force,* which pulls family members away from the family system. Stierlin identified three transactional modes that characterize parent-adolescent relationships. Two of these modes *(binding* and *delegating)* are centripetal, and the third *(expelling)* is centrifugal. These modes are generally functional for families but become dysfunctional when they are inappropriately timed or so excessively intense that only one extreme predominates. He proposes, in essence, that a family system operates most effectively when these two opposing forces operate in a more or less balanced manner.

Considerable interest in extremely high family cohesion continues, as witnessed by recent articles in the literature (Schaffer, 1964; Hoffman, 1975; Karpel, 1976; Klugman, 1976; Haley, 1980; Stanton & Todd, 1982). Hoffman describes the dysfunctional nature of enmeshed or too richly cross-joined family systems. Minuchin (1974, p. 248) calls attention to the often overlooked point that dyadic groupings have difficulty functioning in enmeshed family systems because of interference from another (third or fourth) party: "Dyadic transactions rarely occurred. They become triadic or group transactions that promoted a sense of vagueness and confusion in all family members." Weak family coalitions and parent-child coalitions characterize disengaged and enmeshed family systems, respectively. A strong marital coalition correlates with balanced family cohesion. In this regard Satir (1964, p. 1) states that

> the parents are the architects of the family and the *marriage relationship* is the key to all other *family relationships*. When there is difficulty with the marital pair, there is [sic] more than likely problems in parenting.

Karpel (1976) proposed a model that describes how individuals deal with the duality of distance (the "I") and relation (the "we") and how these strategies vary at different stages of maturity (immature, transitional, and mature). In the immature stage, individuals deal with distance by being "unrelated" or by relating only through pure fusion. Only in the mature stage can individuals maintain both relation (through dialogue) and distance (through individuation). The importance of this "I" versus "We" balance in mature relationships is emphasized in that individuation and dialogue facilitate each other.

Low cohesion has also been described by psychiatrists with a variety of terms, including emotional divorce (Bowden, 1960), disengagement (Minuchin, 1974), pseudohostility (Wynne et al., 1958), and expelling (Stierlin, 1974).

Sociological Definitions

Family sociologists have also identified the cohesion dimension in their work. An early example is Angell (1936), who identified both "family integration" and "family adaptability" (which relates directly to the dimension of family adaptability used in this study) as key elements of cohesion. Hill (1949) also combined the variables of "adaptability" and "integration" to assess dynamic stability in his study of families under stress from war separation and reunion. Hess and Handel (1959) used this concept, calling the extremes "separateness" and "connectedness," as the central theme of their middle-range theory of family behavior. Nye and Rushing (1969) identified six aspects of family solidarity that are conceptually similar to what we are calling family cohesiveness. These six dimensions are associational integration, affectual integration, consensual integration, functional integration, normative integration, and goal integration. Three of these (associational solidarity, affectual solidarity, and consensual solidarity) were later empirically investigated by Bergtson and Black (1973).

Another sociologist, Colette Carisse (1975), developed a typology of leisure styles that utilizes cohesion as one of the major dimensions. The two extremes of her model are similar to those of others. Extreme togetherness is defined as "pathogenic pursuit of consensus, or total identification," and extreme separateness as "pathogenic pursuit of interpersonal distance" (p. 195).

Small-Group Definitions

The cohesion dimension has been used by small-group theorists and researchers to describe ad hoc groupings. They have often used the term "solidarity," defined as the members' attraction to the group (Festinger, Schachter, & Back, 1950; Fiedler & Neuwese, 1965; Thibault & Kelly, 1967). Cartwright and Zander (1962, p. 10) described cohesion as "the resultant of all the forces acting on all the members to remain in the group."

After working with ad hoc groups of individuals in counseling, Yalom (1970) emphasized the importance of cohesion as a therapeutic factor in group psychotherapy. He described "group cohesion" as a precondition for effective treatment and reviewed the relevant literature supporting this idea. He also developed his own scale and found it to be related to positive outcomes in group psychotherapy. He concluded that "cohesiveness is a widely researched, poorly understood, basics property of groups" (p. 37).

Social-Psychiatric Definitions

Social psychologists interested in the family as a small group have also identified the cohesion dimension. Levinger (1965) discusses marital cohesiveness and marital dissolution, utilizing a definition of cohesion similar to that of small group research. He sees marital cohesion as a special case of group cohesion. Marital cohesion is described as a direct function of psychological attraction and barrier forces inside the marriage and is inversely related to the attractiveness of alternative relationships.

Anthropological Definitions

Paul Rosenblatt, whose orientation includes both social psychology and anthropology as applied to the family, has described "togetherness" (time together) and "apartness" (time apart) as the extremes between which families need to find an optimal balance. Basing his work on the fact that American norms assume family togetherness, he has identified the ways in which families avoid togetherness while appearing to be together. Rosenblatt and Titus (1976) described how family members legitimate being away from home and isolate themselves from each other when they are at home. Rosenblatt and Budd (1975) demonstrated how territoriality and privacy are maintained in married versus unmarried cohabiting couples. In another study, Rosenblatt and Russell (1975) described the problems that families have during vacations and how they cope with this pressured togetherness.

Anthropologists have also described the significance of togetherness in our culture in contrast to other cultures (Stephens, 1963). Some cultures maintain such separateness in the family that the husband and wife do not live, sleep, or even eat together. Although our culture encourages individual freedom and autonomy, it also espouses the normative belief that couples and families should spend considerable time together as a unit.

In conclusion, this conceptual review of the literature from various fields demonstrates that the cohesion dimension is an important aspect of both ad hoc and family groups. The relevance of the dimension to several social science disciplines provides a type of cross-validation of its salience and significance. The most recent interest in the dimension has come, however, from family therapists, who have developed numerous concepts that relate primarily to the extreme ends of the dimension. Cohesion, therefore, is one of the two central dimensions for developing the Circumplex Model of Marital and Family Systems.

BALANCE AND COHESION

An important issue in the Circumplex Model relates to the definition of *balance*. The model postulates that a balance on the dimensions is related to more adequate family functioning. Even though a balanced family system is placed at the two central levels of the model, it should not be assumed that these families always operate in a moderate manner. Being balanced means a family system can experience the extremes on the dimensions when appropriate, but they do not typically function at these extremes for long periods of time. For example, families in the central area of the cohesion dimension allow family members to experience being both independent from and connected to their family. Both extremes are tolerated and expected, provided an individual does not continually function at the extreme. Conversely, extreme family types tend to function only at the extremes and members are not expected or able to change their behaviors. As a result, the more balanced family types have a larger behavior repertoire and are more able to change compared to extreme family types.

Family Adaptability

One of the major contributions of general systems theory (von Bertalanffy, 1968; Buckley, 1967) to the family field is that it has demonstrated the value of system adaptability. In describing sociocultural systems like the family, Buckley identifies the significance of both positive and negative feedback (following Maruyama's [1963] distinction of these concepts). Positive feedback provides the family system with constructive, system-enhancing behaviors that enable the system to grow, create, innovate, and change, i.e., system *morphogenesis.* Conversely, negative feedback attempts to maintain the status quo, i.e., system *morphostasis.*

MORPHOGENESIS AND MORPHOSTASIS: CHANGE AND STABILITY

Much of the early theorizing about family systems was done by family therapists who viewed families as primarily morphostatic (Haley, 1959, 1962, 1963; Lederer & Jackson, 1968; Lennard & Berstein, 1969; Riskin, 1963; Jackson, 1957; Satir, 1964). This position was most clearly identified in Haley's (1959, p. 281) First Law of Relationships, which suggests that family systems function primarily to maintain the status quo.

When an organism indicates a change in relations to another, the other will act upon the first so as to diminish and modify the change.

Viewing the family solely as maintenance oriented, however, is restrictive and misleading. Speer (1970), Hill (1971), and Wertheim (1973, 1975) have recently been critical of this morphostatic view of the family system. To be sure, past theorizing has been fruitful in exploring the organization and functioning of families with severely disturbed members. It has enabled professionals to understand family behavior as rule governed and to recognize that the "deviance" of the identified patient often serves the useful homeostatic function of keeping the family together. However, analysis of the full range of normal family interaction is restricted by this morphostatic model of family systems. It has serious limitations in predicting the interaction in any study of nonclinic families. Certainly it does not speak to the current focus on the growth and development in families. We agree with Speer (1970, p. 261) that

> at a time when there is an ever-increasing interest and conceptual investment in interpersonal growth, changing basic social structures and institutions, social innovation, and creativity, there is something paradoxical and incongrument about a family systems approach based on change-resistant or change-minimizing concepts.

Wynne et al. (1958, p. 89) go much further, suggesting that a rigid status-quo orientation is indicative of pathology.

> Families that rigidly try to maintain homeostasis through successive developmental phases are highly disturbed and atypical. Enduring success in maintaining family homeostasis perhaps should be regarded as a distinctive feature of *disorder* in families.

Both morphogenesis (change) and morphostasis (stability) are therefore hypothesized to be necessary for a viable family system. For this reason, the conceptualization of functional and dysfunctional families offered by Miller (1969) is also inadequate. He suggests that the end points on a family functionality-dysfunctionality continuum be defined in terms of morphostatic processes at the dysfunctional end and morphogenic or growth processes at the functional end.

While we agree with Miller that morphogenesis and morphostasis are extremes on the adaptability dimension, we maintain that both of these extremes are dysfunctional to families if they can only function at these extremes. The most viable family systems are those that maintain a *balance* between both morphogenesis and morphostasis. In times of stress families may require greater change while still maintaining some degree of stability. However, no viable system can function effectively for extended periods in morphogenesis. As Wertheim (1973, p. 365) stated:

> Without some optimal degree of morphostasis, the family system could not survive as a cohesive, viable social unit. Extreme morphogenesis, tantamount to constant change, would preclude building up of even a minimal set of common meanings, values and expectations, essential for communication and the survival of an intimate, face-to-face group.

Wertheim also makes a helpful distinction between "forced" morphostasis and "consensual" morphostasis. The former refers to *apparent stability* in the family system maintained in the absence of genuine consensual validation by its members. It contributes to intrafamily and individual alienation and to disturbed system functioning. The morphostasis found in families with schizophrenic members is an example of forced morphostasis. Consensual morphostasis refers to *"genuine stability* of the family system, consensually validated by its members" (1973, p. 365). As an example, Wertheim notes Ferreira and Winters's (1963, 1965, 1966) finding that spontaneous cognitive congruence is higher among normal than abnormal families.

In the last few years, the focus has shifted to morphogenic forces within the family system. Hoffman (1981) has integrated the writings of many system theorists who have broken away from the cybernetic model. She tracks the thinking of Ashby (1960), Bateson (1979), and Dell (1980), who extrapolates on the concept of "evolutionary feedback." This term describes the basic nonequilibrium ordering principle that governs the forming and unfolding of systems at all levels.

The family development approach (Hill, 1971; Hill & Rodgers, 1964) is highly compatible with modern systems theory and our formulations. This approach sees families as capable of change, adaptation, and a reordering of their structures. Given the continuing shifts in age and composition and the need for the redefinition of rules, a family locked into a rigid equilibrial or morphostatic pattern is in trouble. Families must be able to adapt to such normal transition crises (Rappoport, 1962) as parenthood, placement of children in school, the encouragement and acceptance of autonomy in adolescence, the launching of children, and adjustment to retirement. The family development approach has recently been expanded in several family therapy models. Strategic family therapists such as Haley (1980) have highlighted the life-cycle notion in terms of the critical transition points with which families often have difficulty. From the Bohemian camp, Carter and McGoldrick (1980) have proposed a series of developmental tasks that families must master in order to achieve an adequate functioning level in preparation for the following life-cycle stage.

CONCEPTUAL DEFINITION AND SIGNIFICANCE OF FAMILY ADAPTABILITY

Adaptability as defined in this book is *the ability of a marital/family system to change its power structure, role relationships, and relationship rules in response to situational and developmental stress.* The specific variables that are of interest in terms of this dimension are *family power structure* (assertiveness and control), *negotiation styles, role relationships* and *relationship rules,* and *feedback* (positive and negative).

Basically, the most viable family systems are those in the two central levels of the adaptability dimension (see Figure 4.1). It is hypothesized that when there is a more free-flowing balance between morphogenesis and morphostasis, there will be a mutually assertive style of communicating, egalitarian leadership, successful negotiation, positive and negative feedback loops, role sharing and role making, and rule making, with few implicit rules and more explicit rules. Conversely, dysfunctional family systems will fall at the extremes of these variables.

Our definition of adaptability is highly compatible with the definition of family systems proposed by Wertheim (1973, 1975, p. 286). She states that

> an ideal, adaptive family system can be conceptualized as one characterized by an optimal, socio-culturally appropriate balance between stability-promoting, "self-corrective" processes, or *morphostasis* and change-promoting, "self-directive" processes, or morphogenesis.

However, our definition of adaptive family systems is more concrete and specific, for it relates to concepts that can be operationally defined and measured. For example, Angell (1936) identified family adaptability as a significant dimension in understanding family success in coping with the stress of prolonged unemployment. Hill (1949) utilized this concept in his study of war separation and reunion and found that highly adaptable families had the best adjustment to both stressor events.

Family adaptability has been defined as an important dimension by other theorists. In an excellent discussion of family adaptability, referred to as "famila spongia," Clark Vincent (1966) points out that this aspect of the family is often overlooked. He maintains that this function is vital to rapidly changing societies because it serves the mediating function between individuals and other social structures. He states that

> the rapid and pervasive social changes associated with industrialization necessitate a family system that both structurally and functionally is highly adaptive externally to the demands of other social institutions and internally to the needs of its own members. (p. 29)

In another article on family adaptability, Kieren and Tallman (1971, 1972, p. 248) define this dimension more as an individual property: "a spouse's ability to deal effectively with a problematic situation by changing roles and strategies in terms of new or modified assessments of the situation to which he/she is confronted." They maintain that spousal adaptability is composed of three interrelated concepts — flexibility, empathy, and motivation — and they have developed scales for measuring these concepts (1971).

The family therapy literature also speaks to the importance of focusing on the adaptability dimension. A primary goal of the family therapists surveyed (N = 290) by the 1970 GAP report is the provision of more flexible leadership (66 percent) and improved role agreement (64 percent) in the families they treat. Both leadership and role relationships are important aspects of the adaptability dimension.

In summary, the family adaptability dimension appears to be one of considerable interest to family theorists and family therapists. However, there have been a few attempts to clarify conceptually or integrate this dimension with other relevant family concepts.

Family Communication

Communication is generally accepted as one of the most crucial facets of interpersonal relationships. Its prominence in the theoretical construction of interpersonal and family interactions attests to its great importance. Goffman (1959) viewed communication as central to the symbolic presentations that comprise all human interactions. Communication is also important from the viewpoint of family development theory (Nunnally, 1971; Miller, 1971; Corrales, 1974), but its importance is perhaps most fully recognized by systems theory (Buckley, 1967; Russell, 1979). Information is exchanged within and between family systems utilizing established channels of communication. Virginia Satir (1972) writes that "communication is the greatest single factor affecting a person's health and his relationship to others."

In one of the most detailed elaborations of the role of communication in human interactions, *The Pragmatics of Human Communication* (1967), Watzlawick, Beavin, and Jackson define a family as a rule-governed system whose members are continually in the process of negotiating or defining the nature of their relationships. Lewis and Spaniers's (1979) theory of marital quality postulates that effective interspousal communication contributes to the rewards each spouse experiences in his or her interactions.

Moving to a less abstract level, the significance of effective communication between spouses and within families has been recognized by therapists, researchers, and family life educators. Broderick (1976) cited the important diagnostic function of communication and the need to focus on family communication patterns. In their review of recent trends in marriage therapy and divorce, Paolino and McCrady (1978) recommended communication training as an effective initial intervention for mild to moderate marital problems. Further evidence of the belief that good communication skills are crucial to satisfaction with family relationships is offered by large numbers of people involved in the marriage and family enrichment movement who incorporate communication skill training into their enrichment programs (Mace, 1977; Travis & Travis, 1975; Sherwood & Sherer, 1975; Regula, 1975; Miller, Corrales, & Wackman, 1975; Hinkle & Moore, 1971; Schlein, 1971; D'Augelli, Deyss, Guerney, Hershenberg, & Sborlsky, 1974; Van Zoost, 1973; Campbell, 1974; Carnes & Laube, 1975; Miller, 1971; Nunnally, 1971). Dysfunctional patterns of communication have been identified with particular kinds of family systems. L'Abate (1980) integrated Satir's (1972) typology of incongruent communication patterns with various models of individual and family problems.

Despite the widely acclaimed importance of communication to family relationships found in the writings of theorists and family practitioners, research into the nature of family communication presents some challenging difficulties. One of the main difficulties is the complexity of family communication, which presents a wide variety of aspects on which researchers might focus. Due to this variety of formulations and consequent variety of operational definitions, few family communica-

TABLE 4.2   Studies of Family Communication

Researcher(s)	Aspect of Communication	How Measured	Who Measured
Navran (1967)	Communication in general	Self-report	Each spouse
Levinger & Senn (1967)	Self-disclosure	Self-report	Each spouse
Cutler & Dyer (1965)	Selective response to violations of expectations by their spouse	Self-report	Each spouse
Jorgensen & Gaudy (1980)	Relationship of self-disclosure to marital satisfaction	Self-report	Each spouse Reports of other spouse Couple scores
Hawkins, Weisberg, & Ray (1980)	Communication styles	Self-report Observation	Each spouse Reports of other spouse Independent observers
Powers & Hutchinson (1979)	Communication apprehension	Self-report	Each spouse

tion studies are directly comparable. Communication has been studied as a general construct (Navran, 1967); as self-disclosure (Jourard, 1971; Jorgensen & Gaudy, 1980); as a skill-learning process during therapy (Schreiber, 1966); in terms of different styles or patterns of interaction (Corrales, 1974; Miller, 1974; Hawkins, Weisberg, & Ray, 1980); in terms of specific components such as empathy, congruence, and regard (Schumm, 1980; Epstein & Jackson, 1978; Miller, 1971; Nunnally, 1971; Barrett-Lennard, 1962); or in terms of couples' hesitancy to communicate within the context of a close interpersonal relationship (Powers & Hutchinson, 1979). In addition to these approaches, many other researchers have developed scales to measure the particular aspect of communication in which they were interested (Hobart & Klausner, 1959; Van der Veen, 1976; Moos, 1974; Bienvenu, 1970; Olson et al., 1982).

Table 4.2 summarizes some of the studies of interspousal and intrafamily communication. Most studies of communication have relied exclusively on self-report data without any attempt to measure or reconcile the differing perceptions of additional family members. Further, most studies have focused on communication in the spousal relationship only.

Hypotheses Derived From the Circumplex Model

One of the assets of a theoretical model is that hypotheses can be deduced and tested in order to evaluate and further develop the model. The following are hypotheses derived from the model.

Hypothesis 1: *Couples/families with balanced (two central levels) cohesion and adaptability will generally function more adequately across the family life cycle than will those at the extremes of these dimensions.*

An important issue in the Circumplex Model relates to the definition of balance. The model postulates that a balance on the dimensions is related to more adequate family functioning. Even though a balanced family system is located on the two central levels of the model, it should not be assumed that these families always operate in a "moderate" manner. Being balanced means a family system can experience the extremes on the dimension when appropriate but that they do not typically function at these extremes for long periods of time.

Hypothesis 2: *Balanced families have larger behavioral repertoires and are more able to change compared to extreme families.*

Families in the balanced area of the cohesion dimension ("separated" and "connected") allow family members to experience being both independent from and connected to their family. Families in the balanced area of adaptability ("structured" and "flexible") allow family members to be chaotic at times but with some degree of stability. Both extremes are tolerated and expected, but the family does not continually function only at the extremes and are not encouraged to change the way they function as a family.

Hypothesis 1 postulates a *curvilinear* relationship between the dimensions of cohesion and adaptability and effective family functioning. An alternative hypothesis (Hypothesis 3) relates to couples and families whose normative expectations support extreme behavior on these dimensions.

INTEGRATING NORMATIVE EXPECTATIONS OF FAMILIES

Hypothesis 3: *If the normative expectations of a couple or family support behaviors on one of both extremes of the circumplex dimen-*

sions, it will function well as long as all family members accept these expectations.

Although a curvilinear relationship is generally predicted, some important qualifications must be made in terms of the *normative expectations* and *cultural* bias of Hypothesis 1.

The normative expectations in our culture provide two conflicting themes that can create problems for couples and families. One theme is that family members are expected to do things together as a family; the second theme encourages individuals to "do their own thing." The theme of independence becomes more prominent as children approach adolescence and has taken on greater importance for increasing numbers of women in our culture. As a result, it has become difficult for many American families to balance these two themes.

Families in our culture still vary greatly in the extent to which they encourage and support individual development in ways that may differ from the family's values. While parents probably prefer that their children develop values and ideas similar to theirs, most parents allow their children to become somewhat autonomous and differentiated from the family system.

However, a sizable minority of families have normative expectations that strongly emphasize family togetherness, often at the expense of individuation from the family system. Their family norms stress emotional and physical togetherness, and they strive for high levels of consensus and loyalty. Such American ethnic groups as Slovak-Americans (Stein, 1978), Puerto Ricans (Minuchin, Montalvo, Guerney, Rossman, & Schumer, 1967) and Italians (Goetzel, 1973), as well as religious groups such as the Amish (Wittmer, 1973) and Mormons (Schvaneveldt, 1973), have high expectations regarding family togetherness. These expectations are also common, but less predominant, in many other American families, regardless of their ethnic or religious orientation. Many of these families could be described as extreme on the cohesion dimension (i.e., enmeshed), and they function well as long as all family members are willing to go along with those expectations.

FAMILY COMMUNICATION: A FACILITATING DIMENSION

Communication is a critical element of the Circumplex Model because it facilitates movement on the cohesion and adaptability dimensions. This leads to two specific hypotheses linking communication to balanced types and change on cohesion and adaptability.

Hypothesis 4: *Balanced couples/families will tend to have more positive communication skills than Extreme families.*

Hypothesis 5: *Positive communication skills will enable Balanced couples/families to change their levels of cohesion and adaptability more easily than those at the Extremes.*

In general, positive communication skills are seen as helping marital and family systems facilitate and maintain a balance on the two dimensions. Conversely, negative communication skills prevent and minimize marital and family systems from moving into the central areas and, thereby, increase the probability that extreme systems will remain extreme.

Positive communication skills include sending clear and congruent messages, empathy, supportive statements, and effective problem-solving skills. Conversely, *negative* communication skills include sending incongruent and disqualifying messages, lack of empathy, nonsupportive (negative) statements, poor problem-solving skills, and paradoxical and double-binding messages (Olson, 1972). Although many studies have investigated communication and problem-solving skills in couples (Vincent, Weiss, & Birchler, 1975; Sprenkle & Olson, 1978) and in families (Alexander & Barton, 1976; Guerney, 1976; Patterson, 1976), these studies have not specifically tested the relationship of these skills to the hypotheses derived from the Circumplex Model.

FAMILY DEVELOPMENT AND THE CIRCUMPLEX MODEL

Hypothesis 6: *To deal with situational stress and developmental changes across the life cycle, Balanced families will change their cohesion and adaptability whereas Extreme families will resist change over time.*

This hypothesis addresses the issue of change in the family system in response to stress or to accommodate changes in family members, particularly as family members change their expectations. The Circumplex Model is dynamic in that it assumes that individuals and family systems will change, and it hypothesizes that change can be beneficial to the maintenance and improvement of family functioning.

The model is dynamic in that it assumes that changes can occur in family types over time. Families are free to move in any direction that the situation, stage of the family life cycle, or socialization of family members may require. A retrospective look at a family illustrates the dynamic nature of the model.

Steve and Sally were both raised in rather traditional homes. Three years after they were married, they became parents for the first time, and Sally resigned from her teaching job. Because of the dependency needs of their son and their own desire for mutual support during this transition period, they developed a moderately high, but not extreme, level of family cohesion (connected). Also, their upbringing led them to be moderately low, but not rigid, on the adaptability dimension (structured). They were comfortable with a rather traditional, husband-dominant power structure and segregated role relationship, preferring the relative security of these established patterns to the difficulties of continually negotiating them. According to the model, their family type would be described as *structurally connected,* an option that seemed to be satisfying to them at the time.

Years later when Sally and Steve's son became a teenager, Sally began to pursue a career. Both parents experienced a good deal of "consciousness raising" about sex roles through the media and through involvement in several growth groups. Because of their son's needs for more autonomy at this age, as well as the parents' separate career interests, they began operating at a lower level of cohesiveness, moving from being connected to being more separated.

Furthermore, the family power structure shifted from husband dominant to a more shared pattern. Sally exercised much more control in the relationship than previously, and the couple struggled almost on a weekly basis to redefine the rules and role relationship that govern their relationship. Although they occasionally yearn for the security of their earlier, more structured relationship, both find excitement and challenge in this more flexible relationship style. In short, *flexibly separated* best describes their current family organizational pattern.

This brief case history illustrates the dynamic nature of the model, which allows for movement within reasonable limits. It also seeks to recognize diverse values and legitimizes the various organizational ideals of families.

When one family member desires change, the family system must deal with this request. For example, increasing numbers of married women want to develop more autonomy from their husbands (cohesion dimension) and also want more power and equality in their relationships (adaptability dimension). If their husbands are unwilling to understand and change in accordance with these expectations, the marriages will probably experience increased amounts of stress. Another common example of changing expectations is when a child reaches adolescence. Like the wife in the previous example, adolescents often want more freedom, independence, and power in the family system.

The Circumplex Model allows one to integrate systems theory with family development, a proposal made more than a decade ago by Reuben Hill (1971). Building on the family development approach described by Hill and Rodgers (1964), it is hypothesized that families must change as they deal with normal transitions in the family. It is expected, therefore, that the stage of the family life cycle and composition of the family will have considerable impact on the type of family system that exists.

It is hypothesized that at any stage of the family life cycle, there will be a diversity in types of family systems as described in the Circumplex Model. In spite of this diversity, it is predicted that families will cluster together in some types more frequently than in others at different stages of the family life cycle.

In order to test some specific hypotheses, seven stages in this study were collapsed into four. The four new stages were called *Couples Without Children, Families with Children, Families with Adolescents,* and *Older Couples.* The first stage remains unchanged and includes young couples without children. Stages 2 and 3 were combined to form the new stage of families with young children to the ages of twelve years. Stages 4 and 5 were combined to form the adolescent stage, and Stages 6 and 7 were combined to form the older couple group.

At the four newly created stages for this analysis, the following general hypotheses from the Circumplex Model were suggested (Olson et al., 1980). At the Young Couple stage, it was proposed that the couples would tend to fall into the upper-right quadrant of the model. It was also hypothesized that Families with Children would initially tend to fall into this quadrant and then would move to the lower-right quadrant. It was hypothesized that at the Adolescent stage, families that function well would fall into the Balanced types. With Older Couples it was hypothesized that the nondistressed couples would fall into the Balanced area and that distressed couples would be in the lower-left or -right quadrant. These hypotheses will be examined in more detail in Chapter X.

Empirical Studies Combining Cohesion and Adaptability

While there are numerous studies that have studied either cohesion or adaptability (see Olson et al., 1980), this review focuses on studies that incorporated *both* dimensions. There is evidence from these studies that significant gains are made utilizing both dimensions simultaneously. This enables one to classify couples or families into *types,* as has been done within the Circumplex Model.

The first major family study to include both family cohesion and adaptability and to combine them into family types is Angell's (1936) classic book, *The Family Encounters the Depression.* His two central concepts were "family integration," which is very similar to cohesion, and "family adaptability." He defined integration as "the bonds of coherence and unity running through family life, of which common interests, affection, and a sense of economic interdependence are perhaps the most prominent" (p. 15). Family adaptability related to how the family functioned as a unit, their flexibility in meeting difficulties, the family's readiness to adjust to changes, and its manner to making decisions.

Dividing families into high, medium, and low categories on the two dimensions, he formed nine types of families — eight of which he located empirically and described. The conceptual and empirical value of forming family types was discovered after trying many other analyses using single variables and combinations of other variables. The importance of this discovery seemed obvious after it was made (a common characteristic of most discoveries). In this regard, Angell (1936, p. 290) stated that

> I am ashamed of the fact that I did not see clearly from the start that integration alone would be no basis for predicting the effect of a decrease in income from accustomed sources. It seems now perfectly obvious that if one wished to define types in relation to a change of any kind, flexibility or adaptability with reference to that change was a very important consideration.

In two subsequent studies, Reuben Hill used both integration and adaptability and combined them into a measure he called "dynamic stability." Hill (1949) studied *Families Under Stress* to learn how 135 families dealt with war separation and reunion. He also formed family types by cross-classifying family integration and adaptability. He concluded that "taken as a whole, family integration is highly significant in predicting success both in separation and reunion, but . . . its relationship is higher with reunion adjustments than separation adjustments. The most highly integrated families did best in reunion and second best in separation" (p. 132). Family adaptability related more directly to family adjustment to separation than to reunion. The most adaptable families were not the most successful in adjusting to these two situations. In the typological analysis that combined integration and adaptability, it was found that the medium integration and high adaptability types had the best overall adjustment to both reunion and separation.

Hill, Moss, and Wirths (1953) also used these two dimensions in a study of personal and family adjustments to rapid urbanization in a monograph entitled *Eddyville's Families*. Although cross-classification was done with adaptability and other variables, it was not done with integration.

There are few conceptual and empirical studies following up on these early studies that used cohesion and adaptability. Only recently, in a series of studies of military separation by Hamilton McCubbin and colleagues, has there been an attempt to build upon and extend the classic studies of Angell and Hill. McCubbin et al. (1975, 1976, 1977, 1979, 1982) and Boss (1979; Boss, McCubbin, & Lester, 1980), examining occupationally (military and business) induced family separations, underscore the central importance of family adaptability and cohesiveness. They arrived at this conclusion by focusing on the coping behaviors and coping patterns that families employ in the management of stress.

Adaptability and integration emerged as significant factors in three additional studies. A study by McCubbin, Boss, Wilson, & Lester (1979) found in a second-order factor analysis that wives' coping behaviors focused on two dimensions: (1) maintaining family integrity and integration and (2) promoting individual member's independence and self-sufficiency. In summary, they found that the management of family stress involves maintaining a delicate balance between individual development and growth *and* family unity and integration.

A study that demonstrated empirically that cohesion and adaptability are underlying dimensions in assessing family behavior was conducted by van der Veen (1976). He developed the Family Concepts Test (FCT), which contained a nontheoretical set of eighty items that were thought to provide a comprehensive picture of family dynamics. This scale focused on an individual's perception of attitudes, feelings, and expectations toward his or her family to obtain a "family concept" that was analogous to the self-concept. This FCT was administered, using the Q-sort technique, to a large sample of families (parents, adolescents, and siblings) in which some adolescents were disturbed and others were nondisturbed. Using factor analysis to condense the eighty items, fifteen first-order factors with eigenvalues greater than 1 were found. After a second-order factor analysis, the two higher-order dimensions that emerged were *family integration* and *adaptive coping*. Family integration was very similar to cohesion and it was composed of the following first-order factors: family loyalty, togetherness versus separateness, consideration versus conflict, open communication, and closeness versus estrangement. Adaptive coping, which is similar to the adaptability dimension, was composed of the following first-order factors: family actualization, community sociability, and locus of control. The similarity of these second-order factors to the circumplex dimensions is noteworthy since the item pool was not constructed with any theoretical orientation in mind.

Van der Veen's (1976) findings and those of earlier studies (Novak & van der Veen, 1970; van der Veen, 1965) are also very congruent with the hypothesized relationships derived from the Circumplex Model. Members of disturbed families had lower family concepts than did members of nondisturbed families on all of the adaptive coping factors and the first three factors of family integration.

In order to assess what variables would distinguish healthy family functioning from problem functioning, Westley and Epstein (1969) studied 1970 college students and 88 families in Canada. The major variables on which they focused were *problem solving, power, authority,* and *roles,* which are related to the adaptability dimension of the Circumplex Model, and the development of *autonomy,* which is related to family cohesion. They found that the quality of harmony of the husband-wife relationship was critical for the emotional health of the adolescent. Children from mother-dominated and father-dominated homes had more emotional problems and fewer strengths, whereas those from father-led and democratic families had few problems and major strengths. Autonomy dealt with the extent to which individual family members could make their own decisions and were differentiated from the family system. Families that encouraged autonomy had significantly more emotionally healthy adolescents than those that minimized it. This study demonstrates again the importance of the variables related to these two circumplex dimensions.

In a rather systematic study of family interaction with healthy and patient families, Lewis et al. (1976) developed the Family System Rating Scales, which contain several of the variables central to the cohesion and adaptability dimensions in the Circumplex Model. Their sample consisted of 33 nonpatient families and 70 patient families with one member having one of the following three symptoms: behavior disorders (45), psychoses (18), and neuroses (7). Family members were videotaped while they were completing five interaction tasks: (1) discussing what they disagreed about, (2) planning something together, (3) discussing the greatest pain in the relationship, (4) discussing placement of family members on a Family Closeness Board, and (5) discussing family strengths.

The *Family System Rating Scale* (FSRS) used to rate the videotapes has thirteen subscales that relate to the Circumplex Model in the following ways: cohesion dimension (closeness, coalitions, and autonomy — four scales); adaptability dimension (power and negotiation); communication dimension (affect — four scales; Mythology). Their findings are complicated by low interrater reliabilities in part caused by the confusing operational definitions of the variables. However, by using sum scores across these scales, the researchers did obtain interesting findings. The sum total of the FSRS correlated very closely to the one-item Global Family Health-Pathology Scale ($r = .90$), even though that scale also had low interrater reliability. The FSRS also correlated with the sum of the Gossett-Timerlawn Adolescent Psychopathology Scale ($r = .42$); the FSRS intercorrelations with the subscales of this measure were very low but significant. In general, this research was an ambitious study of family interaction and demonstrated the value of the cohesion, adaptability, and communication dimensions in discriminating types of family systems.

Moos and Moos (1976) utilized a Family Environment Scale (FES) with 100 families and identified six typologies of families using cluster analysis of mean scores on family members. Of the ten concepts assessed by the FES, several related directly to the cohesion and adaptability dimensions. The cohesion dimension was measured by two scales (cohesion and independence), adaptability was assessed by two scales (control and organization), and the communication dimension was measured by two scales (expressiveness and conflict). While the scale has been useful in some studies (Druckman, 1979; Fuhr, Moos, & Dishotsky, 1981; Bell & Bell, 1982), a study by Russell (1980) found that the FES lacked construct validity for family cohesion.

In order to determine how important family cohesion, family adaptability, and family communication concepts are to healthy family functioning and as goals for family therapy, Fisher and Sprenkle (1977) conducted a survey of 310 marriage and family therapists. These family therapists made ratings and rankings on the ten family cohesion concepts, seven family adaptability concepts, and seventeen family communication concepts in terms of how important these concepts were to (1) healthy family functioning and (2) goals for guiding their therapeutic interventions with couples and families.

Considering *healthy family functioning*, the mean rating for cohesion and adaptability was 3.9; it was 4.0 for communication, indicating that all three dimensions were seen as *very* important (5 = crucial; 4 = very important; 3 = important; 2 = somewhat important; 1 = not important). In the upper third of the ranking were 30 percent of the cohesion concepts, 29 percent of the adaptability concepts, and 35 percent of the communication concepts. Considering the *goals of therapy*, the mean rating for cohesion was 3.6; for adaptability, 4.1; for communication, 4.0, indicating that these three dimensions are *usually* used to guide therapy (5 = always, 4 = usually; 3 = often; 2 = seldom; 1 = never). In addition, there was considerable congruence between the descriptions of healthy family functioning and goals for family treatment on cohesion (r = .54), adaptability (r = .56), and communication (r = .65). In general, this study demonstrated the value of cohesion, adaptability, and communication dimensions for describing healthy family functioning and for setting goals for family intervention.

Fisher, Gibbin, and Hoopes (1982) completed a questionnaire survey of nonclinical family members about their views on the nature of a healthy family compared with family therapists' perceptions (Fisher & Sprenkle, 1978). There were two notable differences between the two groups. Families ranked some items — such as family identification, physical caretaking, emotional attraction, pleasurable interaction, and loyalty — higher than therapists did. Therapists ranked flexibility, shared leadership, and utilizing feedback considerably higher than families did. Generally, families valued cohesion more, whereas therapists placed a higher value on adaptability.

Another study of family therapists found that the cohesion, adaptability, and communication dimensions offered important goals for treatment. The Group for the Advancement of Psychiatry (1970) conducted a survey of family therapists. Of the 290 respondents, 40 percent were social workers, another 40 percent were psychiatrists and psychologists, and the remaining 20 percent were marriage counselors and other helping professionals. These therapists were asked to indicate the primary goals they had for family therapy from a list of eight. *Improved communication* was rated as primary for 85 percent of the therapists; *improved empathy,* (communication) 56 percent; *improved autonomy and individuation* (cohesion), 56 percent; more *flexible leadership* (adaptability), 34 percent; *reduced conflict* (communication), 23 percent; *individual symptomatic improvement,* 23 percent; and *improved individual task performance* (adaptability), 12 percent. It is interesting that all of the goals selected for this study except improved symptomatic improvement related to the cohesion, adaptability, and communication dimensions. Also, 90 percent of the respondents said that *all eight goals* were either of primary or secondary importance for some families. This study, like the one by Fisher and Sprenkle (1977), indicates the importance of these dimensions as goals for family therapy.

In a recent book, Minuchin (1974) emphasized the importance of the disengaged-enmeshed continuum (cohesion dimension), but he also devoted attention to family adaption (adaptability dimension). Not only did he focus directly on these two dimensions in family therapy, but his comments about the dimensions are very congruent with those presented in this book and will, therefore, be highlighted.

Minuchin indicated that while many families tend toward enmeshed and disengaged subsystems at times in the family life cycle, such as an enmeshed mother-child relationship, the subsystems should move toward disengagement as the children grow older. However, systems that continue to function at the extremes of this dimension often have problems. He stated:

> Operations at the extremes, however, indicate areas of possible pathology. A highly enmeshed subsystem of mother and children, for example, can exclude father, who becomes disengaged in the extreme. The resulting undermining of the children's independence might be an important factor in the development of symptoms. . . . Members of disengaged subsystems or families may function autonomously but have a skewed sense of independence and lack feelings of loyalty and belonging and the capacity for interdependence and for requesting support when needed. . . . Both types of relating cause family problems when adaptive mechanisms are evoked. (p. 55)

In describing family adaptation, Minuchin argued that stress often produces the need for family change. He believes that many families in treatment are simply going through transitions and need help in adapting to the new situations. "The label of pathology would be reserved for families who in the face of stress increase the rigidity of their transactional patterns and boundaries, and avoid or resist any exploration of alternative" (p. 60). Stress could be produced because of external or internal pressures in the family. It usually occurs when new members are added to or dropped from the family system, or because of developmental changes in family members, such as when a child becomes an adolescent.

In conclusion, there are a growing number of studies that have found the two circumplex dimensions to be important for understanding marital and family systems. The earliest work by Angell (1936) and Hill (1949; Hill, Moss, & Wirth, 1953) also demonstrated the value of cross-classifying the dimensions to form family types. Their studies and more recent work by McCubbin, Boss, and colleagues have demonstrated how these dimensions help to describe how families deal with stress.

The empirical potency of these dimensions is demonstrated by the fact that they emerged as second-order factors in the Family Concept Test developed by van der Veen (1976). Variables related to the circumplex dimensions were found to be statistically discriminating in several large studies of family interaction conducted by Westley and Epstein (1969), Lewis et al. (1976), and Moos and Moos (1976). The value of these two dimensions to family therapists was specifically investigated by Fisher and colleagues (Fisher & Sprenkle, 1977, 1978; Fisher et al., 1982) and both emerged as useful for describing healthy family functioning and for goals in family therapy. A survey of family therapists (GAP, 1970) also found that variables related to these dimensions were important, and prominent family therapists like Minuchin (1976) have integrated these two dimensions into their diagnostic and treatment programs.

Empirical Studies Validating the Circumplex Model

The studies reviewed in the previous section demonstrated the salience of the cohesion and adaptability dimensions in describing marital and family systems, discriminating between different groups of couples and families, and in planning and conducting marital and family therapy. While the analysis of the previous studies was post hoc, the studies reviewed in this section used the Circumplex Model as the theoretical base and specifically tested hypotheses derived from the model.

The first study, done by Sprenkle and Olson (1978), compared clinic and nonclinic couples on variables related to the adaptability dimension. Using the SIMFAM interaction game, they found that under stressful conditions, the nonclinic couples tended to share leadership whereas the clinic couples had a wife-leadership pattern. Nonclinic couples were also significantly more creative, more supportive, and more responsive to each other's attempt to exact influence than clinic couples were. This and related findings demonstrated support for the curvilinear hypothesis that shared leadership (balanced adaptability) was related to better marital functioning.

A second study by Russell (1979) focused on both dimensions and compared 31 families with female adolescents divided according to level of functioning (high and low). Using the SIMFAM game, she found that high-functioning families were more balanced on both family adaptability and cohesion, while low-functioning families had extreme scores on these two dimensions. Placing the families into types based on the two dimensions, she found that all of the low-functioning families fell into the Extreme ares. Most (ten of fifteen) of the high-functioning families fell into the Balanced types. These findings generally supported the hypothesis regarding family functioning and the Circumplex Model.

One of the basic assumptions of the Circumplex Model is that the two dimensions in the model are independent. In two separate studies conducted by Russell (1978, 1979) that utilized self-report and behavioral measures of both cohesion and adaptability, factor analysis revealed that measures of these dimensions loaded on separate factors. Hence the independence of the two dimensions was empirically demonstrated and validated.

The first study by Russell (1978) involved thirty family triads and used four behavioral measures of adaptability and one self-report measure. There was also one self-report and one behavioral measure of cohesion, family support, and family creativity. A factor analysis revealed that the first rotated factor contained all four behavioral measures of adaptability (average r = .77) and negative loadings (average r = .54) on the two family creativity measures. The self-report measures of adaptability did not load on any factor. The second factor contained high loadings on both the self-report ($r = .76$) and behavioral ($r = .75$) measures of cohesion and a high loading ($r = .75$) on the behavioral measure of family support, which is conceptually related to cohesion.

The second study by Russell (1979) involved twenty family triads and similar measures of cohesion and adaptability in addition to some relevant measures from Moos's Family Environment Scale (1976). In this study, the four behavioral measures of adaptability and the one self-report measure loaded on the first factor (average $r = .73$). The second factor contained four self-report and one behavioral measure of cohesion (average $r = .53$). As would be expected, the Moos Conflict Scale correlated negatively ($r = -.68$) with the cohesion dimension. In conclusion, this second analysis confirmed and replicated the findings of the first study and indicated the independence of the cohesion and adaptability dimensions.

A study by Druckman (1979) considered the effectiveness of family-oriented treatment for adolescents. Twenty-nine families with female juvenile offenders were assessed using the Moos' Family Environment Scale (1976) on the cohesion and adaptability dimensions before and after family-oriented treatment. As predicted by the Circumplex Model, families at pretesting had low scores on family cohesion ("disengaged") and high scores on adaptability ("chaotic"). At posttesting, both program completers and dropouts became more moderate on both of these dimensions. Those with very high family cohesion had the highest rate of recidivism. In general, these findings offer some support for the model.

Portner (1980) compared 55 families (parents and one adolescent) in family therapy with a control group of 117 nonproblem families. She compared the two groups using FACES and the Inventory of Parent-Adolescent Confict (IPAC). As hypothesized, nonclinic families were more likely to fall in the Balanced areas of the Circumplex Model on cohesion and adaptability than were the clinic families (58 percent and 42 percent, respectively). Clinic families tended to be more toward the "chaotic disengaged" extreme (30 percent) with fewer nonclinic families at that extreme (12 percent).

Bell and Bell (1982) also utilized FACES and the IPAC to study 33 families with runaways and compared them with the same 117 nonproblem families used in the Portner (1982) study. As hypothesized, he found significantly more nonproblem families than runaway families based on descriptions from the mothers and adolescents (but not from the fathers) in the Balanced area. Conversely, he found more runaway families than nonproblem families in the Mid-Range and Extreme types. Also, significantly more runaway families (29 percent) than nonproblem families (7 percent) were "disengaged." A higher percentage of runaway families (23 percent) were more "chaotic" than nonproblem families (7 percent).

Summary

The Circumplex Model was developed in an attempt to integrate the diversity of concepts in the fields of family theory and family therapy. The three dimensions that emerged from a conceptual clustering were *family cohesion, family adaptability,* and *family communication.* The two dimensions of cohesion and adaptability were used to form the Circumplex Model. Communication was considered as a facilitating dimension because it enables movement on the other two dimensions.

The model identifies sixteen types of marital and family systems that can be reduced to three major types: *Balanced, Mid-Range,* and *Extreme.* Hypotheses are derived from the model; the most general hypothesis is that Balanced family types tend to function more adequately than do Extreme types. More specific hypotheses relate family types and family functioning to various stages of the family life cycle. Considerable research focusing separately on the individual dimensions has been conducted: Some studies have generally supported the model, and numerous other studies are currently underway. This model provides the foundation for this entire study. Specific findings related to the Circumplex Model are discussed in Chapters V and XI.

chapter

V

Marital and Family Types

THE CIRCUMPLEX MODEL provides the basic foundation and underlying theme for this entire book. It is used as the dependent variable in much of the analysis. Families can be classified along the two separate dimensions of cohesion and adaptability. Based on this classification, the couple or family can be placed into one of the sixteen types, which are then organized into three main groups, or family types: *Balanced, Mid-Range,* and *Extreme.*

A major focus of this chapter is to examine how families differ in cohesion and adaptability at different stages of the family life cycle. It will also focus on whether the three family types are stable across the life cycle.

In order to classify each family, family members were asked to describe how they perceived their family. These assessments were gathered using the most recent version of the Family Adaptability and Cohesion Evaluation Scales (FACES II). This scale assesses two major areas of family functioning: cohesion and adaptability. To classify families, their scores on each of the two separate dimensions are combined to determine placement on the Circumplex Model (see Figure 5.1).

This study is somewhat unique in that it systematically obtained the views of several family members. The results clearly demonstrate that members from the same family do *not* necessarily hold similar perceptions of the nature of their family life. Indeed, the descriptions presented occasionally make it difficult to believe members are reporting on the same family. As a result, the analysis will be done using both individual and couple scores.

Family Cohesion

Family cohesion is the "emotional bonding that family members have toward one another" (Olson et al., 1982). It is a measure of how

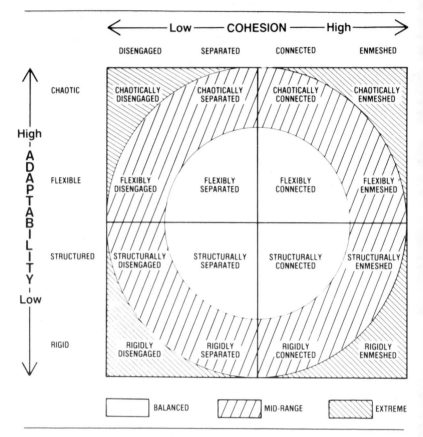

Figure 5.1 Circumplex Model: Sixteen Types of Marital and Family Systems

close to each other family members feel on an emotional level or their sense of connectedness to or separateness from other family members. This study found significant differences between husbands and wives on their perceptions of family cohesion. People at various stages of the family life cycle also reported different levels of cohesion in their families. Thus there were both family member differences and stage differences on the measure of family cohesion.

Wives generally rated their families as more closely knit, or higher on cohesion, than did the husbands across the seven stages of the life cycle. Only with Launching Families (Stage 5) did the wives' average score on cohesion drop slightly below the mean score for husbands (see

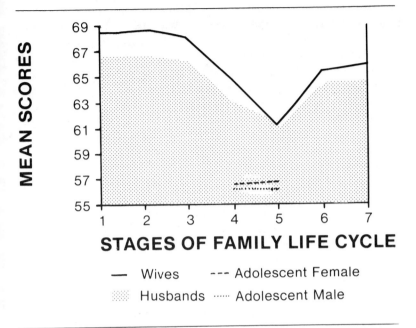

Figure 5.2 Cohesion

Figure 5.2). The differences between husbands and wives were greatest in the earlier stages, converging at the Launching stage (Stage 5) and then separating again at the Empty Nest and Retirement stages (Stages 6 and 7). In these later two stages, wives' scores again significantly exceeded husbands.

Family cohesion appeared to be at its highest among families in the early stages of the family life cycle. Levels of family cohesion were lower among Families with Adolescent Children (Stage 4) and reached the lowest level with families at the Launching stage (Stage 5). Levels of cohesion were higher again at the Empty Nest and Retirement stages. However, these levels of cohesion were still lower than the levels reported by couples at the earliest stages of the family life cycle.

From the perspective of family development theory, it seems appropriate that family cohesion differs by stage. It reaches its ebb during the Launching stage, when adolescents are leaving home and attempting to carve out a life style and identity of their own, independent of their family. These lower levels at the Launching stage reflect the efforts of the adolescent to differentiate him- or herself from the family. The result is a lower sense of togetherness and closeness among all family members at the Launching stage. It also seems appropriate that reported levels of cohesion are at their highest in the earliest stage(s), when romantic and idealistic views of the marital relationship are apt to be at their highest, reflecting a desire for a greater degree of togetherness.

Both male and female adolescents reported significantly lower levels of family cohesion than did either of their parents (see Figure 5.2). Teenagers in both the Adolescent and Launching stages (4 and 5) reported lower levels of family cohesion. This finding is consistent with the interpretation that adolescents are seeking to differentiate themselves from their family. In order for them to accomplish this task, it is often necessary for them to view their family as less cohesive. In general, both the adolescent males and females felt that there was less cohesion in their families than did their parents.

Family Adaptability

Family adaptability is the "ability of a marital or family system to change its power structure, role relationships, and relationship rules in response to situational and developmental stress" (Olson et al., 1982). Thus family adaptability is a measure of the extent to which a family can adapt its structure, rules, and roles to meet the challenges presented by the changing needs of the family and its individual members. This is a measure of the ability of the family to *change* when it is appropriate or necessary.

As with cohesion, perceptions of family adaptability also varied significantly at different stages of the family life cycle and among different family members. Wives reported significantly higher levels of family adaptability than did husbands at all of the stages, except at the Launching stage (Stage 5). The differences on adaptability were not as pronounced as were those on cohesion (see Figure 5.3), but the fluctuations between groups were similar to those on cohesion. Scores on family adaptability progressively decreased from the newly married group (Stage 1) through Families with Adolescents (Stage 4) and then increased again during the two postlaunching stages (Stage 6, Empty Nest Families; Stage 7, Families in Retirement).

Unlike the scores on family cohesion (where group means for husbands and wives both reached their low point at the Launching stage), husbands' assessments of family adaptability reached a low

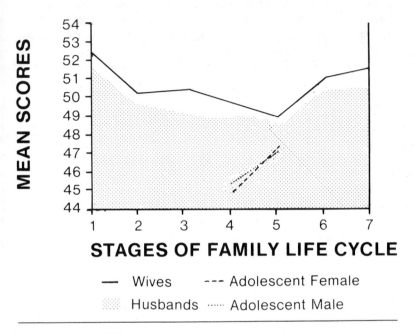

Figure 5.3 Adaptability

point in the Adolescent stage (Stage 4) and became somewhat higher in each of the succeeding stages. In contrast, the mean for wives' scores on adaptability reached its lowest point during the Launching stage and increased in the later two stages.

Adolescents viewed their families as significantly less flexible on adaptability than did their parents. At both the Adolescent stage (Stage 4) and the Launching stage (Stage 5), teenagers' scores on family adaptability were substantially lower than their mothers' or fathers' were. This parent-adolescent contrast was greatest at the Adolescent stage. The discrepancy between the generations decreased somewhat with the older adolescents in the Launching stage (Stage 5), but they were still significantly different.

These parent-adolescent differences are also consistent with the generational differences found on cohesion. It is at this time in their lives that adolescents usually seek greater freedom and autonomy from their families and frequently work toward loosening previous family restrictions. Thus while they are seeking greater flexibility from their families, it is reasonable to expect them to view their families as less flexible. The results reported here on both adaptability and cohesion suggest support for some of the most important developmental tasks that the family development theorists view as germane to the Adolescent and Launching stages.

Family Types: Balanced, Mid-Range, and Extreme Families

The designation of families by type is determined by placement of the scores for cohesion and adaptability on the Circumplex Model. This discussion of family types moves from the consideration of the two dimensions separately, to the simultaneous consolidated assessment of both dimensions. As discussed earlier (see Chapter IV), the three family types are: *Balanced:* scores on both dimensions are in the balanced range; *Extreme:* scores on both dimensions are at extreme levels (either high or low); and *Mid-Range:* the score for one dimension may fall in the balanced range while the score for the other dimension is extremely high or low.

The proportion of families that fell into each of the three types varied across the seven stages of the family life cycle. The percentage of families representing each family type at each stage is shown in Figure 5.4. This distribution is based on the individual scores of husbands and wives. While the frequency of each family type does vary among stages, an analysis of variance indicates these distributions are not significantly different. In other words, there appears to be some consistency regarding the number of Balanced, Mid-Range, and Extreme family types across the life-cycle stages.

Adolescents as a group tended to view their families as more extreme and less balanced. Their perceptions are contrasted with those of the total group of parents (in Figure 5.5). While these differences were not found to be statistically significant, they do reflect the fact that adolescents viewed their families as significantly lower on both cohesion and adaptabiliy than their parents did.

Couple Scores

In order to examine more effectively the differences among couples or families, it is necessary to develop a score that represents the family as a unit. One of the purposes of the Circumplex Model is not only to

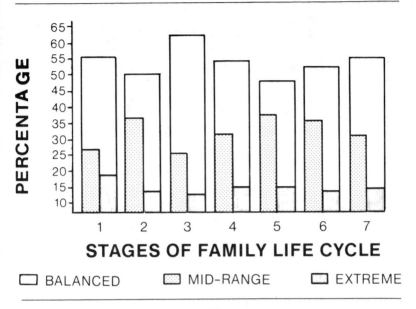

Figure 5.4 Family Type: Husbands and Wives

assess how individuals view themselves within the context of their families, but also to determine how families, as integrated units, view themselves. This is important because it provides the opportunity to explore differences among families as well as differences among members of a single family.

How do couple scores compare with individual scores? The previous analysis of the Circumplex Model was based on the scores of individuals. All the husbands were grouped together and compared with all the wives and all the adolescents. This allowed for comparison among family members and across the stages of the family life cycle. It also allowed us to examine norms for each family member: husband, wife, and adolescent.

Now we will shift our perspective to examine the data for couples rather than for individual husbands and wives. Husbands' scores are combined with their wives' scores to form a *couple mean* (average) score on each of the two dimensions (cohesion and adaptability). As with individual scoring, scores from the two dimensions are combined to form a 4 × 4 matrix that represents the sixteen family categories of the

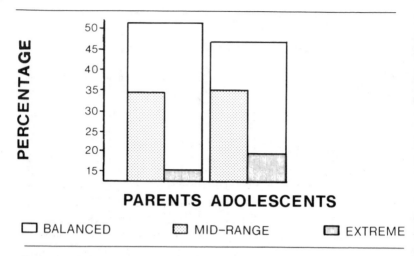

Figure 5.5 Family Type

Circumplex Model (see Figure 5.1). The couple is placed in the cell (family type) appropriate to their couple mean score on each dimension. This placement also indicates whether the couple is classified as Balanced, Mid-Range, or Extreme. (For more details on the development of couple and family scores, see Appendix F.)

The results using couple scores closely parallel the findings based on individual scores. Couples at the seven stages of the family life cycle differed in the levels of cohesion and adaptability in their families they reported. Using a couple mean score on family adaptability and cohesion, significant differences were found among stages for both dimensions. The results using the couple mean were similar to those using the the individual scores.

The sense of closeness in the family unit dropped from the early stages to a low point during the Launching years. A greater sense of family cohesion was reported in the two groups representing couples whose children had left home (Stages 6 and 7). The couple mean cohesion scores for the first two stages were very similiar; they then dropped progressively through the next three stages. They reached their lowest level in couples in the Launching stage (Stage V), when children are either preparing or in the process of leaving home. In the last two stages, couple mean cohesion scores increased but did not achieve the high levels recorded during the early years of marriage. Thus couples in the earliest years of marriage reported the greatest amount of closeness.

Adaptability showed a pattern similar to cohesion. There was a slight but progressive drop through the first five stages and then a rebound in reported levels of adaptability in the last two stages of the family life cycle. As expected, couple mean scores across stages demonstrated a pattern similar to individual scores. The couple data continued to demonstrate significant differences between groups at different stages on each of the dimensions.

In order to classify couples into the three family types, a *couple distance score* was created. The couple distance scores represent the distance of the couple mean from the center of the Circumplex Model. Small couple distances from the center represent the Balanced type, and couples with high distance scores represent the Extreme type. Couples between these two groups are the Mid-Range types. (Norms and formulas for the couple distance scores are presented in Appendix F.)

Using the couple distance scores, the frequency distributions of Balanced, Mid-Range, and Extreme types were again found *not* to differ significantly among the stages. The fact that the same results found using individual scores, couple mean scores, and couple distance scores supports the empirical validity to the findings. In summary, there is considerable consistency in the number of Balanced, Mid-Range, and Extreme families at various stages of the life cycle regardless of whether the results are based on individual or couple scores.

Norms for the Sixteen Family Types

Focusing on the sixteen types, one can gain a more detailed perspective on the cluster of types in the Circumplex Model. Figure 5.6 provides a summary of the actual percentage of adults and adolescents falling into each of the sixteen types. The four center cells represent the Balanced types, and the four corner cells represent the Extreme types. The Mid-Range types are represented by the other eight cells.

Since this sample of families is "normal," the frequency distribution of families in certain Extreme types is rather low. The Extreme types clustered primarily into the lower left ("rigidly disengaged") and upper right ("chaotically enmeshed"), with very few in the other two extremes ("chaotically disengaged" and "rigidly enmeshed"). These findings are

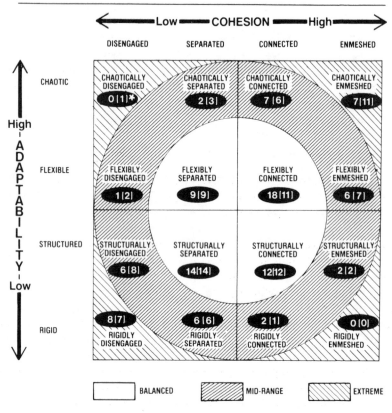

Figure 5.6 Sixteen Types of Families: Parents and Adolescents (in percentages)

not surprising considering this normative sample, but they are also related to the correlation between cohesion and adaptability reported earlier.

It is also questionable whether the families in this study really represent Extreme family types. While they are extreme compared to the other families in this sample, they are probably more accurately labeled as Mid-Range types in comparison with problem families. This issue will be addressed in future studies using FACES II to assess types in the Circumplex Model and is discussed in greater detail elsewhere (Chapter XI).

Summary

Closeness (cohesion) and change (adaptability) within families appear to reach a low point during the adolescent and launching years. They are at their highest levels among the couples at the earliest stages of marriage. Adolescents reported even lower levels of cohesion and adaptability than their parents did. It was suggested that these findings are consistent with a developmental view of family life. It is during the adolescent and launching years, when teenagers are seeking freedom to develop their own separateness from their family and to make the family rules more flexible, that cohesion and adaptability are lowest.

Cohesion and adaptability were at their highest levels among young couples without children (Stage 1). This also seems appropriate, given that this is the time when couples are working to establish a sense of identity for themselves as a marital unit. They are working toward the establishment of greater closeness while also trying to develop roles and rules that appropriately integrate their former separate lifestyles into their couple relationship.

Across most of the stages, wives perceived their families to have greater adaptability and cohesion than their husbands did. Stage differences on *each dimension* were significant at both the individual and the couple levels. Although the blurring of stage differences with possible cohort differences makes a clear interpretation difficult, the differences reported here certainly add credence to the developmental perspective based on family life-cycle stages.

Families were also designated as Balanced, Mid-Range, or Extreme family types. Individual scores, couple mean scores, and couple distance scores produced similar results. While the distribution of the three family types varied among states, the differences were *not* statistically different. Adolescents indicated that they viewed their families as less Balanced and more Extreme than their parents did.

chapter
VI
Marital and Family Strengths

> Although the professional literature is replete with criteria for identify-
> ing "problem families" and criteria useful in the diagnosis of family
> problems or family disorganization, little is known about how we
> might identify a "strong family." Sound research into the dynamics of
> the so-called healthy or normal family is minimal.
>
> *H.A. Otto, 1963*

Even though this statement was written twenty years ago, it still
holds true today. The need to understand how families cope with both
the usual hardships and the unexpected crises in their lives has been
noted by many writers. Yet family researchers have only just begun to
study family strengths for dealing with hardship. Table 6.1 summarizes
the seven major family strengths that have been discussed by various
authors: *family pride, family support, cohesion, adaptability, communication, religious orientation,* and *social support.*

Family strengths have been referred to as resources by family
sociologists. Early work in this area viewed family strengths in the
context of family resources, which were divided into two broad
categories: integration and adaptability (Angell, 1936; Cavan & Ranck,
1938; Koos, 1946). Hill (1949, 1958) identified family resources as a key
component within the ABCX stress framework. Burr (1973) later expanded on the definition of resources to be the "variation in a family's
ability to prevent a stressor event of change in a family social system
from creating some crisis in the system."

Other writers have described family strengths as qualities that help
marriage and family relationships. Pollack (1953) writes about altruism,
a balance of independence and interdependence, positivism, flexibility,
compromise, the ability to foster growth and development of members,
the individuation of members, clear generational boundaries and supportive relationships. Young (1953) states that the most important resource for families to develop is adaptability.

In a pilot project and follow-up study, Otto (1963) attempted to clarify the definition of family strengths from the perspective of families themselves. Twelve major dimensions were produced, which can be grouped into the following abilities (see Table 6.1 for a complete listing):

- To provide a sense of family unity, loyalty, and interfamily cooperation.
- To provide support and security.
- To perform roles flexibly.
- To maintain constructive relationships with the community.

Otto's continued work (1962, 1964; Otto and Griffiths, 1965) flowed into the human potential movement of the 1960s. Family strengths were often highlighted as an important and untapped resources. Much of this work was aimed at helping families enrich their relationships in order to prevent future difficulties. Interaction methods were used as primary tools in enrichment workshops that were designed to increase family strengths. These have been articulated in what Otto (1979) calls characteristics of the "new family" (see Table 6.1).

More recently, a large informal survey examined the strengths of American families as part of the White House Conference on Families (Tanner-Nelson & Banonis, 1981). Families in that survey defined "strong" families as (1) families in which relationships are highly valued, and (2) families whose members support each other through good times and bad. Other family qualities mentioned less frequently included mutual respect, a sense of unity, clearly expressed values, effective communication, and emotional support.

Empirical Studies and Methods

Empirical work on family strengths is still in its infancy. Stinnett and Sauer (1977) described the characteristics of families identified as "strong" by Home Extension Agents and by the families' own self-evaluation. Characteristics included: (1) good communication patterns, (2) spending time together, (3) having a high degree of religious orientation, (4) dealing with crises in a positive manner, (5) being committed to each other, and (6) showing an honest appreciation for each other.

Following this initial study, Stinnet, Chesser, DeFrain, and Knaub (1981) surveyed 430 families with questionnaires and revised their initial categories to five factors: love, religion, respect, communication, and individuality. Beam (1979) reviewed college students' perceptions of their family strengths and found factors similar to those Stinnet outlined.

Davis (1980) isolated *family pride* as a measure of self-esteem and related family strengths. In a study of clinical and nonclinical life-span families, she concluded that family pride is related to other measures of family strengths and that clinical families demonstrated lower scores on a family pride scale than did life-span families.

If we return to the more expansive term of "resources," there is additional research to acknowledge. McCubbin, Joy, et al. (1980), in reviewing the stress research of the last decade, delineated four major types of resources: (1) personal resources, (2) social support, (3) coping, and (4) the family system's internal resources.

This review raises several important issues. First, as was stated earlier, empirical work on family strengths is still in its infancy. No attention has been paid to: (1) how strengths develop and change over the life cycle, (2) how marital strengths compare to family strengths, (3) whether certain kinds of family and marital strengths are associated with specific family types, and (4) how certain strengths are related to levels of stress within the family. The first two issues will be discussed in this chapter, and the last two will be discussed in Chapters XI and XII.

Questions concerning how strengths change over the life cycle may contribute to the process component (Otto, 1963). He proposes that family strengths are "dynamic, fluid, and inter-related" and that they can be measured only by longitudinal studies. Attention also needs to be paid to determining whether *marital* strengths differ from *family* strengths. At present, there is a lack of clarity, both conceptually and empirically, in distinguishing between these two concepts.

Are "family strengths" the same as "family resources," or are they a smaller constellation of attributes, encompassed by the broader term "resources"? Otto (1963) and Stinnet and Saur (1977) have taken the approach of incorporating a potpourri of family attributes, combining behavioral and attitudinal dimensions interchangeably (such as family pride, religiousity, good communication, soliciting social support) to define family strengths.

The increasingly expansive definition of family strengths makes it difficult to measure. Perhaps this explains why few attempts have been made to develop an instrument to measure this dimension. One approach to moving beyond the theoretical stage is to delimit the definition of "strength." This has been done most recently by an interesting study that identified family pride as a family variable contributing to strengths (Davis, 1980). *Family pride* was defined as an "individual

TABLE 6.1 Review of Family Strengths Literature

Major Variables	(1) Angell (1936) (2) Cavan (1938) (3) Koos (1946)	Pollak (1953)	Otto (1963)	Otto (1979)	(1) Stinnett & Sauer (1977) (2) Stinnett et al. (1981)
Family Pride		Positivism	Concern for family unity, loyalty, and interfamily cooperation	Seek out growth in experiences	(1) Ability to deal with crisis in a positive manner
Family Support	(2) Supportive relationships (3) Altruism	Ability to foster growth and development of members To provide support, security, to aid in developing creativity Sensitive to individual member needs	Utilizing consciously fostered ways to develop strong emotional ties	Love and understanding	(1) Spending time together (2) Love
Cohesion	(1) Integration Cohesion (2) Individuation of members (3) Clear generational boundaries	Balance of independence and interdependence	Mutual respect for individuality of members		(1) Appreciation Commitment (2) Respect Individuality

Adaptability (1)	Flexibility	Perform family roles flexibly	
	Compromise	Ability to grow through children	
Communication		Effective communication	(1 & 2) Good communication patterns
		Sensitive listening	
Religious Orientation		Meet spiritual needs of family	Spirituality—Commitment to realizing potential as human being
			(1 & 2) High degree of religious orientation
Social Support		Ability to maintain relationships outside the family; this includes constructive, responsible community relationships in neighborhood, school, town, government	Active participation in community "social responsibility" and ecological interests
		Ability to seek help when appropriate	

family member's perception that his or her family is a worthy group." A worthy group was composed of competent members who usually do things well and who refer to the family as a source of satisfaction. Davis supplied empirical support that family pride was not similar to individual self-esteem but was a group characteristic, reflecting family consensus rather than individual perceptions. Davis's work gives support to the idea of narrowing the definition of family strengths to a constellation of attributes that are part of a family system's internal resources. This approach allows for more adequate linkage between conceptual definitions and future empirical work.

The focus of this study is both family and marital strengths. Family strengths were measured by two scales: family pride and family accord. Marital strengths wree assessed by an inventory called ENRICH, which focuses on twelve different areas in the marriage relationship. Whereas the fathers, mothers, and adolescents all took the Family Strengths inventory, only the couple took ENRICH (which focuses on the marriage relationship only).

Marital and family strengths show clear differences across the family life cycle (Table 6.2). More specifically, eight of the twelve strength areas show significant differences among stages. There are also four strength areas where wives scored consistently higher than husbands (family pride, leisure activities, family and friends, and religious orientation). Husbands scored significantly higher than wives on communication, which indicates that they were more satisfied with marital communication. More details on these and related findings are presented later in this chapter.

Family Strengths Scale

This scale measured two dimensions that were found to be conceptually and empirically important: family pride and family accord. *Family pride* focused on loyalty, optimism, and trust in one's family. *Family accord* dealt with feeling able to accomplish tasks, deal with problems, and get along well together. The total score on Family Strengths (both scales combined) for husbands and wives across the life cycle is indicated in Figure 6.1.

Family strengths show clear differences across the family life cycle (see Table 6.2). These differences are primarily due to differences on family pride and not on family accord. Family accord does not show stage or sex differences. It appears that wives felt more family pride in

TABLE 6.2 Differences Across the Family Life Cycle (ANOVA)

	Stage Differences		Gender Differences		Who Scored Higher
	F	p	F	p	
Family Strengths	3.7	.001	—	ns	
Family pride	6.9	.001	11.4	.001	Wives
Family accord	—	ns	—	ns	
Marital Strengths					
Personality issues	.75	.001	—	ns	
Communication	—	ns	6.5	.01	Husbands
Conflict resolution	—	ns	—	ns	
Leisure activities	4.8	.001	23.2	.001	Wives
Sexual relationship	—	ns	—	.001	
Children	28.7	.001	—	ns	
Family and friends	3.7	.001	19.7	.001	Wives
Egalitarian roles	23.5	.001	—	ns	
Financial management	9.1	.001	—	ns	
Religious orientation	12.3	.001	12.5	.001	Wives

ns = not significant

their families than did husbands. This is consistent with the idea that the wife often feels more responsible for this social aspect of family life.

Adolescents perceived significantly fewer family strengths than did fathers or mothers. There are no differences between the scores of male and female adolescents on family strengths. One consistent pattern does emerge on family and marital strengths: The wives' scores began declining for families with children (Stage 3) and reached their lowest point with families launching children (Stage 5). Husbands had a similar pattern, but the husbands' scores increased when the adolescents were still in the home (Stage 4). This same pattern occurred with family strengths (family pride and family accord) and several areas of marital strengths (communication, conflict resolution, and financial management). This is the same pattern that occurred with marital and family satisfaction (see Chapter X).

Marital Strengths: ENRICH

Because the marriage relationship plays such an important role in how well the family functions, it was considered essential to focus on strengths in the marriage. To tap the marital strengths, an inventory called ENRICH was developed. (More details on the inventory are contained in (Appendix B).

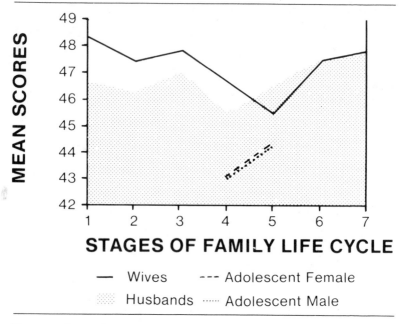

STAGES OF FAMILY LIFE CYCLE

— Wives   --- Adolescent Female

    Husbands   ····· Adolescent Male

Figure 6.1 Family Strengths

Previous research was reviewed in order to decide what content areas to measure. Fournier, Springer, and Olson (1977) summarized major relationship problems reported by couples in various studies into three levels: *personal issues, interpersonal issues,* and *external issues.* Additional conflict areas such as sexual incompatibility, abusive and violent behaviors, and dependency were identified by Fournier (1979). Table 6.3 lists the most salient content categories from ten studies. It also identifies how many times each of the specific issues were listed as a common marital problem.

ENRICH categories reflect the important content issues identified in earlier studies. Assessment of these areas within a marriage can describe potential problem issues for a couple, or it can identify areas of strength and enrichment. The definitions of the categories in ENRICH (provided below) are derived from the actual items developed for each category.

There were significant differences among stages of the life cycle on seven of the ten ENRICH scales. Only three areas (communication, conflict resolution, and sexual relationship) showed no differences across stages. While the husbands were consistently more satisfied with their communication than were wives, wives reported feeling better

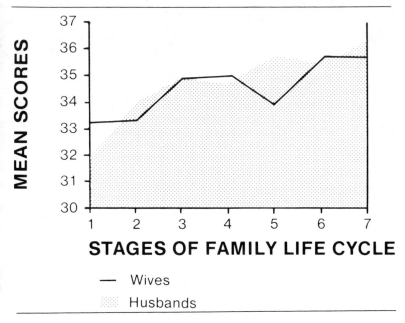

Figure 6.2 Personality Issues (ENRICH)

than husbands in terms of leisure activities, family and friends, and religious orientation (see Table 6.1). Figures illustrating these findings will be included only for those subscales demonstrating significant differences between stages or genders.

PERSONALITY ISSUES

This category assessed an individual's perception of his or her partner with regard to behaviors or traits and the level of satisfaction or dissatisfaction felt on those issues. Items include traits such as tardiness, temper, moodiness, stubbornness, jealousy, and possessiveness. Personal behaviors related to public demonstration of affection and smoking and drinking habits are also addressed. In addition, ENRICH looks at a spouse's general outlook, dependability, and tendency to be domineering. High scores reflect adjustment to partner and satisfaction with the partner's personality. Low scores indicate a low level of acceptance or lack of comfort with the partner's personality and behaviors.

TABLE 6.3 Summary of Problem Areas Mentioned in Ten Studies of Marital Strengths

ENRICH Category	Topic Area	Concepts Identified in Previous Studies	
INTRAPERSONAL ISSUES			
Personality Issues	Personality	personality (4) unstable (1) dependency (2)	immature (1) jealous (2) intelligence (2)
	Personal habits	daily routines (1) habits (2) health (2) neatness (1) energy level (2)	physical problem (2) drinking (1) personal freedom (1) violence (1)
Religious Orientation	Incompatible backgrounds	religion (5) incompatible background (2)	background differences (4)
Leisure Activities	Interests and values	social and political values (1) value differences (1) social life (2) values (2) spare time (1)	interests and values (3) social activities (2) recreation (3)
Conventionality	Expectations	expectations (2)	conventionalization (2)
INTERPERSONAL ISSUES			
Communication	Communication	decision making (1) relationship maintenance (1) affection (1)	communication (6)

Sexual Relationship	Sex	sexual relationship (7) extramarital sex (2) affection (2)	sex (3)
Egalitarian Roles	Marital Roles	household roles (2) external role problems (1) marital roles (5)	internal role problems (1)
Conflict Resolution	Conflict	power struggle (1) deal with anger (1) boredom (1)	arguments (1) dominance (1) conflict resolution (2)
EXTERNAL ISSUES Family Friends	Relatives	partner's family (1) parents (1) in-laws (3)	relatives (2) family (2)
	Friends	friends (7)	out with boys/girls (1)
Children	Children	parenthood (2) no sense of family (1)	family planning (1) children (4)
Financial Management	Money	handling money (4) saving (1)	money (3) house (3)

SOURCE: Adapted with permission from Fournier (1979).

a. Specific categories from reviewed studies: Rausch et al. (1974); Rappoport (1963); Kitson and Sussman (1977); Microys and Bader (1977); Hobart (1958); Hunt & Hunt (1977); Sager (1976); Mace (1972); Stahman & Hiebert (1977); Fournier, Springer, & Olson (1978).

NOTE: The number in parentheses next to each category is the number of times out of ten that each specific category was mentioned in the above articles.

103

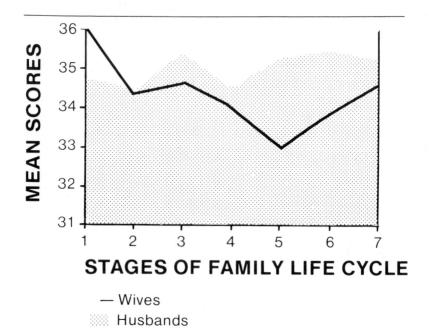

— Wives
░ Husbands

Figure 6.3 Marital Communication

Older couples (Stages 4-7) showed an increasing willingness to rate their spouses' personal behaviors favorably. This was a steady upward trend, with no significant differences between husbands and wives (see Figure 6.2).

COMMUNICATION

This category is concerned with an individual's feelings, beliefs, and attitudes toward the role of communication in the maintenance of the marriage relationship. Items focus on the level of comfort felt by both partners in being able to share important emotions and beliefs with each other, the perception of a partner's way of giving and receiving information, and the respondent's perception of how adequately they communicate with each other. High scores reflect the couple's awareness and satisfaction with the level and type of communication in their relationship. Low scores reflect a lack of satisfaction with their communication; they indicate that the couple may need to work on improving their communication skills.

Husbands tended to rate their marital communication more favorably than did wives (see Figure 6.3). This difference was greatest at the Launching stage (Stage 5), when wives might be expecting more from their partner since their adolescents are leaving home. Generally, there were no stage differences in regard to communication.

CONFLICT RESOLUTION

This category assessed an individual's attitudes, feelings, and beliefs toward the existence and resolution of conflict in his or her relationship. Items focus on the openness of partners to recognize and resolve issues, the strategies and procedures used to end arguments, and partners' satisfaction with the way problems are resolved. High scores reflect realistic attitudes about the probability of relationship conflicts and comfort with the way most problems are handled in the couple's relationship. Low scores suggest an ineffective approach to relationship conflicts and dissatisfaction with the way the conflict is resolved. No significant differences were found among stages or between spouses in conflict resolution.

FINANCIAL MANAGEMENT

This category focuses on attitudes and concerns about the way economic issues are managed within the couple's relationship. Items assess whether individuals tend be spenders or savers, their concern with issues of credit and debts, the care with which financial decisions on major purchases and decisions regarding financial matters and money management are made, and satisfaction with economic status. High scores reflect satisfaction with financial management and realistic attitudes toward financial matters. Low scores indicate various concerns with financial management in the relationship.

Life-cycle trends in the category follow the same pattern as trends in satisfaction with marriage and family life (see Chapter X). The dip at the adolescent stage appears to reflect the strain put on family resources by adolescent children, even when the increased earning power of families at this period of life is taken into account.

LEISURE ACTIVITIES

This category assessed each individual's preferences for spending free time. Items reflect social versus personal activities, active versus passive interests, shared versus individual preferences, and expectations as to whether leisure time should be spent together or balanced between separate and joint activities. High scores reflect compatibility, flexibility, and/or consensus about the use of leisure time activities. Low scores reflect dissatisfaction with how leisure time is used in the couple's relationship.

Wives tended to perceive more satisfaction about how leisure time is used than husbands did, especially when there were school-age children (Stage 3) and after adolescents left home (Stages 6 and 7). Across the life cycle there was a general increase in satisfaction for both spouses with leisure activities.

SEXUAL RELATIONSHIP

This category assessed an individual's feelings and concerns about affection and the sexual relationship with his or her partner. Items reflect satisfaction with expressions of affection, level of comfort in discussion of sexual issues, attitudes toward sexual behavior, intercourse, and birth control decisions, and feelings about sexual fidelity. High scores reflect satisfaction with affectional expressions and a positive attitude about the role of sexuality in marriage. Low scores indicate dissatisfaction with the expression of affection in the relationship, concern about the role of sexuality in marriage, and/or disagreement over decisions regarding birth control. No significant differences were found between husbands and wives or across the life cycle regarding their sexual relationship.

CHILDREN AND MARRIAGE

This category assessed individual attitudes and feelings about having children and agreement on the number of children preferred. Specific items reflect a couple's awareness of the impact of children on the marriage relationship, their satisfaction with roles and with the responsibilities of the parents in child rearing, compatibility in philosophy toward discipline of children, and shared goals and values desired for the children. High scores reflect a consensus regarding decisions to have children and the size of family desired, a realistic perception of the impact of children on the marriage relationship, and satisfaction with how parental roles and responsibilities are defined. Low scores reflect a lack of consensus regarding decisions to have children and the size of family preferred, concern over the impact of children on the relationship, and discomfort with perceptions of parental roles and responsibilities.

Other than a striking increase for both spouses after the childless stage of life (Stage 1), husbands and wives across the life cycle scored similarly on the children and marriage scale. The increase at Stage 2 is probably due to the fact that childless couples had not yet come to decisions about some of the parenting issues.

FAMILY AND FRIENDS

This category assessed feelings and concerns about relationships with relatives, in-laws, and friends. Items reflect the attitudes of friends and relatives toward the marriage, expectations regarding the amount of time spent with family and friends, and perceptions of the situation as either potentially conflictful or satisfactory. High scores reflect comfortable family and friend relationships. Low scores reflect discomfort with family and friend relationships and imply potential areas of conflict.

Family and friendships tended to become more comfortable and less conflictual across the life cycle. There are significant differences betwen stages of the life cycle with a trend toward increasing satisfaction across the stages. Wives saw this area more positively than did husbands at nearly every stage of life.

EGALITARIAN ROLES

This category assessed an individual's beliefs, feelings, and attitudes about various marital and family roles. Items focus on occupational roles, household roles, sex roles, and parental roles. A high individual score indicates more egalitarian values. A low individual score, rather than indicating a lack of satisfaction, indicates that the scorer *values traditional husband-wife roles and areas of responsibility.*

While no sex differences were found with respect to egalitarianism, there were stage differences. As would be expected, older couples were more traditional, while younger couples were more egalitarian in their values and roles (see Figure 6.4).

RELIGIOUS ORIENTATION

This category assessed an individual's attitudes, feelings, and concerns about religious beliefs and practices within his or her marriage. Items focus on the meaning and importance of religion, involvements in church activities, and the expected role that religious beliefs will have in the marriage. High scores reflect a more traditional view that religion is an extremely important component of marriage. Low scores reflect a more individualistic and less traditional interpretation of the role of religion.

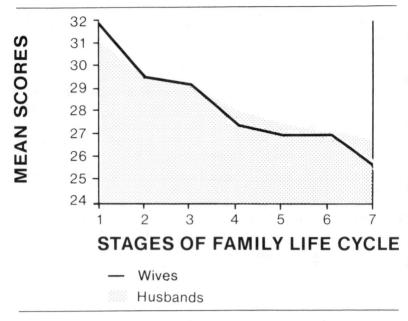

Figure 6.4 Egalitarian Roles (ENRICH)

As on the Egalitarian Roles Scale, older couples scored significantly more traditionally on religious orientation. In addition, husbands were significantly more individualistic and less traditional on religion than were wives.

CONGREGATIONAL ACTIVITIES

Complimentary to the Religious Orientation subscale, the Congregational Activities scale measures active participation in the church. *A Study of Generations* (Strommen et al., 1972) reported normative data on the Congregational Activity Scale for a representative sample of 4745 Lutherans in the United States.

The highest possible scores on the Congregational Activity Scale are received by persons who report they are very active in their congregation. They regularly spend evenings at church, regularly receive communion, keep well informed about their congregation, and find congregational participation to be a major source of life satisfaction. About 56 percent of Strommen et al.'s sample attended worship regularly, and the other 44 percent ranged from being inactive to being very

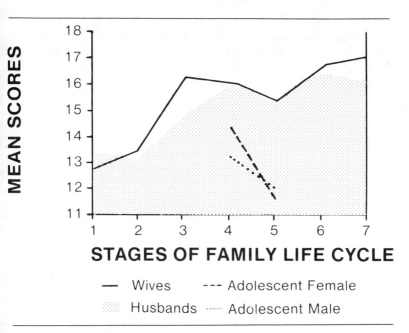

Figure 6.5 Congregational Activity

active. For about half of the group, the congregation was their only contact with an *organized* group life outside of their work.

There were rather dramatic differences in the participation in congregational activities across the life cycle. Younger couples (Stages 2 and 3) participated significantly less than older couples did (Stages 4-7). This trend held for both husbands and wives, and there were no significant sex differences at any stage. Adolescents participated much less than their parents, and there was a significant drop in adolescents' participation after the age of 18 (Launching stage, Stage 5).

Summary

This chapter has attempted to organize and summarize some of the findings regarding marital and family strengths. There were differences across the stages of the life cycle on many of the strengths examined. Wives consistently perceived higher levels of family pride and were more satisfied with their leisure activities and with the relationship they had with relatives and friends, and they were generally more religious. Husbands tended to be more positive about communication in the marriage than wives were. In the chapters that follow, these marital and family strengths will be used to predict family types and to predict high- and low-stress families (Chapters XI and XII).

chapter
VII

Family Stress and Change

THE IMPACT OF CUMULATIVE LIFE CHANGES on the health of individuals has been a major topic of research in the past decade. The concepts of life stress and strains have received increased attention in both the popularized media and the scientific literature. Family stress as described in this chapter has its basic roots in three areas: psychological stress theory, family development theory, and family stress theory.

In the past 25 years, there has been considerable research dealing with the topic of life events and strains. Research has focused on the impact of cumulative stressors upon various somatic and psychiatric disorders and family dysfunction. This content of "cumulative life changes" has been applied only recently in a systematic manner to the study of family stress and the family's response to these stressful conditions.

The purpose of this chapter is to define stressors, stress, and strain and to determine how they are distributed across the family life cycle. As we strive to understand how families respond and adapt to life transitions and unexpected hardships, it is essential to gain a fuller appreciation of what families perceive as "typical" or "normative" stressors and strains at each stage of the family cycle. It would be useful to counselors and family life educators if we could document what stressors and strains families can expect and when families may be experiencing an unusual accumulation or "pile-up" of demands.

Psychobiological Stress Research

Cannon (1929) is credited with early experimental work demonstrating that stimuli (e.g., life events) associated with emotional arousal cause changes in physiological processes. Meyer (cited in Leif, 1948), using a "life chart" in medical diagnosis, demonstrated the relationship between ordinary life events and illness. He pointed out that the human body attempts to maintain homeostasis. Any life change that upsets the body's state calls for readjustment. Excessive changes tax the body's capacity for readjustment and, thereby, produce stress. Thus life events are conceived of as "stressors" that require change in the individual's ongoing life pattern (Holmes & Rahe, 1967). Stress is the organism's physiological and psychological response to these stressors, particularly when there is a perceived imbalance between environmental demands (life change) and the individual's capability to meet these demands.

Most of the research showing a positive relationship between life events and illness has used an instrument developed by Holmes and Rahe (1967) that lists 43 events of a family, personal, occupational, or financial nature that require some change or readjustment. In the earliest version, The Schedule of Recent Experience (SRE; Hawkins, Davies, & Holmes, 1957), an individual's score was the number of events experienced in a given time period (usually six months to two years). Subsequently, proportional weights were assigned to each event based on the relative amount of readjustment (in terms of intensity and length of time) required by an individual experiencing each event. An individual's score was the sum score of each event experienced times that event's weight.

The Holmes and Rahe scale has been used in a number of prospective and retrospective studies over the past decade. Positive relationships have been found between the magnitude of life changes and various symptoms such as heart disease, fractures, childhood leukemia, pregnancy, beginning of prison terms, poor teacher performance, low college grade point average, and college football players' injuries (Holmes & Masuda, 1974).

Efforts to extend life stress research to children have also been undertaken. Most notable are the efforts of Coddington (1972), who developed life events questionnaires for children at preschool, elementary, junior high, and senior high levels. Using a weighting scheme similar to that of Holmes and Rahe, he found a consistent increase in life change units with age. Gersten, Langner, Eisenberg, and Orzeck (1974), using their own life event checklist developed for children, found a positive correlation between life events, particularly undesirable events, and measures of psychological impairment in children.

Recently, a research team at the University of Minnesota Family Stress and Coping project developed A-FILE (the Adolescent Family Inventory of Life Events and Changes; McCubbin, Patterson, Bauman, & Harris, 1981). A-FILE is used to assess the pile-up of life events and changes in a family from the perspective of an adolescent member. This instrument is designed to record those salient life events and strains that may have an impact on the emotional, social, and personality development of adolescents. Initial tests of A-FILE revealed a strong association between the pile-up of family-adolescent stressors and adolescent substance use and abuse (McCubbin & Patterson, 1981b).

Individual and Family Development

Family members grow up and change, and families may move from one community to another. Children become young adults and leave home, and parents may become grandparents. These life events and transitions are relatively predictable, and all of us may experience them in the course of our lives.

Despite the predictability, the move from a familiar and stable state to the unknown often does not come with ease. Historically, family development theorists (Hill & Rodgers, 1964) and more recently by family therapists (Haley, 1980; Carter & McGoldrick, 1980) have emphasized the difficulty that many families have in making transitions. Typically, these transitions are marked by psychological and interpersonal conflicts and confusion.

Family transitions, such as the family moving from one city to another, may involve a relatively limited change in one family member but have repercussions on the entire family. Because families function as a total unit, the impact of a seemingly minor event (for example, a child entering school for the first time or a child becoming an adolescent) may trigger other major changes in the family unit.

Some transitions may require a sweeping reorganization of the family unit and its social network. In the case of divorce the family unit will struggle with the loss of a member, social status, and income and with the need to reestablish the family in a new community of friendships. While some transitions may be anticipated (e.g., the parents who prepare for their first child), others may be very unexpected (e.g., a wife becoming pregnant at age 40).

Many transitions are "normal" in that they are expected to happen in a family unit over the life course. Their significant common denominator is that they encompass a transition period often marked by feelings of uncertainty, anxiety, and sense of loss. Also, marital, parent-child, and child-child conflicts are difficult to resolve easily. This period involves the processes of adjustment, reorganization, consolidation, and adaptation (McCubbin & Patterson, 1982).

Families are called upon to change established patterns of behavior and bring stability to the family unit, both in terms of family relationships among members and in terms of the family's relationship to the community. While these transitions may be commonly experienced, little attention has been paid to the content and process of these changes until recently. Considerable interest has now moved the topic into a prominent area of professional research and thinking.

It is not possible to describe all the issues of individual and family development and transitions over the life span. However, it is useful to note some of the most salient observations in order to emphasize the importance of family transitions as a major stressor on family life.

Individual Family Members Change Over Time

Erik Erikson (1976) views each life stage as a key "psychosocial crisis," which he defines *not* as a threat or catastrophe but as a turning point, a crucial period of increased vulnerability and heightened potential. The way in which an individual family member resolves the crisis can either enhance or weaken his or her ability to master crises in subsequent stages.

From a family perspective, the individual member's life stages can be viewed as "cogwheeling" with stages of others in the family. In the language of family systems theory this quality is called "interdependency." The major psychosocial crises in the individual family member's life cycle are presented in Table 7.1. Specifically, family members are called on to resolve personality and psychosocial crises such as building trust, becoming more autonomous, establishing interpersonal relationships, and developing a sense of personal integrity. Family members develop over time in pursuit of human goals of hope, competence, love, and wisdom.

Family Systems Change Over Time

Paralleling individual development tasks and responsibilities, the family unit assumes a separate set of responsibilities and tasks created by its own shifts in structure, roles, and rules. Family transitional events such as marriage, parenthood, launching, and middle age call for family reorganization and adaptation. They impose new responsibilities, open up new opportunities, and pose new challenges for the family unit.

TABLE 7.1 Individual Family Member Crises over the Life Cycle

Developmental Stage	Psychosocial Crises	Developmental Goals
Infancy	Trust vs. Mistrust	Hope
Early Childhood	Autonomy vs. Shame, Doubt	Will
Play Age	Initiative vs. Guilt	Purpose
School Age	Industry vs. Inferiority	Competence
Adolescence	Identity vs. Identity Confusion	Fidelity
Young Adulthood	Intimacy vs. Isolation	Love
Maturity	Generativity vs. Self-Absorption	Care
Old Age	Integrity vs. Despair, Disgust	Wisdom

SOURCE: Adapted from Erikson (1976, p. 25).

The developmental tasks for families are presented in Table 7.2. The family unit struggles with changes in structure (e.g., movement of members in and out of the family system), shifts in family roles (e.g., from couple to parent to grandparent), and tension created by changes in the needs of individual members as they navigate their personal course of development.

Family stress emerges as a consequence of ongoing development and evolution, structural reorganization, and unpredictable disruptions. Additionally, stress and strains emerge out of the individual family member's thoughts, actions, and emotions, interacting with and influencing changing events in the family and the outer world. Conversely, changing events in the community and society influence the changing events within the family member.

Klaus Riegel (1975) has attempted to describe these interrelated sources of stress (see Table 7.3). He noted the distinction between the timing of events that happen to males and those that happen to females. He describes differences in the influences of psychosocial and biological factors on each sex. For example, he views the birth of children as having a powerful biological effect upon mother and primarily a social effect upon father. His description of the interrelated sources of stress in the family as a result of adult and family developmental processes is presented in Table 7.3.

Family Stress Research

Within the family field, a considerable body of theory and research has evolved quite independently of the psychobiological stress and the

TABLE 7.2 Family Developmental Tasks Through the Family Life Cycle

Family Life Cycle	Stage-Critical Family Development Tasks
Married couple	• Establishing a mutually satisfying marriage. • Adjusting to pregnancy and the promise of parenthood. • Fitting into the kin network.
Childbearing and Preschool-Age	• Having, adjusting to, and encouraging the development of infants. • Establishing a satisfying home for both parents and infant(s). • Adapting to the critical needs and interests of preschool children in stimulating, growth-promoting ways. • Coping with energy depletion and lack of privacy as parents.
School-Age	• Fitting into the community of families of school-age children in constructive ways. • Encouraging children's educational achievement.
Teenage	• Balanced freedom with responsibility as teenagers mature and emancipate themselves. • Establishing postparental interests and careers as growing parents.
Launching center	• Releasing young adults into work, military service, college, marriage, and so on with appropriate rituals and assistance. • Maintaining a supportive home base.
Middle-Aged Parents	• Rebuilding the marriage relationship. • Maintaining kin ties with older and younger generations.
Aging Family Members	• Coping with bereavement and living alone. • Closing the family home or adapting it to aging. • Adjusting to retirement.

SOURCE: Adapted from Duvall (1977).

TABLE 7.3 Levels and Events in Adult Life

Level (Years)	Males Psychosocial	Males Biophysical	Females Psychosocial	Females Biophysical	Sudden Changes
1 (20-25)	College/first job; First child; Marriage		First job/college; Marriage	First child	
2 (25-30)	Second job; Other children; Children in preschool		Loss of job; Children in preschool	Other children	
3 (30-35)	Promotion; Move; Children in school		Without job; Move; Children in school		
4 (35-50)	Promotion; Departure of children; Second home		Second career; Departure of children; Second home		
5 (50-65)	Unemployment; Isolation; Grandfather; Head of kin	Incapacitation	Unemployment; Grandmother; Head of kin	Menopause	Loss of job; Loss of parents; Illness; Loss of friends
6 (65+)	Deprivation	Sensory-motor deficiencies	Widowhood	Widowhood; Incapacitation	Retirement; Loss of partner; Death

SOURCE: Riegel (1975, p. 107).

developmental stress research briefly summarized above. Beginning with the early work of Hill (1949), who studied the stressors of war separation and reunion, family scholars have made an effort to understand why it is that families faced with a single stressor event as loss, illness, or separation vary in their ability to adjust or adapt to the situation. Hill (1958) advanced the ABC-X Family Crisis Model, which states that

A (the stressor event)
    interacting with
B (the family's crisis meeting resources)
    interacting with
C (the definition the family makes of the event)
    produces X (the crisis).

In this model, Hill defined a *stressor* as a "situation for which the family has had little or no prior preparation" and *crisis* as "any sharp or decisive change from which old patterns are inadequate." These definitions are analogous to those used in life events research to define stressors and stress, respectively. Hill further described stressors in terms of their *hardships,* which he operationalized as the number of changes that were required by the stressor event. This concept of hardships corresponds to the weights or life change units assigned to life events in psychobiological stress research.

Building on this ABC-X Model, McCubbin and Patterson (1982) have advanced a Double ABC-X model (see Figure 7.1) to describe more adequately family adjustment and adaptation to stressors or family crises. In Hill's original model, the "a" factor was the stressor event. The Double ABC-X Model relabels the "a" factor as "Aa," or "Family Pile-Up," which includes the stressor (Hill's "a" factor), family hardships, and prior strains that continue to affect on family life.

In the context of the Double ABC-X Model a *stressor* is defined as a life event (normative or nonnormative), affecting the family unit at a discrete point in time, that produces change in the family social system. *Family hardships* are defined as those demands on the family unit specifically associated with the stressor event (e.g., increasing family financial debts when a parent loses a job). *Prior strains* are the residuals of family tension that linger from unresolved prior stressors or that are inherent in ongoing family roles such as being a parent or a spouse (Pearlin & Schooler, 1978).

When a new stressor is experienced by a family unit, prior strains are exacerbated and families become aware of them as demands with

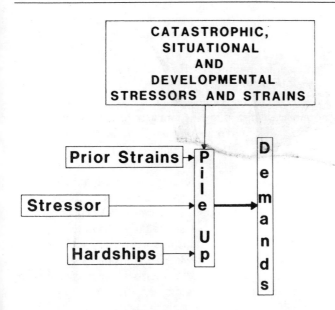

DOUBLE ABCX MODEL
OF
FAMILY STRESSORS AND STRAINS

SOURCE: McCubbin & Patterson (1982).

Figure 7.1   Double ABC-X Model of Family Stressors and Strains

which the family must also cope. For example, marital conflict may intensify when parents disagree about how to manage the care of a child just diagnosed to have a chronic illness. Unlike stressor events, which occur at discrete points in time, prior strains may not have a specific onset and may emerge more insidiously in the family. Just as their onset is unclear, the resolution of strains is often also unclear to families, which makes them even more difficult to deal with.

Demands on the family produce internal tension that requires management skills (Antonovsky, 1979). When this tension is not overcome, stress emerges. *Family stress,* as distinct from a stressor, is defined as a state of tension that arises from an actual or perceived demand that calls for adjustment or adaptive behavior. Consequently, *distress* is defined as stress that is perceived as unpleasant or undesirable by the member(s) of the family unit (McCubbin & Patterson, 1982).

McCubbin and Patterson (1982, 1983) have advanced the concept of the "pile-up" of family life stressors and strains as an important factor in predicting family adjustment over the family life cycle. Specifically, behavioral scientists have hypothesized that an excessive number of life changes and strains occurring within a brief period of time (one year) have a high probability of disrupting the family unit. This would contribute to deterioration of the family unit and of the emotional and physical well-being of its members. Golan (1981) offered a similar hypothesis in an attempt to explain why some families have so much more difficulty adapting to a war disaster such as a bombing. The family that is already struggling with other life changes such as a developmental transition, which is subjectively perceived as more urgent, may lack the resources to cope with any additional stressors.

If a family's resources (to cope with stressors) are already depleted, overtaxed, or exhausted from dealing with other life changes, the family unit may be less able to make further adjustments when confronted with additional social or interpersonal stressors. In other words, family life changes and strains are *additive* and may push the family unit to its limit. At this point in time, one would anticipate some negative consequences (e.g., marital discord, conflicts) in the family system and/or for its members (e.g., illness, emotional strain).

Consequently, family social scientists have attempted to link stress-illness research and family stress theory. This linkage is predicated on understanding the family as a "system" in terms of the interconnectedness of its members. What affects one person in the family also affects the others to some degree. Change in any part of the system requires some readjustment by the whole system and by individual members. Life events, both normative and nonnormative, that are experienced by the family as a whole or by any one member are all added together to determine the magnitude of a family's life change.

It is hypothesized that the pile-up of family stressors and strains would be positively associated with a decline in family functioning and the well-being of its members. However, we remain relatively unclear as to what are the "normal" life events and strains the family unit can anticipate or handle over the family cycle.

Normative Stressors and Strains over the Life Cycle

Families face many demands throughout the family life cycle. These demands are often described in terms of *family transitions, family pas-*

sages, family developmental tasks, and *family life events.* But past research has not documented in any systematic way the specific demands and most frequent family life stressors at each stage of the family cycle. In this section we will describe what various family members identify as their major family life stressors.

Husbands and wives were asked to identify the stressors and strains that their "family" had experienced during the past year. These stressors and strains were recorded on FILE and summarized by adding the number of times each stressor or strain was recorded with a "yes." The ten most frequently cited stressors or strains were identified within each of the seven stages of the family cycle. The results of this analysis are presented below.

To begin the discussion of stressors, an overall picture of how the pile-up of stressors and strains change developed over time. The actual number of stressor events that husbands and wives indicated at different steps of the life cycle is indicated in Figure 7.2. Our overview of family life stressors as presented in Figure 7.2 indicates: (a) the relative persistance of stressors and strains over the family cycle; (b) the major pile-up of stressors and strains occurring at the Adolescent (Stage 4) and Launching (Stage 5) stages of the family cycle; (c) the discernible drop in demands (stressors and strains) at the Empty Nest (Stage 6) and the Retired Couple (Stage 7) stages of the family cycle; and (d) the differences between husbands and wives in their assessment of the number of "demands" the family unit struggles with.

Specifically, wives reported more "demands" during the Childbearing (Stage 2), School-Age (Stage 3), Launching (Stage 5), and Empty Nest (Stage 6) stages of the family life cycle. This brief overview encourages us to probe more deeply into the distribution of specific stressors and strains that affect families at each stage of the family cycle.

Analysis focused on the cluster of stressors and strains most characteristic of *each stage* of the family cycle and on clusters that were consistently mentioned *across all stages* of the family cycle. By identifying the ten most frequently cited stressors and strains (recorded by either parent at each stage) and grouping them into their major categories (e.g., losses, illness, intrafamily strains), we can begin to understand more clearly the "pile-up" distribution of stressors and strains across the family cycle. (A more complete listing of all the stressors and strains and their frequencies is presented in Appendix E.)

The ten most frequently cited stressors and strains are presented in Table 7.4. First of all, there was a rather persistent struggle with financial

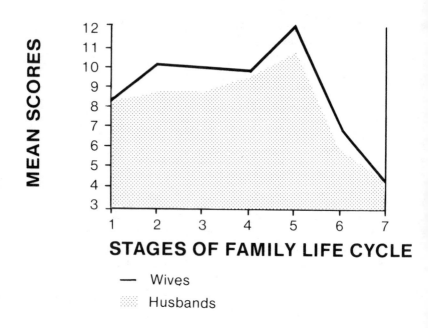

Figure 7.2   Life Events and Changes

stressors and strains across all stages of the family cycle. Financial strains are clearly problematic for families at the Childbearing (Stage 2), Adolescent (Stage 4), Launching (Stage 5), and the Retirement (Stage 7) stages.

Intrafamily strains were also problematic across the family cycle. However, intrafamily strains (e.g., father's time away, husband-wife conflict, chores not getting done) are most apparent during the School-Age (Stage 3) and Adolescent (Stage 4) stages of the family cycle. It comes as no surprise that work-family strains are also persistent across the family cycle. These strains (e.g., increased work responsibilities) are most apparent for the Young Couples (Stage 1) and the School-Age (Stage 3) stages of the family cycle.

Losses of relatives, family members, and close friends and illnesses appear to be associated with the Empty Nest (Stage 6) and Retirement (Stage 7) stages of the family cycle. However, it is important to note that

TABLE 7.4 Top Ten Stressors and Strains over the Family Life Cycle

Stressor	Young Couple (1)	Child-bearing (2)	Stage School-Age (3)	Adolescent (4)	Launch-ing (5)	Empty Nest (6)	Retire-ment (7)
Intra Family Strains	20[a]	20	50	30	20	10	10
Financial Strains	30	50	20	60	40	30	40
Work-Family Strains	40	10	30	10	10	10	10
Illnesses	10	10			10	20	20
Marital Strains						10	
Pregnancy		10					
Family Transitions					20		
Losses						20	20

a. Percentage of families reporting strain/stressor.

illnesses are also cited as major stressors during the Young Couple (Stage 1), Childbearing (Stage 2), and Launching (Stage 5) stages.

As expected, pregnancy stressors and strains are associated with the Childbearing (Stage 2) stage, and family transitions (e.g., children moving in and out of the family) are associated with the Launching (Stage 5) stage of the family cycle. It is surprising to note that marital strains emerges as a major stressor at the Empty Nest (Stage 6) stage.

STAGE 1: YOUNG COUPLES WITHOUT CHILDREN

Young couples indicated the most struggle in four areas of family stressors and strains: work-family strains (40 percent), finance and business strains (30 percent), intrafamily strains (20 percent), and illness and family "care" strains (10 percent). Specifically, the couple struggle with husband absence, incomplete home tasks, financial debts, and increased expenses. Additionally, the couple face changes in job/work situation and intrawork-related strains of dissatisfaction and worker conflicts. Surprisingly, the couple also experience illness of a relative or friend.

TABLE 7.5 Profile of Family Stressors and Strains: Stage 1 (Young Couples Without Children)

Stressor/Strain	Percentage Reporting Strain
Intrafamily Strains	
Increase in husband/father's time away from the family	32
Increase in the number of tasks or chores that do not get done.	36
Finance and Business Strains	
Took out a loan or refinanced a loan to cover increased expenses.	38
A member purchased a car or another major item.	50
Increased strain on family "money" for food, clothing, energy, home care.	50
Work-Family Strains	
A member changed to a new job/career.	46
Decrease in satisfaction with job/career.	44
A member had increased difficulty with people at work.	40
A member promoted at work or given more responsibilities.	54
Illness and Family Care Strains	
Close relative or friend of the family became seriously ill.	30

In general, these couples are called upon to adjust to the demands of shaping a lasting relationship, managing financial burdens, and handling work-related hardships, all of which place a burden upon younger couples. Table 7.5 provides the percentage of husbands and wives who identified specific stressors as problematic.

STAGE 2: CHILDBEARING STAGE

It comes as no surprise to note the increased demands of a child entering the family unit. Families at the childbearing stage of the family cycle struggle with financial and business strains (50 percent), intrafamily strains (20 percent), pregnancy and childbearing strains (10 percent), work-family strains (10 percent), and illness in the family unit (10 percent). Stressors associated with the advent of children include greater involvement in outside activities, decrease in satisfaction with job, and illness of a relative or friend.

TABLE 7.6   Profile of Family Stressors and Strains: Stage 2 (Childbearing Families)

Stressor/Strain	Percentage Reporting Strain
Intrafamily Strain	
Increase in the amount of "outside activities" in which the children are involved.	40
Increase in the number of tasks or chores that do not get done.	42
Pregnancy and Childbearing Strains	
Wife gave birth to or a member adopted a child.	34
Finance and Business Strains	
Took out a loan or refinanced a loan to cover increased expenses.	38
Change in conditions (economic, political, weather) that hurts family investments and/or income.	32
A member purchased a car or other major item.	50
Increased strain on family "money" for medical/dental expenses	20
Increased strain on family "money" for food, clothing, energy, home care	50
Work-Family Strains	
Decrease in satisfaction with job/career.	41
Illness and Family Care Strains	
Close relative or friend of the family became seriously ill.	30

The increase in financial strains was most notable at this stage. Some financial strains, such as loans, car purchases, medical expenses, financial debts, and related changes in economic, political, and weather conditions, were noteworthy. Table 7.6 lists the top ten stressors at this stage and the percentage of couples who saw these events as troublesome.

STAGE 3: FAMILIES WITH SCHOOL-AGE CHILDREN

Familes involved in the day-to-day routines of raising school-age children appear to struggle with a different grouping of family life stressors and strains. While financial strains (20 percent) of taking out a loan and increased expenditures continue, the majority of life events and strains are associated with intrafamily (50 percent) and work-family strains (30 percent). Specifically, these families face an increase in family-related demands such as children's outside activities, chores that do not get done, child-child conflicts, and child management difficulties

TABLE 7.7 Profile of Family Stressors and Strains: Stage 3 (Families with School-Age Children)

Stressor/Strain	Percentage Reporting Strain
Intrafamily Strains	
Increase of husband/father's time away from the family.	30
Increase in conflict among children in the family.	34
Increased difficulty in managing school-age children (6 to 11 years old).	32
Increase in the amount of "outside activities" in which the children are involved.	70
Increase in the number of tasks or chores that do not get done.	50
Finance and Business Strains	
A member purchased a car or other major item.	49
Increased strain on family "money" for food, clothing, energy, home care.	46
Work-Family Transition and Strains	
Decrease in satisfaction with job/career.	29
A member was promoted at work or given more responsibilities.	35
A member changed to a new job/career.	29

along with father-husband absence. Additionally, the parents appear to experience difficulty at work in terms of less satisfaction, more responsibilities, and changes to a new job/career.

STAGE 4: FAMILIES WITH ADOLESCENTS

Families struggling with the demands of raising an adolescent member appear to face yet another cluster of family demands. Specifically, these families face intrafamily strains (30 percent), financial strains (60 percent), and work-family strains (10 percent). This stage of the family cycle is characterized by difficulty managing teenage children, but even more important is the noteable increase in family finances and business strains. These families face not only loans and changes in economic and other conditions that hurt family investments and/or income, but also strains on family "money" matters and on funds for medical/dental expenses, food, clothing, and home care, as well as the child(ren's) education. The data clearly indicate that at the Adolescent stage of the family cycle, the family is pressured by economic and business strains.

TABLE 7.8   Profile of Family Stressors and Strains: Stage 4 (Families with Adolescents)

Stressor/Strain	Percentage Reporting Strain
Intrafamily Strains	
Increased difficulty in managing teenage children.	30
Increase in the amount of "outside activities" in which children are involved.	68
Increase in the number of tasks or chores that do not get done.	48
Finance and Business Strains	
Took out a loan or refinanced a loan to cover increased expenses.	33
Change in conditions (economic, political, weather) that hurts family investments and/or income.	34
A member purchased a car or other major item.	43
Increased strain on family "money" for medical/dental expenses.	31
Increased strain on family "money" for food, clothing, energy, home care.	62
Increased strain on family "money" for children's education.	30
Work-Family Transitions and Strains	
A member was promoted at work or given more responsibilities	330

STAGE 5: LAUNCHING FAMILIES

Families in the process of launching young adults continue to face the demands of financial and business strains (40 percent). Specifically, loans or refinanced loans, purchases of major items, and increased expenses for food, clothing, energy, home care, and child(ren's) education continue to be important sources of stress for the family unit.

Predictably, families at this stage struggle with young adult members leaving home (20 percent) and beginning post-high school education/training. Additionally, these families face the intrafamily strains (20 percent) of an increase in children's outside activities, an increase in tasks or chores that do not get done, and a member changing to a new job/career (10 percent), as well as the serious illness (10 percent) of a close relative or friend of the family.

TABLE 7.9 Profile of Family Stressors and Strains: Stage 5 (Launching Families)

Stressor/Strain	Percentage Reporting Strain
Intrafamily Strains	
Increase in the amount of "outside" activities in which the children are involved.	49
Increase in the number of tasks or chores that do not get done.	45
Finance and Business Strains	
Took out a loan or refinanced a loan to cover increased expenses.	35
A member purchased a car or other major item.	51
Increased strain on family "money" for food, clothing, energy, home care.	54
Increased strain on family "money" for children's education.	51
Work-Family Transitions and Strains	
A member changed to a new job/career.	34
Illness and Family Care Strains	
Close relative or friend of the family became seriously ill.	36
Transition "In and Out"	
Young adult member left home.	38
Young adult member began college (for post-high school training).	45

STAGE 6: EMPTY NEST FAMILIES

As the children/young adults exit from the family to assume new roles and responsibilities, the remaining couple face additional demands. Specifically, at this stage, the couple face a full range of stressors and strains in areas of intrafamily strains (10 percent), marital strains (10 percent), financial strains (40 percent), work-family strains (10 percent), illness (20 percent), and losses (20 percent).

To be specific, these families struggle with chores not getting done, difficulty with sexual relationship between husband and wife, financial hardships or threats to family investments, major purchases, and financial strains on purchasing food, clothing, energy, and home care. Additionally, there is a decrease in satisfaction with job/career, serious illness of relative or friend, and death of spouse's parent, close relative, or close friend of the family.

TABLE 7.10   Profile of Family Stressors and Strains: Stage 6 (Empty Nest
Families)

Stressor/Strain	Percentage Reporting Strain
Intrafamily Strains	
Increase in the number of tasks or chores that do not get done.	36
Marital Strains	
Increased difficulty with sexual relationship between husband and wife.	19
Finance and Business Strains	
Change in conditions (economic, political, weather) that hurts family investments and/or income.	27
A member purchased a car or other major item.	32
Increased strain on family "money" for food, clothing, energy, home care.	30
Work-Family Transitions and Strains	
Decrease in satisfaction with job/career.	27
Illness and Family Care Strains	
Close relative or friend of the family became seriously ill.	34
Family member experienced menopause.	31
Losses	
Death of husband's or wife's parent or close relative.	22
Close friend of the family died.	22

STAGE 8: FAMILIES IN RETIREMENT

With the children launched, the adult members of the "empty nest" move out of the work role into retirement and face another set of family stressors and demands. Financial strains (40 percent) continue to be major sources of stress. The couple face threats to family investments or income, major purchases, and increased expenses for medical and dental expenses as well as financial strains related to food, clothing, energy, and home care. Additionally, they are called on to cope with intrafamily strains (10 percent); a parent/spouse, close friend, or relative becoming seriously ill (20 percent); and work-family transitions (10 percent). They also face the death of husband's or wife's parent (20 percent), close relative, or close friend.

SUMMARY

In general, it would appear that family stressors and strains are both uniform and unique across stages of the family cycle. Family stressors and strains associated with financial demands, intrafamily struggles,

TABLE 7.11   Profile of Family Stressors and Strains: Stage 7 (Retirement Families)

Stressor/Strain	Percentage Reporting Strain
Intrafamily Strains	
Increase in the number of tasks or chores that do not get done.	23
Finance and Business Strains	
Change in agriculture market, stock market, or land values that hurts family investments and/or income.	14
A member purchased a car or other major item.	23
Increased strain on family "money" for medical/dental expenses.	17
Increased strain on family "money" for food, clothing, energy, home care	15
Work-Family Transitions and Strains	
A member retired from work.	23
Illness and Family Care Strains	
Parent/spouse became seriously ill or injured.	14
Close relative or friend of the family became seriously ill.	22
Losses	
Death of husband's or wife's parents and/or close relative	21
Close friend of the family died.	28

and work-family difficulties persist across all stages of the family cycle. While marital strains may be common, they are most evident at the latter or empty nest stage of the family cycle. Contrary to our common-sense notion of family losses associated with the latter years of the family cycle, we discovered that the loss of relatives and close friends affect families at the couple and childbearing stages of the family cycle as well.

Specific Stressors and Strains Across the Life Cycle

These analyses of stressors and strains across the family cycle provide us with a feel for the complex and relatively uneven manner in which life events punctuate family life. While these data focus our attention on difficulties families face, we need a more in-depth examination of these stressors to grasp fully the impact of life events and strains on family functioning (see Table 7.12).

TABLE 7.12   Specific Stressors and Strains Across the Family Cycle

Stressor/Strain[a]
Intrafamily and Marital Strains
Increase in the number of tasks or chores that do not get done.
A member appears to have emotional problems.
Increased difficulty with sexual relationship between husband and wife.
Finance and Business Strains
Change in conditions (economic, political, weather) that hurts family investments and/or income.
Change in agriculture market, stock market, or land values that hurts family investments and/or income.
A member purchased a car or other major item.
Increased strain on family money for medical/dental expenses.
Increased strain on family money for food, clothing, energy, and home care.
Work-Family Transitions and Strains
A member changed to a new job/career.
A member lost, quit, or retired from a job.
Illness and Family Care Strains
Parent/spouse became seriously ill or injured.
Close relative or friend of the family became seriously ill.
Losses
Death of husband's or wife's parents and/or close relative.
Close friend of the family died.

a.   At least 10 percent across all seven stages.

By identifying those life events and family strains that 10 percent or more families record as affecting them, we can begin to construct a rather vivid picture of those common threads of "demands" that shape the course of family adjustment and adaptation across all stages of the family cycle.

Tasks that do not get done. Contrary to popular belief that well-functioning families are efficient and effective, the data clearly indicate that in the context of modern America, families are faced with the stressor of incomplete tasks. This apparently is a source of strain, particularly during the School-Age, Adolescent, and Launching stages of the family cycle.

Emotional difficulties in family life. Families called attention to the fact that some members experience emotional problems. This was true for families across all stages of the family cycle. It was a particularly important issue for families at the Launching stage of the family cycle.

Sexual difficulty between husband and wife. While this may be an extremely private matter, families are also willing to note that the husband-wife sexual relationship is a source of strain across all stages of the family cycle. However, this is more likely to be reported as an issue during the Young Couple, Childbearing, Adolescent, and Launching stages of the family life cycle.

Unstable economic conditions. In this era of economic distress, it comes as no surprise to note the frequent mention of family difficulty with changes in conditions (economic, political, or weather) that hurt family investments and /or income. This is a particularly important issue for families in the Childbearing, Adolescent, Launching, and Empty Nest years of the family cycle. Interestingly, the issue of the economy as a stressor appears to affect couples deciding to or beginning to raise children; families in the middle years; families sending their young ones off to college, school, or the work force; and families preparing for retirement.

Major economic investments and purchases. As families face an unstable economic climate, they are also called on to make major investments in an automobile or other important items. This stressor is most prevalent before the Launching stage of the family cycle.

Medical and/or dental expenses. With rising interest rates, and the associated higher cost of living, families note the difficulty of paying for increased medical and dental expenses. This stressor is particularly noticeable during the Childbearing and child-rearing stages of the family cycle. This matter gains added importance when we take into consideration the General Mills report on *Stress and Health* (1979), which indicated that low-income families will sacrifice quality and preventative health care as a means of coping with economic stressors. This stressor appears to affect families at all stages of the family life cycle but is particularly threatening to parents during the early stages of rearing infants and young children.

Money for basics of family living. No family escapes the impact of economic instability. Families in this study point to the stressor of less money today for food, clothing, energy, and the like. Newly formed families (young couples), families raising children, and families with adolescents call particular attention to this stressor.

Changing jobs and/or careers. Families noted the transition of members from one job or career to another; this was true across all stages of the family cycle. However, this stressor was most prevalent during the Young Couple stage and the Launching stage of the family cycle. Young couples are in search of their careers; families in the middle years often face wives entering the work force after raising children, and men are possibly in search of a new job and/or career.

Lost, quit, or retired from a job. A family member's departure from the work force on the basis of choice or as a result of an employer's decision is a stressor that has an impact on all families across all stages of the family cycle. This stressor is particularly prevalent during the Young Couple and the Launching stages of the family cycle. In other words, the loss of work for whatever reason has a marked affect on young families and families in the middle years. When we consider that families in the middle years are already loaded with other normative stressors and strains and are called upon to support their young adults, we can begin to picture a family unit "at risk."

Illness in the family. A serious illness for a close relative or family member is obviously not confined to the later years. Families across stages face the prospect of serious illness affecting them. However, this stressor is particularly prevalent at the Launching and Empty Nest stages of the family cycle.

Death in the family. As was true for illness in the family, the death of a family member or close friend also affects families throughout the life cycle. However, it is equally true that this loss of a significant other is most prevalent during the Adolescent, Launching, Empty Nest, and Retirement stages of the family cycle.

These stressors and strains do not appear to occur with sufficient frequency to indicate that they are ubiquitous and therefore normal aspects of family life. However, it is reasonable to argue that although infrequent, these stressors and strains do affect families across all stages of the family cycle. They occur with sufficient regularity to note their importance.

Conclusion

It seems reasonable to conclude from these observations that families struggle with both normative and nonnormative stressors and strains. Balancing financial demands with work-family strains and intrafamily struggles in an effort to maintain harmony is a difficult challenge throughout the life cycle. Given that the families involved in this study have responded to these challenges in a relatively constructive and enduring fashion, it would be helpful for us to examine further the resources and coping strategies they have used in responding to these demands and strains over the life span.

chapter
VIII
Family Coping Strategies

TRADITIONALLY, FAMILY STRESS has been viewed as a problematic situation to be contrasted with the smooth operation of a family unit. As a result, the study of family stress has focused on documenting the numerous psychological, interpersonal, and social changes in the family's response to stressors and related hardships.

Currently, most investigations appear to be shifting away from this "dysfunctional" view of family stress to an interest in accounting for why some families are better able than others to endure hardships over the life span. This recent emphasis, which views "demands" as prevalent and predictable but not necessarily problematic, has led to our increased interest in coping behavior. We believe that understanding how families cope with stress is just as important as understanding the frequency and severity of life changes and transitions themselves. This notion is supported by the accumulating empirical evidence that links coping to successful individual and family adjustment.

Considering coping styles in families, three general questions emerge. First, *how do members use the resources available within their family to cope?* This question can be approached from the perspective of both resources used by individual family members and resources that are combined to form a collective set of internal strategies. Of particular interest is the differences between coping styles of families who report low levels of stress versus those who experience higher levels of stress.

Second, *how do families use resources from outside their system to cope with stressful life events?* This question explores the family's use of external community and social support systems. Third, *are there differences among families in their use of internal versus external coping strategies and are these differences related to their stage of the family life cycle?*

This chapter addresses these questions by reviewing the conceptual literature on coping in both individuals and families. A rationale for the use of F-COPES, an instrument designed to assess internal and external coping strategies, is presented and described. The chapter concludes with an examination of families' current use of specific community programs and services. It also explores the types of programs and services they would like to have available to help them cope with problems.

The present interest in family coping signals an important shift in our priorities in the study of family behavior under stress. We have moved from a simple "fight versus flight" notion of coping to the study of the complex processes of acquiring, building, exchanging, and using resources to resist and adjust to the impact of demands.

Four basic hypotheses have been suggested from the limited number of family-oriented coping studies conducted to date. Coping behaviors can potentially: (1) decrease the family's vulnerability to stress, (2) strengthen or maintain those family resources that serve to protect the family from the full impact of problems, (3) reduce or eliminate the impact of stressor events and their specific hardships, and (4) involve the process of actively influencing the environment by doing something to change the social circumstances to make it easier for the family to adjust to the difficult situation (McCubbin, Joy, Cauble, Comeau, Patterson, & Needle, 1980).

We would add a fifth hypothesis that coping strategies will differ with stages of the family life cycle. What may be used to handle family demands at an early stage, such as the transition to parenthood, may not be used or useful at a later stage, such as retirement.

Prior Research and Theory About Coping

Over its relatively brief history of study, coping has acquired a rich variety of definitions, which despite a common thread have varying degrees of generality and abstraction (Meneghan, 1983). Often these definitions have been used interchangeably (Pearlin & Schooler, 1978), leading to considerable confusion among both researchers and practitioners. We have highlighted three basic themes from the literature: (1) coping as a process, (2) coping efficacy, and (3) individual and family coping.

COPING AS A PROCESS

Coping is a life-long process that has no fixed beginning or endpoint. Coping can occur at both the individual and family levels, but most individual problems have an impact first on other family members and then become a family concern. Much of the earlier work on coping was done on the individual level, but increasing attention is being given to coping in the family.

Beginning at the individual level of coping, we go to the classic work of Lois Murphy (1974), whose longitudinal studies of young children have provided a wealth of knowledge in the field of child development. Murphy insightfully captures some of the complexities of coping, emphasizing the process dimension of this concept. Murphy contrasts coping with simple problem-solving skills that resolve the difficulties of daily living with relative ease. Coping goes beyond the confines of problem solving and includes the trial-and-error attempts that follow when resolution is not apparent.

Thus coping *emerges* from a stressful context, illustrated by Robert White (1974, p. 48), who quotes Shakespeare: "when the sea was calm all boats alike show mastership in floating," and then extends the metaphor, "only in a storm were they obliged to cope." Coping, therefore, is a response to change and calls forth creativity and production of new behavior (Coles & Coles, 1978).

From a more sociological perspective, Klein (1983) makes a similar comparison to Murphy's, examining two rather separate fields of study — family problem solving and family stress and coping. In comparing the two, he sees stress as more severe, more disruptive, the event as more unclear and more difficult to control.

Linking these two concepts together in another way, McCubbin, Joy, et al. (1980) describe problem-solving abilities as an important resource that may be drawn on to develop a coping strategy in times of stress. Other authors, such as Pearlin and Schooler (1978), place less emphasis on the crisis as the precipitating factor and instead emphasize the protective function of coping. This buffering or insulating effect serves to alleviate the associated strains and emotional stress that typically come with a stressor event.

Meneghan (1983) has elaborated on the definition presented by Pearlin and Schooler and introduces a categorical scheme for coping. The three broad groupings are: (1) *resources,* generalized attitudes about oneself and the world, and *skills,* both intellectual and interpersonal; (2) *coping styles,* the habitual preferences for problem-solving plans; and (3) *coping efforts,* the specific actions that are taken in specific situations to resolve the issue.

While this definition of coping is comprehensive, one must guard against the concept becoming too global. This problem of global and expansive definitions is a common one for many key concepts in the stress field. Our resolution of this problem will be presented later on in this chapter when we provide our own definition of coping with the description of F-COPES.

EXAMINING COPING EFFECTIVENESS

The measurement of "optimal" or successful coping is another area of controversy in the study of coping. Meneghan (1982, p. 94) writes, "Implicit in the concept of coping at all levels is the notion of effectiveness." Yet how do we know what kinds of coping are most effective? Pearlin and Schooler (1978, p. 11) were among the first to introduce criteria for assessing successful outcome. They define coping efficacy as "the ability of coping behaviors to reduce the causal impact of the stressor event upon the definition of the event as a crisis."

This definition must be qualified, however, with the knowledge that efficacy is always framed by its cultural context. Reiss (1981) for example, describes some of what makes up our Western ideology in terms of successful adjustment. The component parts of successful coping include rationality, objective appraisal, and a sense of control or mastery. Optimal coping is determined by the variety of solutions that a culture provides (Mechanic, 1974). Hansen and Hill (1964) describe the role of the community in dealing with stress, offering "blueprints for behavior."

Other authors cautiously warn against making judgments that imply that the researchers might know what successful coping includes. Reiss and Oliveri (1980, p. 443) write: "In our fledgling science of family stress and coping we may be rushing to judgment, on very slender evidence concerning which strategies are 'best.' " They explain that coping may at times be "creative and inspired" but at other times "banal and tragic."

While the process dimension of coping is theoretically intriguing, it does make it more difficult to identify what is successful coping. What may be effective at one time in a given process may not be at all helpful at another point in time. Furthermore, coping that may not look at all useful may eventually turn out to be much more fruitful than another strategy that initially looked ideal. Establishing coping efficacy may dangerously oversimplify the construct and may offer "a finality which blinds us to longer range consequences and to the capricious aspects of family life" (Klein, 1983). To conclude, we borrow from Meneghan (1983), who stated: "The effectiveness of coping varies considerably, depending on one's choice of outcome criteria and time frame in which effects are examined."

INDIVIDUAL AND/OR FAMILY COPING

There is an increasing amount of interest in how individual coping extends to family coping after some stressor event occurs. David Reiss and colleagues have also struggled with the notion of family coping. They define it as a response when "the family is called upon to exert unusual effort to observe, to experience, to define, to understand and to take some kind of special action so that it can return to the more orderly routines of daily life" (Reiss & Oliveri, 1980, p. 431).

Investigations have revealed that a family's strategy for coping is not created in a single instant but is progressively modified over time. Because the family is a system, coping behaviors involve the management of various dimensions of family life simultaneously: (1) maintaining satisfactory internal conditions for communication and family organization, (2) promoting member independence and self-esteem, (3) maintenance of family bonds of coherence and unity, (4) maintenance and development of social supports in transactions with the community, and (5) maintenance of some efforts to control the impact of the stressor and the amount of change in the family unit. Coping then becomes a process of achieving a balance in the family system that facilitates organization and unity and promotes individual growth and development (McCubbin, Joy, et al., 1980).

Shifting from the individual level to a family level of coping, coping becomes much more complex. This has been cautiously attempted by only a few due to the enormous number of theoretical and methodological problems involved. This explains why researchers have focused mainly on the individual level of coping. Klein (1983) suggests that it is dangerous to assume theoretically that groups have the same properties as individuals. The issues of measurement are especially cumbersome in terms of accounting for individual members and the family as a whole.

Despite these problems, inroads into family coping have been made. Reuben Hill's (1949) family separation study is a classic example. Hill borrowed Koos's (1946) description of coping as a roller coaster process of adjustment that involves initial disorganization, followed by recovery and reorganization.

McCubbin (1979) expanded upon Hill's ABC-X stress framework, arguing that coping behavior is an "integral part of a family's total repetoire of adaptive behaviors." He integrates the reaction portion of coping and the active responses a family makes with its environment. This definition takes a somewhat different slant, emphasizing the family's response to stress as both an intrafamily (member to member) and a transactional (family and community) process. These active processes of family adjustment and adaptation involved have only recently received attention (McCubbin & Patterson, 1983; Meneghan, 1981).

Therefore, in making the shift to the family level of analysis, several dimensions emerge. First of all, in addition to the individual's perspectives, the subjective reality of the family becomes an entity in its own right. Reiss (1981) describes this as the family's "paradigm," or group construction of reality. Hansen and Johnson (1979) also indicate that the family must be considered as a complex group.

Second, the interactional nature of coping becomes far more important in a family. Coordination between family members emerges as a critical variable. Since family coping is a *collection of individual responses,* it is reasonable to assume that some specific strategies may be more important than others, especially at given points in the life cycle and in connection to specific stressor events.

Certain coping strategies, such as compromise, may require more equal input from all family members. Other strategies may depend more on the parents than on the children. An example of this might be establishing who will make certain kinds of decisions in times of crisis. Lastly, certain coping strategies may operate effectively for the family when only one member is "assigned" the task. The role for one member may be to acquire social support from outside networks to aid the family in dealing with a crisis. The role for another may be to stabilize the family by reframing the situation. It is clear that family coping needs to be defined differently than individual coping in order to encompass the internal and external family processes.

Recent discussions of the role of coping in the family's response to stressful circumstances focus on two basic sets of coping patterns: resistance coping and adaptive coping. *Resistance coping* is the family's collective efforts to minimize or reduce the impact of a stressor. *Adaptive coping* is the family's collective efforts to reorganize and consolidate itself and return to orderliness should a stressor disrupt the family unit. Family efforts at coping are designed to change the stressful circumstances, reduce family tension, and maintain family unity and balance in the face of stress and distress (McCubbin & Patterson, 1983).

Family coping is viewed as more than the family's responses to a stressor. Rather, it is viewed as a set of interactions *within* the family and transactions *between* the family and the community. Within this framework, coping changes over time and varies as a result of the stressor, the severity of the stressor, the extent of the "pile-up" of other demands, the amount of disturbance in the family system, and the availability and use of intrafamily and community resources (McCubbin & Patterson, 1983). While it is highly unlikely that any single study could capture or measure the highly complex nature of family coping, we have attempted to understand the underlying dimensions of coping and how these dimensions vary across the family life cycle.

Assessing Family Coping

In the last decade, family researchers have continued to develop coping inventories to measure various strategies that emerge from a host of stressful contexts (McCubbin & Patterson, 1982). The inventory on Family Coping Strategies (F-COPES) represents another attempt in this series. It was created to identify effective problem-solving approaches and behaviors used by families in response to problems or difficulties. It was initially designed to integrate family resources and the meaning perception factors identified in family stress theory (Hill, 1964; Hill & Hansen, 1965; Burr, 1973; McCubbin & Patterson, 1983).

While the five coping strategies presented in Table 8.1 are considered important to families, it should be noted that these strategies represent only a small sampling of the expansive repetoire of coping responses actually used by families. For this study, these strategies were used to discern whether their use made a difference in a family's adjustment to stressors, hardships, and strains. In addition, we investigated the type and amount of coping strategies used in different types of families (Balanced, Mid-Range, and Extreme) and at different stages of the family life cycle.

INTERNAL FAMILY COPING STRATEGIES

We will now review each coping strategy more carefully and examine how frequently each is used over the family life cycle. We will begin with the *internal* (intrafamily processes) strategies: reframing and passive appraisal. Both strategies assess the family's ability to define the stressor event as a challenge that can be overcome (reframing) or as something that will take care of itself over time (passive appraisal). Families can often cope with stress more effectively if they can develop

TABLE 8.1 Description of Family Coping Strategies (F-COPES)

Strategy	Description
Internal	*The ways in which individual members deal with difficulties by using resources residing within their own family.*
Reframing	The family's ability to redefine stressful experiences in a way that makes them more acceptable and manageable. Reframing assesses how families view change, with respect to their confidence in being able to handle problems.
Passive Appraisal	To balance the more active behaviors included in other factors, this scale focuses more on the less responsive approaches a family might employ when faced with stress. By adopting a more passive approach, responsibility and self-initiative are minimized for dealing with difficulties.
External	*The behavior individual members employ to acquire resources outside their family.*
Acquiring Social Support	The family's ability to engage actively in utilizing resources from relatives, friends, neighbors, and extended family.
Seeking Spiritual Support	The family's ability to acquire spiritual support.
Mobilizing Family to Acquire and Accept Help	The family's ability to seek out community resources and accept help from others.

explanations for how the event happened, why the event happened, and how their social environment could be rearranged to overcome the undesirable situation (Reiss, 1981; Gerhardt, 1979).

Reframing Over the Family Life Cycle

The strategy described as reframing looks at different types of *meanings* the family uses to describe the stressor event. Watzlawick, Weakland, and Fisch (1974, p. 95), who first coined the term, write:

> To reframe means to change the conceptual and/or emotional setting or viewpoint in which a situation is experienced, and to place it in another frame which fits the "facts" of the same concrete situation equally well or even better; and thereby change its entire meaning.

The importance of this strategy is also explained by Marris, who states that people change or adjust to difficulties after they have established *meaning* or made sense of the change. Lazarus (1966, 1977) argues that it is the cognitive processes that determine the intensity of emotional reactions. In particular, he emphasizes the notion of control that comes through perception. The "cognitive appraisal" of an event or strain may help neutralize the impact by minimizing the danger and bolstering one's confidence in mastering certain tasks.

Other authors write about similar kinds of cognitive appraisal processes e.g., Haan, 1977; Antonovsky, (1979). Antonovsky describes "coherence" as an appraisal process that goes beyond a specific coping strategy, resembling more of a world view. Coherence includes a sense of confidence that one's environment is predictable and understandable. The difference between coherence and cognitive appraisal is that coherence plays down the mastery notion and incorporates the belief that a certain degree of fatalism is also important.

Fatalism is defined here as knowing when certain events are beyond one's control and accepting this with minimal discomfort. Pearlin and Schooler (1978) underscored the importance of this coping strategy. They found that when people faced situations over which they had little control (such as being laid off or financial stresses), a sense of mastery and confidence in taking charge were not useful. However, in dealing with problems that resided in interpersonal difficulties (such as parent-child struggles) these same strategies were critical.

The strategy we call reframing represents an attempt to capture the ideas of these various authors. It is the family's ability to redefine a demanding situation in a more rational and acceptable way in order to make the situation more manageable. It assesses the family's ability to tackle obstacles, to display confidence publically, and to initiate

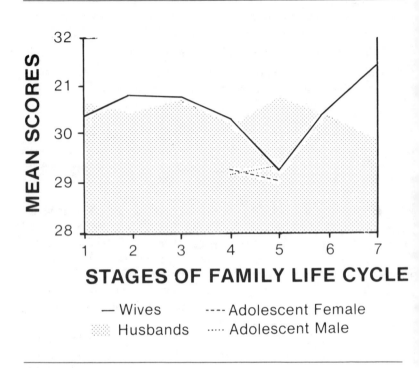

Figure 8.1   Reframing

problem-solving strategies early on in the experience. Equally im-portant, reframing assesses the family's ability to identify selectively which events can be successfully altered and which are beyond one's control. Those that are beyond one's control are redefined in a way that makes it easier to accept. Reframing is similar to what Pearlin and Schooler (1978) identify as "positive comparisons" and "selective ig-noring."

Our analysis of family reframing over the life cycle in Figure 8.1 reveals that both husbands and wives emphasize its importance over time. There were no differences in scores over the seven stages. The average score suggests that parents utilize this strategy more often than other strategies assessed in this inventory. However, while husbands consistently refer to reframing as the coping strategy of choice, wives indicate less emphasis on reframing during adolescence and more use of it during the retirement stage of the family cycle. As expected, adolescents seem less likely to indicate reframing as a strategy used by their families in stressful situations.

Passive Appraisal Over the Family Life Cycle

Whereas reframing reflects an accepting and optimistic orientation toward issues, passive appraisal operates more as an avoidance response to problems. This strategy tends to reflect a more pessimistic attitude toward resolving issues, similar to what Pearlin and Schooler (1978) identified as "helpless resignation." Pearlin and Schooler suggest this strategy is a complementary asset to other coping behaviors. Hansen and Johnson (1979) have also alluded to the idea that "misperception" might make a stressful situation more tolerable by delaying any active or immediate response. It may protect the family from becoming overwhelmed or creating unrealistically high expectations about controlling the outcome of a crisis.

Our analysis of passive appraisal over the family life cycle indicates relatively minimal emphasis upon this strategy by both husbands and wives (see Figure 8.2). Adolescents, however, are inclined to respond slightly more passively than their parents. While there are no differences between husbands and wives in their reported use, there are differences between life-cycle stages. We can note a gradual increase in the use of this strategy by both husbands and wives particularly during the Launching, Empty Nest, and Retirement stages (Stage 5, 6, and 7) of the life cycle.

In contrast, husbands and wives seem to be more responsive and less likely to sit back and wait a crisis out during earlier stages (such as Child Rearing). More secifically, in making comparisons between the various stages, we found no differences between husbands and wives. Scores were significantly lower at the first three stages of the life cycle than at the last two stages.

It is possible that the major stressful life events and strains that occur during the earlier stages can be managed best by acknowledging one's responsibilities and taking charge more quickly. In contrast, it appears that in the later stages greater acceptance of circumstances and less reactivity are the more useful and pragmatic responses.

EXTERNAL FAMILY COPING STRATEGIES

Social support networks such as extended family members (Caplan, 1976), friends, and neighbors (Litwak & Szelenyi, 1969) make up a large portion of the family's bank of resources. Family resources can also include such factors as the family's approaches to problem-solving (Aldous, Condon, Hill, Straus, & Tallman, 1971; Klein & Hill, 1979).

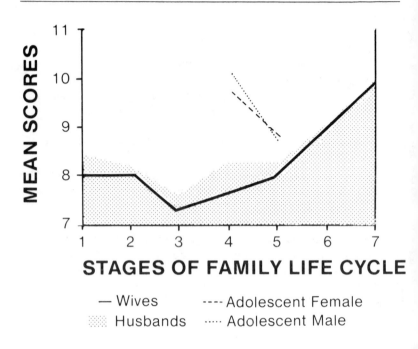

Figure 8.2 Passive Appraisal

Our goal is to identify how a family *uses* the external resources it has at its disposal. This contrasts with the focus of most studies, which have tended to deal more with the description of social support and support networks as resources. Later in this chapter we will also examine some specific resources in which people at various stages of the family life cycle expressed an interest.

There is considerable controversy regarding how valuable social support from others is in coping with stress. Croog, Lipson, and Levine (1972) maintain that the role of social support networks has remained ambiguous. Hansen and Hill (1964) point out the fact that social networks are not always helpful. In fact, in some instances they may intensify the stressfulness of the situation and increase dependency and produce conflict. This fits with what Pearlin and Schooler (1978) found in respect to self-reliance versus help seeking. Self-reliance was far more effective in reducing stress, especially in family relationship problems, than in soliciting help from others.

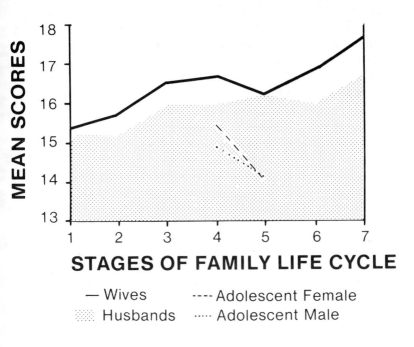

MEAN SCORES

STAGES OF FAMILY LIFE CYCLE

— Wives   ---- Adolescent Female

Husbands   ····· Adolescent Male

Figure 8.3 Seeking Social Support

Do families benefit from specific kinds of support when faced with a specific stressor event? Are there certain types of social support that are temporarily helpful but not useful in the long run? Unger and Powell (1980) argue that families employ different kinds of support networks for different kinds of needs. Pearlin and Schooler (1978) again remind us that successful coping depends not only on *what* we do, but also on *how much* we do it.

To respond to some of these issues, various types of social support have been identified and reviewed. These include: spiritual support, social support, friends, kin and neighbors, and the more formalized support networks available in the community.

Seeking Spiritual Support

This coping strategy identifies family efforts to seek and rely on spiritual support in the face of stressors and strains. Several studies have indicated the importance of spiritual resources in dealing with problematic situations. McCubbin and Lester (1977) found that religious beliefs were a critical coping strategy in managing long-term separations. McCubbin, Dahl, Lester, Benson, and Robertson (1976) also report that religion aided families in tolerating more chronic conditions of father absence. They suggest that spiritual support contributes to maintaining the family unit, and individual self-esteem. It may also serve to decrease the social ambiguity by acting as a reference point for social norms and expectations that guide the family in stressful situations.

Families who use this strategy seek advice from ministers, attend church services, participate in church activities, and have faith in God. This coping strategy is considered important by both husbands and wives throughout the family life cycle. However, the analysis revealed that wives emphasized this coping strategy to a greater degree than their husbands did (see Figure 8.3). There were significant differences between partners, and adolescents were significantly lower than either parent.

There were also significant differences in how members utilize this strategy at various stages of the life cycle. There was significantly less use of spiritual support during the two earliest stages than at the five later stages.

Wives, who showed more stage differences than their husbands did, appeared to employ this coping strategy to a greater extent during the Empty Nest and Retirement stages. Given the increased probability of illness and losses at later stages, one can anticipate a greater reliance on religious beliefs to cope with such stressful life circumstances.

An additional explanation for these findings may be the fact that there are differences between cohorts, i.e., the period in which subjects were born and the social and economic circumstances they faced and experience. The data may reflect a greater dependence on traditional religious organizations for support among older couples because this strategy is less predominant among younger couples today.

Acquiring Social Support

Past research (Koos, 1946; Hill, 1949; Bott, 1957) confirms the overall value of support networks that help people pool or exchange resources for the betterment of the total group. Cassel (1976) and Cobb (1976) emphasize more informal network sources of support such as family, friends, and co-workers. These are considered to be the most predominant sources of support. People generally use these informal networks more readily than they use more formal networks such as community agencies and professional services (Croog, Lipson, & Levine, 1972; Cobb, 1979).

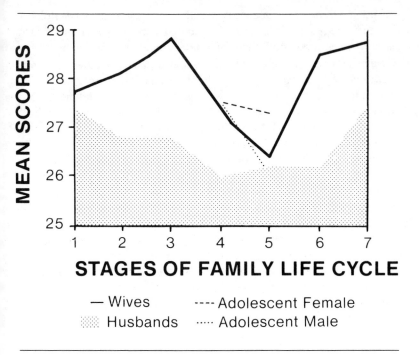

MEAN SCORES (y-axis: 25, 26, 27, 28, 29)

STAGES OF FAMILY LIFE CYCLE (x-axis: 1 2 3 4 5 6 7)

— Wives   ---- Adolescent Female
░ Husbands   ····· Adolescent Male

Figure 8.4   Acquiring Social Support

House (1980) summarizes the findings from many studies and concludes that the most important kind of social support is *esteem* support, or interpersonal transactions that show emotional concern. The ability to ask for and receive this kind as well as other types of support has been found to have a positive influence on health (Cobb, 1976). Other studies have produced similar findings, noting that families are more able to cope with normative and unanticipated stressors when they are: (1) connected to a supportive network and (2) actively involving this network in the problem-solving process (Croog et al., 1972; Burke & Weir, 1977; Hamburg & Adams, 1967). The impact from these sources of support has often been minimized.

To use these untapped resources more fully, certain ecological therapies actively recruit support networks and engage them in the therapeutic process. Speck and Atteneave (1971) herald the practicality of these support systems as being not only more effective in problem solving but also more psychologically respectful. The underlying assumption behind informal networks is that they are reciprocal, implying a mutual obligation for all parties involved. People may be more able to ask for help if they know they may have something to offer someone else at a later date. House (1981) notes that support from these informal networks may seem more genuine because it is not role related. People may offer support more spontaneously, based on their relative status equity.

Our examination of the acquisition of social support indicates that families seek and maintain friendships and community ties during difficult times. Families who emphasize this strategy seek advice from relatives, neighbors, and friends; encouragement from friends; and information from persons who may face similar situations.

There are some overall differences in the use of this strategy between stages (see Figure 8.4) and between husbands and wives. Specific differences were found between Stage 1 (Couples Without Children) and Stage 4 (Families with Adolescents) and between Stage 4 and Stage 7 (Retirement). In general, husbands consider this strategy to be a less important part of their coping repetoire than their wives do. Husbands emphasize its importance only at the early Couples Without Children and Retirement stages (Stages 1 and 7).

In contrast, wives appear to value and use social support more than husbands do across all seven stages. Social support is particularly important for wives at Stage 3 (Families with School-Age Children) and Stages 6 and 7 (Empty Nest and Retirement). Even though this strategy is valued and used by wives, a significant "drop" occurs during the Adolescent and Launching years of the family life cycle (Stages 4 and 5). This drop suggests that during these most demanding years of the family cycle, time constraints and extensive commitments may curtail the extent to which this strategy may be used by both men and women.

It is interesting to note that adolescents fall somewhere in between their parents' scores. The differences exist more between females (mothers and daughters) and males (fathers and sons) than between parents and children (see Figure 8.4).

Females appear to be more actively soliciting help from informal networks, confirming past research that identifies differences in how people understand and use their family and friendship relationships. Women, for example, are considered to have "affectively richer" friendships than men are (Booth, 1972; Wheeler & Nezlek, 1977; Rubin & Shinkers, 1978).

Mobilizing Formal Supports

The role of more formal social support networks, such as community agencies and professional persons, in helping families to weather

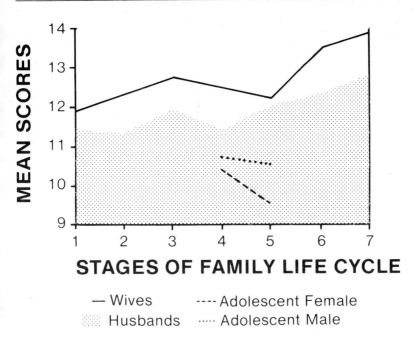

Figure 8.5   Mobilizing To Acquire Help

stressful periods has been shown to be important as a supplemental resource to the informal networks (Caplan, 1974; Caplan & Killilea, 1976). These networks have been found to be critical when the more informal supports are exhausted. Often they are referred to as the "safety net" resource a community provides to those families experiencing prolonged periods of stress.

This coping strategy assessed the extent to which families make an effort to seek assistance from more formalized networks of support such as community agencies and from professional persons. Our analysis of this important coping strategy revealed that both husbands and wives turn to this coping strategy rather sparingly, but with an increasing emphasis over time (see Figure 8.5). Specifically, husbands and wives emphasize its importance and use during the Empty Nest and the Retirement stages of the family cycle. Both husbands and wives used these resources significantly more during the last two stages than during the first two.

Wives made greater use of this coping strategy throughout all stages of the family cycle, but particularly during the Empty Nest and Retirement stages. Adolescents used this mode of coping far less than their parents did. These findings suggest that families are more willing to use help during these later years, particularly in response to illness and losses in the family.

Conclusion

ASSESSING THE MOST USEFUL COPING STRATEGIES

Of the five strategies presented, some were considered more useful than others. In this sample, the most important coping strategy overall was "seeking spiritual support." Considering the strong religious orientation of the sample, this finding makes sense

The second strategy most often reported as helpful was "reframing." Families tended to use this response to not only minimize problematic situations as they experienced them, but also to ward off potential problems that might emerge.

Two strategies placed third in terms of their acceptability and usefulness to families. These included using informal social support from friends, extended family, and neighbors, and formal supports such as professional agencies, family physicians, and therapists. The data indicate that these support networks were called on during stressful times in family's lives and used as a temporary measure to deal with crises. In general, it appears that the more formalized networks of support are not the preferred resources and that the informal networks such as extended family and friends are far more useful. Lastly, families reported that "passive appraisal" was not a strategy they saw as general useful.

ASSESSING COPING STRATEGIES AT LIFE-CYCLE STAGES

Our general hypothesis was that different coping strategies would be used in varying amounts at certain stages of the life cycle. The only exception to this hypothesis was reframing, which showed no significant differences across life-cycle stages. This suggests that reframing is a coping strategy that is less sensitive to *specific* stressors. It may be that reframing has an overall utility in dealing with problematic situations, relationship strains, and more chronic difficulties that families face.

In comparison, stage differences were found with the use of passive appraisal. This strategy was considered less useful at the earlier stages than at later stages. It makes sense that older couples are less hurried and more accepting of the fact that things will take care of themselves over time.

The strategy of seeking spiritual support also showed stage differences. Older couples report this strategy to be much more useful than younger families do. Although older families utilize this strategy more frequently, it is interesting to note a slight dip at the Launching stage (Stage 5). Spiritual resources are possibly less useful for dealing with the unique problems at this stage, such as children leaving home, caring for the older generation, and increased financial hardships.

The strategy of acquiring social support showed some stage changes, particularly with the wives. A decline began at the child-rearing stages (Stages 2 and 3), reaching its lowest point at the Launching stage and then returning to higher use during the Empty Nest and Retirement Stages.

The strategy of mobilizing to acquire help showed significant stage differences, again with greater use during the later two stages of the life cycle (Stages 6 and 7). This may be due to the increasing health concerns couples have as they reach their 60s.

ASSESSING DIFFERENCES IN COPING STRATEGIES AMONG FAMILY MEMBERS

One of the important findings in this chapter pertains to the discrepant perceptions of family members. Husbands, wives, and adolescents assess their family's coping strategies in very different ways. In addition to the fact that individuals have different "worlds," the data suggests that family coping involves the *collection* of various skills and abilities from individual members. Integrated together, they produce the family's coping strategies, which change and develop as the family moves through the life cycle.

Significant differences were found in the use of three strategies dealing with support from various *external resources:* church, extended family and friends, and professionals. Wives always scored higher on these items, implying that they viewed these strategies as more useful than their husbands did. As suggested earlier, the data may be showing that acquiring support is considered more "women's work" and a critical role in maintaining the family during periods of stress. The two internal family strategies, reframing and passive appraisal, showed no gender differences.

Programs and Services

Some external resources, such as mental health agencies or community education programs, are organized into formal support systems or networks. Whether or not families use these external resources may depend to a large extent on the quality, variety, and availability of the programs. Family use may also depend on the appropriateness of the kind of support offered, i.e., does the program meet what the family feels is its need?

Families who responded to the surveys in this study were asked to answer additional questions that were developed to provide information related to three specific issues:

(1) What kinds of programs and services did families use to cope with family problems?

(2) How useful did they find these external resources?

(3) What types of programs were couples and families interested in at different stages of the life cycle?

One set of questions listed *30 programs* that individuals or families might have attended in the past. Individuals were asked if they participated in these workshops, courses, or services, and if so, how useful they were. Second, individuals were asked if they would be interested in attending programs or reading information about 22 potentially relevant topic areas for couples and families.

PROGRAMS AND SERVICES USED

What kinds of programs had families included in the survey used in the past? How useful were these programs to them? Participants were asked to indicate the length of time and usefulness of workshops, programs, courses, or counseling related to the following topics: preparation for marriage, preparation for childbirth, parenting skills, marriage enrichment, family participation as a group in a planned workshop, retirement planning, grief, aging, stress management, medical self-care, weight control, chemical usage control, financial planning, individual counseling, family counseling, and marriage counseling.

In general, individuals had *not* participated in most of the programs listed in the survey. With the exceptions of premarital counseling and childbirth preparation, which had high participation in the age appropriate stages, responses indicated that no more than 15 to 25 percent had participated in any of the programs. It is not known, however, which of these programs were available to those surveyed and which were not available.

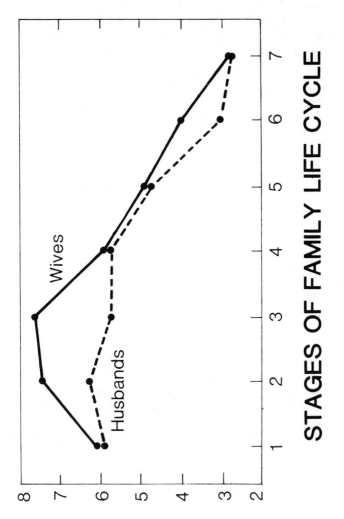

Figure 8.6 Overall Interest in Programs

155

Those who did participate in the programs tended to find them useful although males in the Empty Nest and Retirement stages (Stages 6 and 7) found the programs less useful than did respondents in other stages. As a rule, however, the programs received solid endorsement from those who had used them.

INFORMATION OR PROGRAMS DESIRED

Individuals were asked to indicate their interest in either reading information or attending programs dealing with a variety of topics such as money management, discipline of children, career planning, physical fitness, and numerous others.

In order to determine the total number of programs in which husbands and wives were most interested at each stage of the family life cycle, a sum score across all programs was assessed. Figure 8.6 shows the average number of programs in which individuals were interested across the seven stages.

Younger couples were interested in significantly more programs than older couples were. More specifically, younger couples were interested in an average of 7 to 8 of the 22 programs compared to only 2 to 3 among older couples (see Figure 8.6) While wives were more interested in programs than husbands were, the differences were not significant.

Of the 22 types of programs and information included in the survey, respondents expressed *greatest* interest in programs dealing with marriage enrichment, physical fitness, coping with stress, and planning a will or estate. They also expressed *great* interest in family financial planning, family communication, and family enrichment. *Least* interest was expressed in programs about dealing with divorce; making choices about alcohol, tobacco, and drugs; and career planning.

In order to assess whether the 22 topics clustered into interest areas, a factor analysis was performed. Results of this analysis clearly demonstrated that the topics clustered into three groups, or factors, with conceptually related programs. These three groups were labeled: *coping with changes, parenting issues,* and *enriching relationships.* All 22 of the topic items loaded high on one of these three groups (see Table 8.2).

The *coping with change* factor was so named because it focused on numerous issues with which families must deal over time, including medical problems, aging parents and relatives, death, preparing for retirement, planning a will, and possibly dealing with divorce. The *parenting issues* factor contained a variety of topics related to frequent

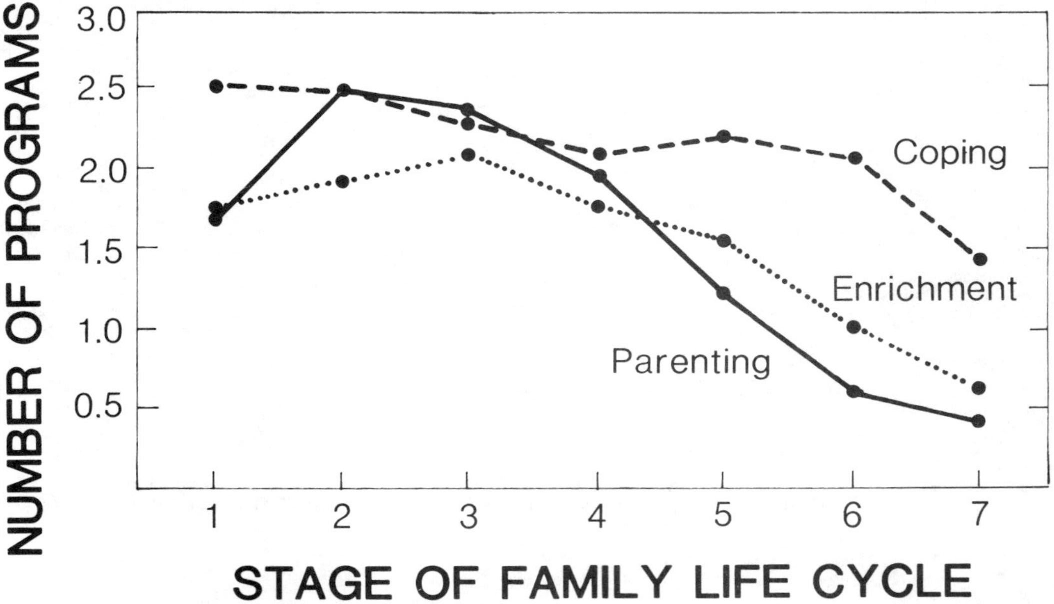

Figure 8.7   Interest in Programs by Factors

157

TABLE 8.2 Programs That Elicited High Interest From More Than 30 Percent of the Sample

	1 H	1 W	2 H	2 W	3 H	3 W	4 H	4 W	5 H	5 W	6 H	6 W	7 H	7 W	Factor Loading
Factor 1: Coping with Change															
Coping with change	31					32									.72
Family medical problems						40									.71
Death and grieving						31									.70
Aging parents and relatives	45	46	42	48	32	44	35	34							.62
Improving physical fitness								34	39	35		34			.55
Preparation for retirement	32							31	44		40	30			.53
Feeding the family nutritiously	38	38				45									.52
Planning a will or estate	49	32	38	56	43	38	44		40	40	42	38	30	31	.46
Dealing with divorce															.39
Factor 2: Parenting Issues															
Handling discipline		34	34	56	36	55									.75
Teaching children about sex		33	59			54	30								.72

Being parents of teenagers				38	45	40	43			.64
Use and abuse of TV			30		30					.52
Making choices about alcohol, etc.										.51
Preparing children for marriage				30	38	46	32	35		.50
Rearing infants and young children	41	47	53	74						.48
Career planning	30				30					.46
Factor 3: Enriching Relationships										
Enriching your marriage	44	51	46	59	57	40	39	34	38	.72
Improving communication skills			39	39	47	32	35	37	30	.71
Coping with stress	38	44	34	39	47	32	34	37	36	.57
Enriching family time	31	30	33	46	54	43	37			.54
Family financial planning	42	35	36	32	33	31	36			.45

a. In percentages.

issues faced by parents. These include rearing infants, handling discipline, teaching children about sex, abuse of television, choices about drugs, and preparing children for marriage. *Enriching relationships* reflected interest in marriage enrichment programs, improving communication skills, coping with stress, enriching family time, and family financial planning.

While interest in all the programs was lower among older couples, there was greater interest in some areas than in others. One way of viewing the differences is to focus separately on the three groups: enrichment, coping, and parenting. Enrichment programs had the most interest across the family life cycle, followed by coping programs (see Figure 8.7). Interest in parenting naturally dropped the most at the later stages. More specifically, younger couples were interested in roughly three coping programs, two marriage and family enrichment programs, and three parenting programs (total 7 to 8). At later stages, couples' interest dropped to less than one enrichment and parenting program and one to two coping programs (total 2 to 3).

Coping with Change

Table 8.2 provides an overview of the programs desired by at least 30 percent of the individuals at each stage. One of the most popular interest areas for both husbands and wives across the life cycle was planning a will or estate. There was considerable interest among younger couples in improving physical fitness and among older couples in preparing for retirement. Wives with young children (Stage 3) were interested in more of the coping with change programs than was any other group.

Parenting Issues

As expected, younger families with children (Stages 2 and 3) indicated the most interest in parenting programs, although Young Couples Without Children (Stage 1) appeared to be anticipating parenting responsibilities (see Table 8.2). Levels of interest between husbands and wives were fairly similar.

Couples actively engaged in child rearing indicated strongest interest in topics that corresponded to developmental needs of their children. For example, Families with Preschool and School-Age Children (Stages 2 and 3) were markedly more interested in discipline and guidance topics (handling discipline, teaching children about sex, use and abuse of television).

Families with Adolescents (Stage 5) were interested in programs about preparing children for marriage and being the parents of teenagers. Career planning was of greatest interest to Young Couples and Families with Young Children (Stages 1 and 2). This is understandable in light of the background data demonstrating a higher frequency of two-career families in these stages. Young adults in these stages are also actively engaged in exploring long-term career goals and in building professional backgrounds.

It is clear that programs targeting the concerns of respondents interested in parenting issues can be directed at both husbands and wives. Services that address the development of cooperative parenting skills as well as specific parent-child issues would maximize the impact and usefulness of parenting programs to these families.

Responses of husbands and wives in the study seemed to reflect changing roles within the family. Apparently, younger fathers or males anticipating parenthood are just as interested as wives in parenting issues. They tended to be interested in fewer parenting topics, but those they were interested received ratings as high as the wives' in the study. More specifically, husbands in parenting stages were strongly interested in 1 to 2 programs, while wives were strongly interested in 3 to 4 programs.

This provides a clear message to program planners to solicit actively the participation of fathers as well as mothers by: (1) ascertaining specific areas of interest to parents via needs assessments so planned programs deliver pertinent information; (2) efficiently and effectively providing needed information in dynamic and concise formats that allow audience participation, and (3) providing free or low-cost childcare to parents who participate in planned programs.

Enriching Relationships

There was considerable interest across the life cycle in programs on enriching your marriage, coping with stress, enriching family time, and family financial planning (see Table 8.2).

Again, younger families (Stages 1 and 2) were most interested in programs like marriage enrichment and coping with stress, although families with school-age children (Stage 3) were most interested in enriching family time and improving communication skills. These interests are probably related to the increased level of activity outside the home during school-age years. Couples interested in relationship topics were also interested in family financial planning, with husbands significantly more interested than wives.

Summary

As was mentioned earlier in this chapter, families do find the use of *external supports* helpful as a coping strategy. It appears that external resources are used where the family does *not* have sufficient internal resources to cope with its problems. Seeking resources such as social support appears to be used when a family experiences an increased amount of stress. In times of low stress, these resources may not be apparent and surface only when there are difficult stressors. This finding confirms a host of past studies (House, 1981; Kaplan et al., 1977; McCubbin, 1979).

The survey of programs and services *used* and *desired* by the families in this study provides some clues about the use of external resources. When community resources address specific family developmental tasks (such as parenting issues) or offer information about a particular stressor event, they can be a source for improving coping strategies at particular stages of the family life cycle. Families at some stages of the life cycle, such as those actively engaged in rearing children, are more interested in acquiring coping abilities from more formalized programs. Families at the later stages seem to receive more support from either internal family resources or informal social networks and less frequently rely upon more formal programs and services offered through various community organizations.

Family interest in external programs has another, as yet unexplained, complementary relationship to coping strategies. The provision of timely information or formalized programs that introduce families to a variety of sources of support could, in turn, influence the family's development of intrafamily and interactional coping styles throughout remaining stages of the family life cycle. Families that successfully enlarge their repertoire of coping skills through involvement in external programs might also increase their ability to use flexibly the coping skills at their disposal. In addition, programs that recognize and respect coping tendencies at various stages among husbands and wives, but that also present alternative coping strategies, would seem to also contribute to the family system's responsiveness to the challenges of stressor events, strains, and hardships.

chapter
IX
Personal Health Behaviors

IN THE LAST DECADE, a wealth of information on the incidence of health problems and risk factors associated with specific diseases has been produced. The benefits of good health habits have been extensively communicated to the public through the various media for several decades but with little evidence regarding impact (Belloc, Breslow, & Hochstim, 1971; Mechanic, 1979; General Mills, 1979). Very little is known about how family members respond to this information (Mechanic, 1979).

On a more positive side, there has been an increasing amount of emphasis placed on prevention. *Healthy People,* the Surgeon General's Report on Health Promotion (U.S. Department of Health and Human Services, 1979) has noted an increase of over 700 percent in annual health expenditures during the last two decades. In spite of these dramatic expenditures for treatment of diseases and disabilities, the improvements do not justify the increased costs. As a result, the report claims that further improvements in the health of the American people will only be achieved, not simply through the increased medical care and greater health expenditures, but through greater efforts designed to *prevent disease* and *promote health.*

Medical care is still primarily oriented toward sickness and crises rather than prevention. The same can be said of families. The General Mills *American Family Report* (1979) stated that

> while Americans pay lip service to the need for good prevention habits, very few actually have the self discipline and real personal commitment to practice them on a regular basis.

The report suggests several reasons for this: (1) To deal with inflation, families are cutting back in health care expenses. (2) Americans show a tendency toward denial of illness; culturally, we define sickness (including mental illness) as a sign of weakness. (3) Sedentary jobs and various

163

forms of popular entertainment tend to diminish the opportunity for physical activity. (4) Only one in four families feels well informed about good health practices. (5) Americans take health for granted and do not take responsibility for their own health.

Numerous studies support these findings. For example, in discussing the attitudes and behaviors of college students, Cafferata (1980) suggested that young adults and adolescents tend to be even more irresponsible about practicing wise health habits than those younger or older. In a study with volunteers over the age of 60, an association was found between exercise, keeping moderate weight, avoiding smoking, and longevity (Palmore, 1970). A Canadian study produced a conservative estimate that 18 percent of years lost between ages 1 and 70 were attributable just to cigarette smoking and alcohol consumption (Ouellet, Romeder, & Lance, 1977). Pratt (1971) examined the relationship between various health practices (sleep, exercise, dental hygiene, smoking, alcohol consumption, nutrition, and health) with a sample of 401 mothers. She found that poorer personal maintenance practices were significantly related to lower levels of health. Low-income women were also found to experience a disproportionately high number of health problems.

Perhaps the landmark study in this area is by Belloc and Breslow (1972), who found a relationship between seven health habits and longevity. These seven health behaviors were: eating regularly and moderately, no cigarette smoking, moderate exercise and moderate or no use of alcohol, and 7 to 8 hours of sleep. Moreover, there was a cumulative effect in that those who followed all of these practices were in better health than were those who did not. This association was found to be independent of age, sex, and economic status.

A follow-up study of men at age 45 who followed four to five of the habits had a life expectancy of 73 years, and those who followed six to seven of the habits had a life expectancy of 78 years (Breslow, 1980). Breslow reminds the reader that this difference of 11 years in life expectancy should be considered in reference to the fact that the total gain in life expectancy from 1900 to 1970 for men in the United States, age 45, was less than 5 years. He argues that these findings have continued to provide support to the premise that health habits (as well as biological factors such as age and sex) constitute "risk factors for diseases that are addictive and in some cases may be synergistic . . . small differences in risk factors appear to have significant impact."

Healthy People (1979) also documents how the lifestyle of an individual can have a significant positive or negative effect on his or her personal health. In comparison to other factors — environment, biology, and the lack of health care — lifestyle represents the major mediating variable. Similar findings are provided in various studies, demonstrating that the dimension of social support is a critical intervening variable with mortality and health behaviors (Berkman & Syme, 1979; Breslow & Engstrom, 1980; Breslow, 1980).

Berkman and Syme (1979) describe the social network index as based on four types of social relationships: (a) marriage, (b) contact with close friends and relatives, (c) church membership, and (d) informal and formal group associations. Each of the four types predicted mortality independently of the other three. The strongest predictors were the more assumed intimate ties of marriage and relationships with friends and relatives.

To date, most studies have focused primarily on the individual level and neglected the issue of family health. Fewer studies have attempted to broaden their scope in order to understand how families contribute to the physical and psychological well-being of individuals.

One study that focused on the relationship between health and marital experiences was done by Renne (1971). A survey analysis of 5373 respondents suggested that divorced people were somewhat more likely than married people to report physical and/or emotional illness. However, those who had remarried and were happy in their new relationship were less likely to report health problems than were the unhappily married who had never divorced. To summarize, marital happiness appeared to be related to both psychological and personal health.

Pratt (1976) explored the impact that family life had on health and concluded that

> from a societal point of view, the family is a basic unit within which health behavior is organized and performed. Families pay most of the direct costs of health care and, in addition, contribute significantly to the support of the entire societal health care system through voluntary giving. Families maintain a societal network of health service plants within which almost all preventative health care and the major share of sick care is carried out. Families have principal responsibility for initiating and coordinating the health services performed by the professional sector.

In examining how the family performs these activities, Pratt noted a number of inadequacies. She argued that the level of health knowledge and the value placed on good health are not strong enough to reinforce good health habits; failures are so widespread that answers must be sought in basic structural features of the society — both in the structure of the medical system and the structure of the family. Pratt proposes an "energized family" model, which she predicts will be more effective for carrying out health care tasks.

The General Mills (1979) study also assesses family health behaviors, comenting on the contradictions between attitudes and behaviors relating to health practices. To cite a few examples:

- Accidents are a prime concern, yet 63% of American families do not fasten their seat belts.
- 46% would like to see more emphasis placed on eating a good breakfast, but 41% often skip it.
- While nutrition is a topic of growing interest, 32% agree that they often eat what they want and do not pay much attention to nutritional values.

Not only are there contradictions in what we say and do, but there is very little consistency on both dimensions over a period of time. In a follow-up study with 302 adults and 350 children, positive health patterns showed low levels of continuity over a 16-year period (Mechanic, 1979). These studies remind us of the complexity of the issue and raise new questions for further followup research.

Personal Health Behaviors

After reviewing the research literature, it was concluded that the seven-item health behavior list developed by Belloc and Breslow (1972) was the best available index for assessing health practices of family members (see Table 9.1). Whereas Belloc and Breslow had used a "yes" or "no" response choice, we developed a five-point scale to increase response choices and to provide more detailed information.

RESULTS OF THE SURVEY

The primary results from this survey will be described for each of the seven items in the scale. Figure 9.1 illustrates the total scores for the parents and adolescents on the Personal Health Practices Scale. The possible range in scores was from a low of 7 to a high of 35. Wives had

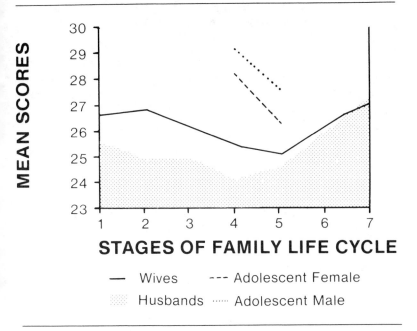

Figure 9.1 Personal Health Practices

significantly higher health practices scores than did husbands, and adolescents had significantly better health practices than their parents did. There were also significant differences across stages of the life cycle. Wives started out with better health practices than husbands at the early stages of the life cycle and they ended up at similar levels at the later stages. Health practices for adolescents (Stage 4), while significantly better than for their parents, dropped somewhat at the Launching stage (Stage 5).

The seven items used to survey the personal health practices of the family members are listed in Table 9.1. Parents' and adolescents' responses are summarized separately for each item. The percentages indicate how frequently each item was practiced by parents and adolescents.

In general, the results indicate that these family members had generally good personal health practices but some improvement could be made in all seven areas.

Item 1. A majority of parents (60 percent) and adolescents (52 percent) almost always eat breakfast, but about one-third of parents and adolescents seldom eat breakfast.

Item 2. Keeping within 10 pounds of their ideal weight was frequently or always done by over half (57 percent) of the adults and two-thirds (64 percent) of the adolescents. On the other hand, one-third (33 percent) of the adults seldom or never kept within 10 pounds; only 14 percent of the adolescents had this problem.

Item 3. Keeping weight down was a problem partially due to the fact that over half (54 percent) of the adults seldom or never exercised vigorously for 15 to 20 minutes at least three time per week. About one-third (30 percent) of the adolescents seldom or never exercised this much. Conversely, over half (55 percent) of the adolescents and about one-quarter (28 percent) of the adults frequently or always did this much exercise.

Item 4. Drinking two or more alcoholic beverages per day was not a problem for most of the adults or adolescents in this sample. About three-quarters of the adolescents and the adults almost never had this much to drink, and only 6 percent of the parents and 4 percent of the adolescents frequently or always drank that much.

Item 5. Smoking tobacco or pot was not a common practice among either parents or adolescents. By far the majority of the parents (81 percent) and adolescents (90 percent) seldom or never smoked tobacco or pot. On the other hand, 17 percent of the adults and 6 percent of the adolescents frequently or always smoked.

Item 6. Eating between meals was very common among adolescents and less frequent among parents. More specifically, over half (54 percent) of the adolescents frequently or always ate between meals, while about one-third (31 percent) of the parents followed that practice. Conversely, over a third (36 percent) of the parents and one-fourth (23 percent) of the adolescents seldom or never ate between meals.

Item 7. Sleeping 7 to 8 hours each night was practiced by the majority of the adults (73 percent) and adolescents (75 percent), while only 14 percent of the adults and 9 percent of the adolescents seldom or never got that much sleep.

TABLE 9.1 Personal Health Practices

Item	Almost Never	Once In A While	Sometimes	Frequently	Almost Always
(1) I eat breakfast.	14[a] (15)[b]	9 (10)	8 (10)	9 (13)	60 (52)
(2) I keep within 10 pounds of my recommended ideal weight.	24 (09)	9 (05)	11 (12)	14 (19)	43 (55)
(3) I exercise vigorously for 15 to 20 minutes at least three times per week.	35 (16)	19 (14)	18 (16)	12 (17)	16 (38)
(4) I drink more than two alcoholic beverages per day.	73 (78)	15 (12)	6 (05)	4 (02)	2 (02)
(5) I smoke tobacco/pot	79 (86)	3 (04)	2 (04)	6 (02)	11 (04)
(6) I eat between meals.	13 (04)	23 (17)	33 (26)	21 (29)	10 (25)
(7) I get 7 to 8 hours sleep each night.	6 (02)	8 (07)	13 (17)	27 (26)	46 (49)

a. Adult responses in percentages in (n = 2,453).

b. Adolescent responses in percentages (n = 433).

COMPARISON OF 1000 FAMILIES AND THE HARVARD STUDY

A survey of personal health practices was recently completed of doctors on the Harvard Medical School faculty (N = 595). To compare the specific responses of these doctors and the families in this study, five items from the two studies were compared. While the study of families used a five-point scale and the Harvard study used a "yes/no" response, the five-point scale was collapsed into two categories. The "yes" category included three responses (sometimes, frequently, and almost always), and the "no" response included two responses (once in a while and almost never). The results of the comparison of the two studies are presented in Table 9.2.

Some differences in the two samples should be mentioned. While the Harvard study included all adults, the vast majority of which were male, the family study included an equal number of husbands and wives who were married. The income and education of these two groups are also quite different, with the doctors being better educated and having higher income levels.

In spite of these differences, the results from these two independent surveys are strikingly similar. In fact, there is less than a 5 percent

TABLE 9.2   Comparison of Harvard Medical School Faculty and 1000 Families

Survey Questions	Harvard Medical School Faculty[a]		1000 Families[b]	
	Yes	No	Yes	No
(1) I eat breakfast	78	22	77	23
(2) I keep within 10 pounds of recommended ideal weight.	71	29	68	32
(3) I exercise vigorously for 15 to 20 minutes at least three times per week.	49	51	46	54
(4) I drink more than two alcoholic beverages per day.	7	93	12	88
(5) I smoke tobacco/pot	19	81	19	81

a. There were 595 faculty in the Harvard study. Responses in percentages.

b. There were 2280 adults in the sample. Responses in percentages.

difference between the two groups on any of the items, and most of the responses are almost identical. This similarity suggests that there is considerable consistency across adults on these personal health behaviors.

Summary

The results of this survey of personal health behaviors indicates that adolescents generally follow better health practices than their parents do. While the health practices of these families are generally good, there is considerable room for improvement, especially in the areas of keeping weight down and increasing exercise levels. It also appears that the personal health practices of adults are almost identical to those of professionals in the field of health, i.e., doctors. It is clear, however, that improvement could be made on most of these health practices and that adolescents could be useful models for their parents in some of these areas.

chapter
X

Marital and Family Satisfaction

MARITAL AND FAMILY SATISFACTION are primary outcome variables because they reflect the mood and happiness with the overall functioning of the family. In this chapter, we will explore how satisfaction varies across stages for husbands, wives, and adolescents. Questions to be explored include: Do couples become less satisfied with their marriages when they become parents, and even *less* satisfied when their children enter adolescence? Also, are Balanced families on the Circumplex Model more satisfied than Extreme families? Have dissatisfied couples experienced more life stress than satisfied couples, and do they have fewer resources to handle that stress?

Three interrelated areas of satisfaction will be explored: the satisfaction of family members with their marriages, with their family lives, and with the overall quality of their lives. Figure 10.1 provides an overview of this chapter and shows how these three areas of satisfaction are embedded within each other: Marriage satisfaction is embedded within family satisfaction, which is embedded in the context of the overall quality of life.

The chapter examines the overlap between these three kinds of satisfaction and describes ways in which these kinds of satisfaction change with respect to stages of the family life cycle, life stress, family resources, and the Circumplex Model. While we explore the relationships among these variables, we will *not* be able to discover any causal connection; hence our discussion will be limited to a description of these relationships.

Marital Satisfaction

There are many ways to define marital satisfaction; one that is useful was provided by Hawkins (1968b, p. 164), who defined it as

the subjective feelings of happiness, satisfaction and pleasure experienced by a spouse when considering all current aspects of his mar-

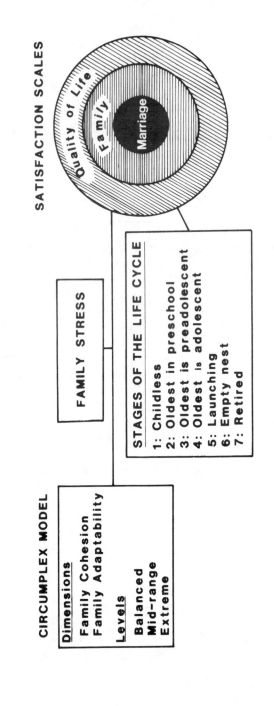

CIRCUMPLEX MODEL

Dimensions

Family Cohesion
Family Adaptability

Levels

Balanced
Mid-range
Extreme

FAMILY STRESS

STAGES OF THE LIFE CYCLE

1: Childless
2: Oldest in preschool
3: Oldest is preadolescent
4: Oldest is adolescent
5: Launching
6: Empty nest
7: Retired

SATISFACTION SCALES

Quality of Life
Family
Marriage

Figure 10.1 Conceptual Overview of Circumplex Model, Family Stress, and Satisfaction

riage. This variable is conceived of as a continuum running from much satisfaction to much dissatisfaction. Marital satisfaction is clearly an attitudinal variable and thus, is a property of individual spouses.

Early descriptions of variables related to marital quality have often taken the form of typologies or ideal types. Burgess and Locke (1945) described insitutional and companionship marriages, with the latter emphasizing affection rather than traditional roles. Hicks and Platt (1970) provided a decade review of research in the 1960s. During the 1970s, marital satisfaction was the major variable in several hundred studies.

In the present study, marital satisfaction is measured separately by two different scales. (The use of two independent measures of marital satisfaction reflects marital satisfaction research's central place in the study of families during the last thirty years; Lewis & Spanier, 1979; Burr, Leigh, Day, & Constantine, 1979). One measure is the short form of the Locke-Wallace Marital Adjustment Scale (Locke & Wallace, 1959). Since the Locke-Wallace scale was employed extensively during the 1960s and 1970s its use allows us to compare our results to many other studies. The second measure of marital satisfaction is from ENRICH; it was developed as a short scale that would be relevant and sensitive to changes in families across the life cycle. Each of the ten items in the scale relates to one of the important content areas in the ENRICH Inventory. (A copy of the ENRICH scale and its reliability scale are contained in Appendix B.)

While these couples were generally satisfied with their marriage, approximately 13 percent of the males and 16 percent of the females indicated that they had considered separation or divorce. At all stages of the family life cycle fewer husbands than wives had considered separation or divorce (see Figure 10.2). The tendency to contemplate separation or divorce was higher for couples in Stage 2 (Families with Pre-School Children) through Stage 5 (Launching Families). Older couples (at the later two stages) are probably more conservative; these are also the couples who have managed to remain married for 25 or more years.

Family Satisfaction

Although a wealth of theorizing and research has been done on marital satisfaction, family researchers have rarely concerned them-

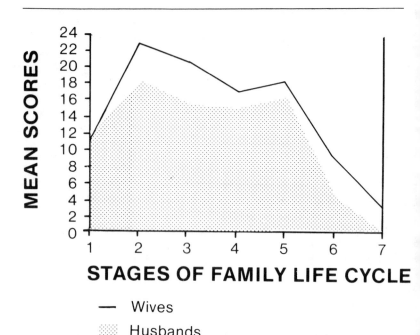

Figure 10.2 Have Considered Divorce

selves with *family satisfaction*. Campbell, Converse, and Rodgers (1976) explicitly differentiated satisfaction with one's family from other forms of satisfaction. For this reason, we developed a Family Satisfaction Scale for this family survey. A pool of items was compiled to (a) assess family satisfaction on each of the specific subscales of family cohesion and of family adaptability and (b) measure satisfaction on these dimensions in a valid and reliable manner.

Because of the integrative nature and the clinical relevance of the Circumplex Model, the Family Satisfaction Scale was designed to assess satisfaction on each of the fourteen subscales of the model. Each subject's satisfaction was measured on the eight *cohesion* subscales of emotional bonding, family boundaries, coalitions, time, space, friends, decision making, and interests and recreation. Also, their satisfaction on the six adaptability subscales of assertiveness, control, discipline, negotiation, roles, and rules was assessed. (A copy of the final 14-item scale and its reliability data are contained in Appendix B.)

Quality of Life

Quality of life can be measured using two distinctly different methods: an assessment of the *objective* quality of one's life or an assessment of one's *subjective* sense of satisfaction with that objective reality. An objective measure of quality of life can be obtained from statistics about specific social and economic indicators (average income, amount spent on education, air quality, availability of parks and recreation facilities, and the like). Such objective data may reveal nothing about a person's satisfaction with his or her life, which is the central theme of subjective approaches.

French, Rodgers, and Cobb (1974) outline the importance of the subjectively defined environment in their discussion of adjustment. They describe adjustment as the fit between an individual and his or her environment as he or she perceives it. While an examination of the individual's objective reality may provide a more standardized indicator of the quality of his or her life, the important consideration is that persons respond to their own perceptions of that reality. Thus when considering the quality of life within a geographical area, objective measures might be most appropriate. However, when discussion focuses on the quality of life of individuals, their subjective perceptions are considered more salient.

This chapter deals with *subjective satisfaction* with the quality of one's life rather than with the objective aspects of the quality of life. Campbell and colleagues (1976) relate these by viewing satisfaction as the difference in level between objective attributes and one's expectations and aspirations with respect to important aspects of one's life.

A common feature of quality-of-life studies is the measurement of satisfaction within particular domains. Each domain focuses on a specific facet of the life experience such as marriage and family life, friends, home and housing, education, employment, religion, and so on. Taken collectively, these domains will encompass a major portion of the life experiences of a large population. Satisfaction within each domain is an individual, subjective judgment of the extent to which individual needs and interests are met by the individual's personal environment.

This study further examines the impact of several of the domains identified in the earlier studies. A *Quality of Life* scale was developed that includes marriage and family life, friends, extended family, home, education, time, religion, employment, financial well-being, and neighborhood and community. Two additional domains of particular interest were added to this study. The first was health, because it was found in a Minnesota study (Stoeckler & Gage, 1978) that satisfaction with health care services was closely linked to the global assessment of satisfaction with quality of life. This study, however, focuses on health rather than health care. The second domain added assessed the impact of mass media on the quality of life. (A complete copy of the Quality of Life Scale and its reliability are included in Appendix B.)

Marital and Family Satisfaction

Several studies have found that marital satisfaction overlaps with overall life satisfaction as much or more than with satisfaction with any other part of life (Andrews & Withey, 1974; Campbell et al., 1976; Glenn & Weaver, 1981). Campbell and colleagues found that satisfaction with family life overlapped with overall life satisfaction even more highly than did marital satisfaction.

In the current study, family and marital satisfaction overlapped a great deal with life satisfaction as a whole, and family satisfaction accounted for even more of life satisfaction than did marital satisfaction. These correlations were found to be higher than in previous studies. For example, Campbell et al. (1976) found the correlation between marital satisfaction and life satisfaction to be .36. The current study finds the same correlation to be .50[1] using the data from individual husbands and wives, and .54 using husband-wife couple means (see Table 10.1). The analogous correlations for family satisfaction with life satisfaction are .68 for individuals and .67 for couple means, compared to Campbell's figure of .41 for individuals. Both the current study and Campbell's study sampled subjects across the life cycle.

Marital satisfaction accounts for about as much of family satisfaction as family satisfaction accounts for quality of life. In the present study, marital satisfaction and family satisfaction correlated about .70, and family satisfaction and quality of life correlated .67 using couple means. Stated another way, marital satisfaction accounts for up to half the variance ($r = .70$, $r^2 = .49$) of family satisfaction, which in turn accounts

TABLE 10.1 Intercorrelations of Satisfaction Variables

	Marital Satisfaction (L-W)	Marital Satisfaction (ENRICH)	Family Satisfaction	Quality of Life	
Marital Satisfaction (Locke-Wallace)	.48	.73	.66	.50	Individual Data
Marital Satisfaction (ENRICH)	.81	.45	.64	.51	
Family Satisfaction	.70	.71	.35	.61	
Quality of Life	.52	.55	.67	.35	Husband-Wife Correlations
		Couple Means			

177

for almost half the variance of life satisfaction overall ($r = .67$, $r^2 = .45$). These figures support the notion illustrated in Figure 10.1 that satisfaction within each of these areas overlaps with satisfaction in others.

The high correlations that are obtained between the satisfaction measures, especially with the couple mean scores, are accented by the relatively low correlations between husbands' scores and wives' scores, as shown on the diagonal in Table 10.1. The low husband-wife correlations for the satisfaction variables highlight the fact that we are measuring individual *perceptions* rather than single-family realities. Couple mean scores can be seen as a kind of couple consensus. It is noteworthy that these "consensus" scores correlate more highly than do the individual data.

Satisfaction Across the Life Cycle

The present study confirms the findings of a great deal of other recent work indicating that adults' satisfaction with marriage tends to have the shape of a very shallow U-curve (Glenn & McLanahan, 1982; Rollins & Galligan, 1978; Schram, 1979; Spanier & Lewis, 1980; Spanier, Lewis, & Cole, 1975; Waldron & Routh, 1981). Previous research has focused on the decline in satisfaction following the birth of the first child and the subsequent rise in satisfaction as the children are launched from the nest. Figures 10.3, 10.4, and 10.5 confirm these general trends for this group of couples.

However, these data also make clear that these trends in the change of satisfaction across the family life cycle represent slight changes in levels of satisfaction. The most dramatic difference in marital and family satisfaction occurs between the Launching (Stage 6) and Empty Nest (Stage 7) stages. A detailed analysis (t tests) of changes across all stages showed significantly higher scores at Stages 6 and 7 than at Stages 2, 3, and 4 for both husbands and wives. Lower levels of satisfaction at these stages of the life cycle have been found in other studies as well.

It is important to remember that these differences in satisfaction levels are small. A multiple regression analysis indicates that stage of the life cycle accounts for only about one one-hundredth of the variance in the satisfaction scores, even when both linear and U-curve trends are included in the analysis.

Although differences in marital satisfaction across life stages are statistically significant with this large sample, they are, with one excep-

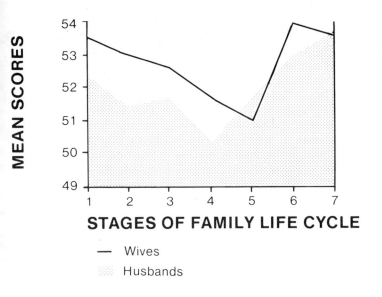

MEAN SCORES

STAGES OF FAMILY LIFE CYCLE

— Wives

Husbands

Figure 10.3 Marital Satisfaction (Locke-Wallace)

tion, of little practical value. The exception occurs between Launching and Empty Nest stages. However, there are factors that cloud the interpretability of this finding. First, the Empty Next stage has a greater variance in ages of subjects than does any other stage. Second, the increase in satisfaction would be reduced by adding data from those marriages that had dissolved. In addition, Schram (1979) argues that the increase in satisfaction at this "postparental" stage can be interpreted as a result of the relaxation of sex roles between the parents. Women in this group see themselves as freer to look for work or organizational roles outside the home, and men find themselves with decreased financial responsibility and more ability to be passive and dependent.

Husband and wife differences were even less pronounced than were differences across the family life cycle. The size of sex differences that did exist were not related to stage of life cycle, with the exception of overall quality-of-life satisfaction. Husbands tended to rate their satisfac-

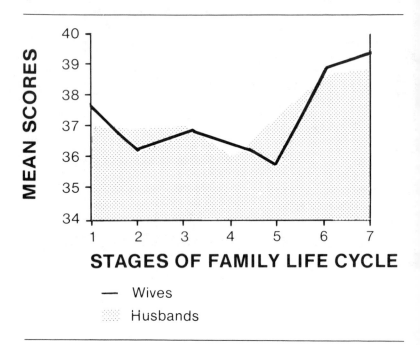

Figure 10.4 Marital Satisfaction (ENRICH)

tion with their overall quality of life higher than their wives did, but again, the difference was small.

Family satisfaction at different stages of the family life cycle is illustrated in Figure 10.5. As with marital satisfaction, wives' family satisfaction starts out higher than husbands' in the early years of marriage. Both husband and wife scores drop, with husbands reaching their lowest point at Stage 4 when adolescents are at home. Wives reach their lowest levels of satisfaction (both marital and family) when the adolescents are leaving home (Stage 5). Family satisfaction increases for both husbands and wives during the Empty Nest and Retirement stages. A more detailed analysis (t tests) indicates that satisfaction at the earlier couple stages (1 and 2) was significantly higher than at the child-rearing and adolescent stages (4 and 5) for both husbands and wives.

It is interesting to note that reports of adolescent family satisfaction differ little from those of adults. This is partly because group mean

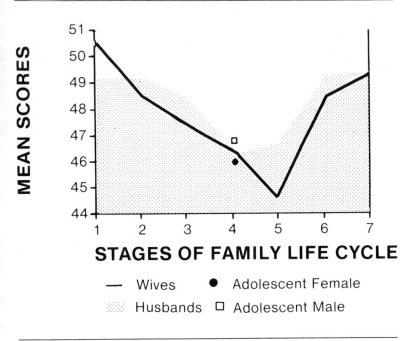

Figure 10.5 Family Satisfaction

scores are used, and the level of agreement between a father, mother, and adolescent within the same family is very low (r = .32). While male adolescents' assessments are significantly higher than females', they are not significantly different from adults'.

Quality of life generally follows the same pattern as do marital and family satisfaction across the life cycle (see Figure 10.6). The primary exception is that quality of life for both husbands and wives starts out rather low compared to the other satisfaction measures. Like the other measures, it increases gradually, reaching its highest point at the Empty Nest and Retirement stages. As with the other measures, there is a drop in husbands' satisfaction at Stage 4 and in wives' satisfaction at Stage 5. A more detailed analysis (t tests) indicated that satisfaction was significantly higher at Retirement stage (Stage 7) than at the Younger Couples stages (Stages 1 and 2).

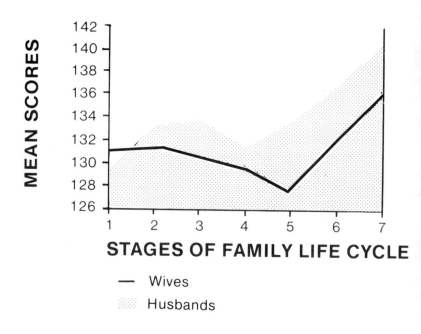

Figure 10.6 Quality of Life

Figures 10.3 through 10.6 display a striking and consistent finding across the satisfaction measures. Until the oldest child is in grade school (Stage 3) changes in different kinds of satisfaction differ. After Stage 3, changes are consistent across all three types of satisfaction: as the oldest child enters adolescence, the satisfaction of both parents declines. When the oldest child leaves home, the father's satisfaction picks back up, but the mother's satisfaction continues to drop. When all the children have left home, the mother's level of satisfaction increases also. Following this point, both parent's satisfaction continues to rise as they move into the Retirement stage.

This differential dip between the parents may indicate a period of adjustment for the wives as their children are beginning to be launched. Similar adjustment may not be required by the husbands, who have spent less time parenting in the home. Longitudinal data will need to be examined in order to specify further these developmental hypotheses.

Satisfaction and the Circumplex Model

All four satisfaction measures indicate that the further a person is from the center of the Circumplex Model, the less satisfied he or she is with his or her marriage, family, or overall quality of life. This pattern holds true whether individual responses or couple mean scores are used. In addition, the more that a husband and wife agree on where they are located on the Circumplex Model, the more satisfied they tend to be and the more they also agree on their level of satisfaction. All of the above findings are both statistically significant and consistent across the four satisfaction scales. However, the correlation coefficients are all small in absolute value, ranging between .09 and .25.

Much larger and theoretically more striking are the strong relationships between the satisfaction measures and the two specific dimensions of the Circumplex Model: family cohesion and family adaptability. Table 10.2 indicates that the more satisfied couples tend to assess their families as more cohesive and more adaptable. The findings hold true for individuals and for couples both across all stages and within each stage. In addition, partialing out either conventionality (social desirability) or life stress makes only a slight impact on the strength of the above relationships. This indicates that the relationship of satisfaction to cohesion and adaptability is significant even when social desirability and stress are controlled for. The correlations between cohesion and adaptability are strongest with family satisfaction for couples who have children still in the home. For those couples, family satisfaction correlates .71 with cohesion and .62 with adaptability.

Family cohesion and adaptability are each clearly predicted by a combination of the four satisfaction measures. Correlation coefficients of .71 and .65 are obtained when predicting cohesion and adaptability, respectively, using individual data with all stages combined. Family satisfaction is by far the most useful satisfaction measure when making predictions. The other satisfaction measures have about half the weight of family satisfaction in the standardized prediction equation.

Interestingly, using couple scores to make predictions increased the significance of our findings. This increase may result from the fact that the Circumplex Model measuring instrument, FACES II, specifically targets the entire family as the unit to be rated. This family unit focus may also account for why Family Satisfaction is the satisfaction scale that best predicts the Circumplex dimensions. These findings are also not surprising since the Family Satisfaction instrument specifically rates

TABLE 10.2   **Means on the Satisfaction Variables of the Individuals in Each Category of Family Cohesion and Family Adaptability**

	Rigid	Structured	Flexible	Chaotic
Family Adaptability (mean score)				
Marital Satisfaction	45.8	50.9	54.1	56.4
(Locke-Wallace)	(294)*	(676)	(637)	(311)
Marital Satisfaction	31.3	36.0	39.1	41.4
(ENRICH)	(320)	(742)	(697)	(331)
Family Satisfaction	40.7	45.6	49.6	54.4
	(315)	(715)	(674)	(328)
Quality of Life	122.0	129.6	134.9	140.7
	(295)	(671)	(629)	(304)

	Disengaged	Separated	Connected	Enmeshed
Family Cohesion (mean score)				
Marital Satisfaction	45.2	50.5	54.1	59.0
(Locke-Wallace)	(292)	(585)	(755)	(286)
Marital Satisfaction	31.3	35.7	39.1	41.3
(ENRICH)	(318)	(642)	(837)	(293)
Family Satisfaction	39.9	44.8	49.8	55.4
	(304)	(626)	(807)	(295)
Quality of Life	121.4	128.7	135.2	140.8
	(283)	(584)	(754)	(278)

*Sample size in parentheses.

satisfaction with the content areas addressed by the Circumplex Model subscales.

Analyses were done to discriminate Balanced families — those in the center of the Circumplex Model — from Extreme families. In each discriminant analysis, the four satisfaction variables were weighted to create the single discriminant function that best differentiates Balanced and Extreme families on the Circumplex Model. Using only the four satisfaction variables, it was possible to classify correctly 64 percent of couples and 62 percent of individuals into the Balanced or Extreme groups.

Furthermore, when all four satisfaction measures were combined to differentiate Balanced from Extreme families, results varied widely among stages of life and between couple-mean versus individual data.

One way to account for the above data might be to hypothesize that being at one place on the Circumplex Model might be the most satisfying at one stage of life, whereas another place on the Circumplex Model might be the most satisfying at another stage of life. This idea is explored in greater depth in Chapter XI.

Another way to account for this is to note that Extreme families ("enmeshed") may not be able to voice dissatisfaction. This relates to Wynne and colleagues' (1958) notion of pseudomutuality. They spoke of the "subjective tension aroused by divergence or independence of expectations, including the open affirmation of a sense of personal identity" (p. 575). We see this subjective tension as a component of the kinds of marital and family dissatisfaction that are measured by the scales in the present study. Wynne identifies pseudomutuality as dealing with this tension by "maintain(ing) the idea or feeling, even though this may be illusory." In other words, enmeshed families will exaggerate their feelings of satisfaction with their marriage and family life.

Family Satisfaction and Family Stress

One important aspect of this study that deserves attention is the relationship between stress and satisfaction. Both have been used as outcome variables in several of the analyses. In order to more fully understand the relative strength of family satisfaction, a series of discriminate analyses was performed.

Satisfied families were not stressed families, and families under stress were, indeed, dissatisfied. The results are clear and consistent that couples under stress are equally dissatisfied with their marriages, with their family lives, and with the quality of their lives. The four satisfaction measures all correlate between $-.33$ and $-.40$ with family stress (see Appendix C).

The first analysis focused on using family strengths and family resources to discriminate between families that were low and high in family satisfaction. The findings clearly demonstrated the striking differences between groups, with families high in satisfaction also being high on the major variables of family strengths and family resources. Furthermore, these relationships are not affected by the family's level of stress. Using these family resources as predictors, it was possible to predict with a high level of accuracy (93 percent) which families were low in satisfaction and which were high. Table 10.3 lists the resources that predict the level of satisfaction for families. It may be that the high

TABLE 10.3   High Satisfaction Groups (vs. low) Are Higher on These Major Family Resources*

Family Types	Family Strengths	Marital Strengths	Family Coping
Cohesion	Pride	Conventionality	Social support
Adaptability	Accord	Communication	Reframing
		Conflict resolution	Spiritual support
		Personality	Seeking help
		Leisure	
		Sexual relationship	Health practices
		Children and marriage	
		Family and friends	
		Financial management	
		Religious orientation	

*High equals upper one-third; low equals lower one-third.

use of resources by satisfied families prevents or reduces their level of stress.

Summary

The results of this study suggest that satisfaction in a variety of domains is pivotal in the understanding of stress, family resources, and family dynamics. Satisfaction with one's marriage, family, and overall quality of life are interwoven and interrelated. These measures of satisfaction also vary by stage of the family life cycle, and certain patterns are consistent across these different measures.

The findings indicate that family satisfaction is very strongly associated with family adaptability and family cohesion. In addition, moderate relationships were found with distance from the center of the Circumplex Model and with family stress and resources. In sum, families that describe themselves as very satisfied also describe themselves to be very adaptable and very cohesive, and they tend to use a large number of resources and to experience low stress levels.

NOTE

1. Average of the Locke-Wallace/Quality of Life correlation coefficient with the ENRICH/Quality of Life correlation coefficient.

chapter
XI
Predicting Family Types

HOW ACCURATELY CAN WE PREDICT family types? What types of families seem to function better at different stages of the family life cycle? Are Balanced versus Extreme family types distinctive in terms of levels of stress, resources, coping, and satisfaction? This chapter focuses on providing a more comprehensive picture of the variables that discriminate among family types at various stages of the family life cycle.

The developmental framework for this study hypothesizes that changes in life-cycle stages will be reflected in various types of family systems. This idea has a long history, initially introduced in the late 1940s by Duvall (1970) and Hill and Rodgers (1964). A key assumption, later to be considered equally important in systems theory, is that of the interdependence of parts. An individual's growth and development was connected to other members progress in the family.

The specific tasks that Duvall (1970) proposed as necessary for families to complete complement those Erikson (1950) proposed for individual development. More recently, Carter and McGoldrick (1980) have elaborated on these tasks in terms of emotional processes with which family members must deal in order to make the transition to another stage. Certain completed tasks serve as markers that prompt the family to move to new structural arrangements. Using the language of family systems theory, it has been argued that these varying structural arrangements are produced by morphogenic forces, producing second-order change (Hoffman, 1981; Hill, 1971). These structural arrangements can also be called "family types."

One of the primary hypotheses in the Circumplex Model is that couples and families will change their levels on cohesion and adaptability to deal more adequately with situational stress and changes in the family life cycle. Specific hypothesis were proposed for several stages of the family life cycle (Olson et al., 1980; Table 1). These hypotheses focused on general location of families at various stages and differences between stressed and nonstressed couples and families.

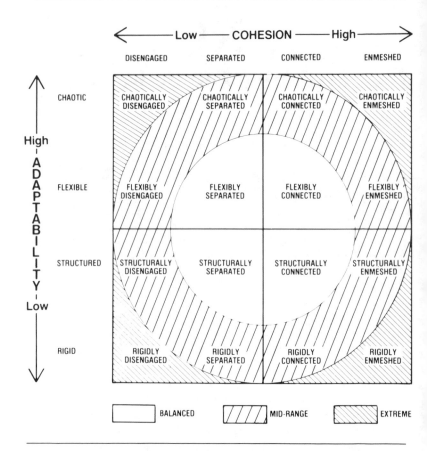

Figure 11.1 Circumplex Model: Sixteen Types of Marital and Family Systems

As a reminder, the three types of families described in this study are Balanced, Mid-Range, and Extreme. Balanced families are those that have moderate levels on cohesion and adaptability. Overall, Balanced families were hypothesized to have more family strengths that would help them cope with stress more effectively and, therefore, they would end up having higher levels of marital and family satisfaction. More specific hypotheses were created for various stages of the life cycle; these will be discussed later.

In order to simplify the analysis and discussion of the findings, it was decided to contrast two of the three major family types, Balanced and

Extreme, and to exclude the Mid-Range types. Dividing the families into Balanced and Extreme types artificially created an Extreme group. Since this study represents a more "normal" sample, these families might more accurately be described as Mid-Range types. A more clinical sample of families (schizophrenic, sexual abuse, drug abuse) might contain more families that would fall into the Extreme family types.

To obtain a large enough sample for this analysis, some stages were combined and the original seven stages were collapsed into four. The four new stages were called: *Couples Without Children, Families with Young Children, Families with Adolescents,* and *Older Couples.* The first stage remains unchanged and includes Young Couples Without Children. Stages 2 and 3 were combined to form the new stage of Families with Young Children to the ages of twelve years. Stages 4 and 5 were combined to form the Families with Adolescents stage, and Stages 6 and 7 were combined to form the Older Couples group.

The following general hypotheses from the Circumplex Model were proposed for the four newly created stages for this analysis (Olson et al., 1980). It was proposed that couples at the Young Couple stage would tend to fall into the upper-right quadrant of the model. It was also hypothesized that Families with Young Children would tend to fall into this quadrant initially and then would move to the lower-right quadrant. It was hypothesized that well-functioning families at the Adolescent stage would fall into the Balanced types. With Older couples, it was hypothesized that nonstressed couples would fall into the Balanced area and stressed couples would be in the lower-left or -right quadrant. These specific hypotheses will be examined in more detail later in this chapter.

Family Types at Four Stages of the Life Cycle

In order to provide another way of looking at the differences in family types across the life cycle, an analysis was done to determine how frequently families fell into each quadrant (I-IV) of the Circumplex Model (see Figure 11.2). For this analysis, the Circumplex Model was divided into four quadrants, and the stages of the life cycle were reduced from seven to four as previously discussed.

While more families at all four stages fell into Quadrants I and IV, there was considerable variation in the percentage of families in each quadrant across the four stages. While a majority (57 percent) of the Couples Without Children (Stage 1) fell into Quadrant II, about one

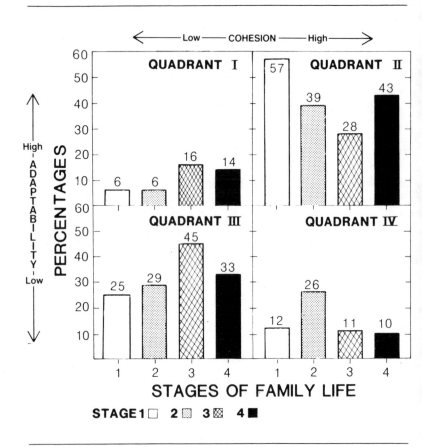

Figure 11.2 Circumplex Model

quarter (25 percent) fell into Quadrant III, with very few families in Quadrants I and IV. In contrast, almost half (45 percent) of Families with Adolescents (Stage 3) fell into Quadrant III, and about one-quarter (28 percent) were in Quadrant II.

Even though fewer families fell into Quadrants I and IV, some stages did have considerably more families in these Quadrants than other stages did. More specifically, about one-quarter (26 percent) of Families with Young Children (Stage 2) fell into Quadrant IV. There were more families from Stages 3 and 4 than from Stages 1 and 2 in Quadrant I.

In conclusion, this analysis provided an overview of the distribution of families in each quadrant of the Circumplex Model. This analysis clearly demonstrates the differences in family types across the four stages of the life cycle and sets the stage for the in-depth predictive analyses that follow.

Individual, Couple, and Family Scores

One of the most perplexing problems in this study pertained to the computation of couple and family scores. How are the couple and the family best represented as units? Researchers have generally relied on only one family member to represent the entire family (Safilios-Rothchild, 1969; Olson et al., 1980). As discussed, there are limitations to this practice; in fact, one of the most important conclusions from this project is that differences among family members in how they describe their own families are important.

Methodologically, this chapter describes how well a variety of *individual, couple,* and *family* scores helped discriminate between and predict Balanced and Extreme types. The alternative methods of scoring used in the discriminant analysis are indicated in Table 1. Initially, individual scores were used for both the predicting variables and the description of family types. Second, couples' mean scores were used to predict couples' types. Lastly, family scores were computed and used at the Adolescent stage (see Chapter XIII for a complete description and discussion of family scores). Family mean z scores and family discrepancy scores for the independent variables were used to predict family types based on a family mean score for cohesion and adaptability. The purpose of these analyses was to discover what variables were most descriptive of Balanced and Extreme families.

Accuracy of Predicting

Predictability is often seen as the ultimate criterion in science since it indicates an understanding of the relative significance of the variables. It does not necessarily mean causality, although this is often implied. Discriminant analysis was the statistical method chosen to determine how well the various family resource variables predicted family types at various stages of the life cycle.

As expected, the accuracy of predicting the family types varied according to the type of scores used (see Table 11.1). The data indicate that couple and family scores offer some added accuracy in prediction

TABLE 11.1 Accuracy of Predicting Balanced and Extreme Types of Families (percentages)

Stage	Individual Scores	Couple Scores	Family Scores
Childless Couples (Stage 1)	94	100	na
Families with Young Children (Stages 2 & 3)	73	82	na
Families with Adolescents (Stages 4 & 5)	80	82	82
Older Couples (Stages 6 & 7)	83	86	na
TOTAL (stages combined)	68	71	na
Average within stages	83	88	82

na = not applicable.

compared to individual scores. The predictions were generally very good, and accuracy increased to very high levels at certain stages of the family life cycle.

The very best predictions occurred when they were made separately for each stage (rather than for all stages combined), using the subscales separately for each of the scales (rather than the total scale scores) to distinguish Balanced versus Extreme family types (excluding Mid-Range types). Conversely, the least accurate predictions in discriminating Balanced from Extreme types occurred when total scale scores were used to predict all stages combined into one group.

One very clear conclusion from this analysis is that there are distinct differences among families at various stages of the life cycle. These unique differences are masked and results are less clear when all stages are combined in the analysis. Second, the findings indicate that the accuracy of predictions also improves when more discrete subscales, rather than the total score for each scale, are used. In other words, the more specific subscale analysis, focusing on separate stages of the life cycle, helps to describe more clearly and to predict Balanced and Extreme family types.

Predictive Analysis

The variables that appear to be the most useful in predicting family types are family and marital strengths, family stress, and marital and family satisfaction. Family coping strategies, with the exception of two subscales (soliciting spiritual support and reframing), are less useful in making predictions. Personal health behaviors are *not* useful in discriminating among groups. Table 11.2 lists the variables that predicts Balanced and Extreme family types. Table 11.2 does not include Older Couples (Stages 6 and 7) because there were no specific variables (but rather the total cluster of variables) that distinguished Balanced from the Extreme family types at these stages.

When the analysis was done on the entire sample, the major hypothesis was supported. Balanced families had the highest levels of marital and family strengths, lowest levels of stress, highest levels of coping, and highest levels of marital and family satisfaction. This supports the general hypotheses from the Circumplex Model that Balanced families are more able to deal with stress because they have more resources and coping skills and, therefore, that they end up more satisfied. The specific variables are indicated in Table 11.2. Some caution in interpreting these data should be noted because the findings vary by stage of the family life cycle.

The following sections will describe the specific findings for each stage of the family life cycle. The data in Table 11.2 clearly indicate that while some of the predictor variables are the same across the various stages of the life cycle, others differ by stage. While the Adolescent stage has the highest number of specific predictor variables, the Older Couple stage has no specific variables, but rather the total cluster of variables.

STAGE 1: YOUNG COUPLES WITHOUT CHILDREN

Couples at this stage are often described as juggling a set of competing demands. Optimally, individuals at this stage have successfully "left home" (Haley, 1980) or in Bowen's terms, differentiated. Carter and McGoldrick (1980, p. 13) indicate that one should "become a self before joining another to form a new family subsystem," and McGoldrick (1980) later claimed that this transition is one of the most complex and difficult to make.

At this beginning stage, the accuracy of predicting the Extreme and Balanced types of families was 100 percent for these couples. However, the families that seem to function best at this stage are the Extreme types rather than the Balanced ones. The decision as to which type functions best was made by looking at scores on family resources, family stress, and family satisfaction. Those families considered to be functioning most adequately have more positive family resources, lower levels of

TABLE 11.2 Family Resources and Stress Levels of Balanced and Extreme Families Across the Life Cycle

Across all Stages (Balanced higher on)	Couples Without Children (Extreme higher on)	Families with Young Children (Extreme higher on)	Families with Adolescents (Balanced higher on)
Family Strengths			
Family Pride	Family Pride		Family Pride
Family Accord	Family Accord		Family Accord
			Parent-Adolescent Communication
Marital Strengths			
Marital Communication		Marital Comunication	Marital Communication
Conflict Resolution	Conflict Resolution	Conflict Resolution	Conflict Resolution
	Personality	Personality	Personality
Sexuality			Sexuality
Children			Children
	Family and Friends	Family and Friends	Family and Friends
Financial Management		Financial Management	Financial Management
			Religious Orientation
Congretational Activities			Congregational Activities
Stress Scores			
Low Stress	Low Stress		Low Stress
Coping Scales			
Spiritual Support			Spiritual Support
Reframing			Reframing
Satisfaction Scales			
Family Satisfaction	Family Satisfaction	Family Satisfaction	Family Satisfaction
Marital Satisfaction	Marital Satisfaction	Marital Satisfaction	Marital Satisfaction
		Quality of Life	Quality of Life
Conventionality	Conventionality	Conventionality	Conventionality

family stress, and, most important, high levels of marital and family satisfaction.

At this stage, Extreme types have higher levels of family strengths, including family pride and loyalty. They also have higher levels of marital strengths, indicating that they have more skill in resolving conflict, like the personality of their partner, and agree on their relationship with family and friends. They also have lower levels of stress and higher levels of marital and family satisfaction, but also higher levels of conventionality (see Table 11.2).

The majority of the Extreme couples fell into the *upper-right* quadrant of the Circumplex Model (see Figure 11.3). The Extreme type in this quadrant is labeled "chaotically enmeshed," a label that is, in reality, too exaggerated for this group. As we are dealing here with a "normal" group of families, Balanced and Extreme distinctions are somewhat artificial. The Extreme group in this analysis might normally fall more into the Mid-Range area of the Circumplex Model, while "problem" families (those with runaways, delinquents, or chemically dependent members) might fall into the more extreme types. Also, couples that in this analysis were considered Extreme had high conventionality scores that would inflate their cohesion scores and thus make them appear more "enmeshed." This would also increase their scores on adaptability and make them appear more "chaotic." This is because there is a positive correlation of about .35 between conventionality and cohesion and adaptability.

Because these are normal couples and because of high levels of conventionality, it is understandable why Extreme types artificially created for this analysis would more accurately be described as Mid-Range families. Couples at Stage 1 might actually fall into the "flexibly enmeshed" and "chaotically connected" types (see Figure 11.3).

As previously hypothesized by the Circumplex Model, the young couples that seem to be functioning well did fall into the *upper-right* quadrant, a finding that is not surprising given that these couples are expected to be higher in cohesion and adaptability. Young couples may be higher in cohesion (connected and enmeshed types) because they are still idealistic, and they may be higher in adaptability (flexible and chaotic) because they are attempting to work out their role relationship, leadership patterns, and relationship rules.

At this early stage of marriage, it makes a great deal of sense that these couples are more connected. Young couples often have extended "honeymoons" and experience an excessive amount of closeness for a period of time. Concurrently, they are struggling to create a new "family" by negotiating a new relationship, a task that demands some

Stage 1: Young Couples

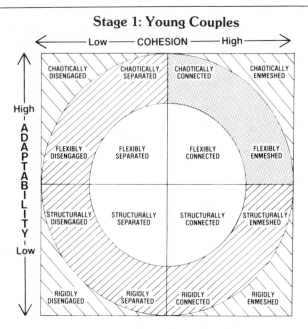

Stage 2: Families with Young Children

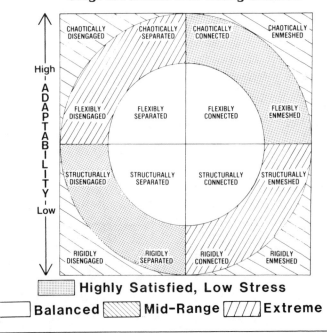

Figure 11.3 Highly Satisfied and Low-Stress Families

flexibility. Often, individual partners are also dealing with career issues (mastering work skills, identifying goals and objectives, acquiring competency), which can consume more time than might be required at a later point in their lives.

The majority of these couples are dual-career, reflecting the trend among young couples today. The literature in this area has certainly illustrated how difficult it is to balance the demands of the work world with family life (Skinner, 1980). Without children, couples can more easily involve themselves in less structured and more flexible life styles. Perhaps it is these variables that contributed to the more "flexible" and "chaotic" behaviors identified by FACES II.

STAGE 2: FAMILIES WITH YOUNG CHILDREN

The next stage is initiated with the entrance of children into the family. The wealth of literature detailing this transition to parenthood (LeMasters, 1957; Russell, 1974) has also produced considerable controversy regarding the levels of stress and marital satisfaction. This study systematically compares these variables with families at various stages of the life cycle.

Our findings indicate that families with younger children also appear to function best as Extreme, as opposed to Balanced, family types (see Table 11.2). This group reported greater marital and family satisfaction and lower stress than Balanced families did. These families reported fewer problems related to the classic descriptors of this life-cycle stage (e.g., the transition to parenthood). Their resources — including greater skill in communicating, resolving conflict, and managing financial affairs; utilizing friends and family for support; and more satisfaction with their partner's personality — are significantly greater than those of Balanced families. Like couples at the earlier stage, they also had high scores on conventionality.

A more careful review of the four Extreme types shows that these couples basically fall into two regions: the upper-right quadrant and lower-left quadrant. One should again be cautious about labeling families in these quadrants as Extreme for the same reasons discussed for Stage 1. Considering the sample, it is certainly possible that we have artificially created Extreme groups when in reality they are Mid-Range types. Therefore, families in the upper-right quadrant would probably best be described as Mid-Range types of "flexibly enmeshed" and "chaotically connected." Those in the lower-left quadrant would represent the Mid-Range types of "rigidly separated" and "structurally disengaged" (see Figure 11.1).

As previously hypothesized in the circumplex Model, it is expected that with the birth of the first child, families will tend to move into the *upper-right* quadrant; there would naturally be some initial increase in levels of cohesion, moving the family toward the "connected" and "enmeshed" types. There might also be increasing levels of adaptability created as the couple deal with the new demands placed on them by the infant. This would make their relationship more "flexible" and perhaps even "chaotic."

As the child(ren) get older, the family type may shift for some couples to the *lower-left* quadrant. The couple may find less time, energy, and interest to be together as much as a couple. This would tend to decrease their level of cohesion, moving them toward the "separated" or "disengaged" types. In terms of adaptability, their roles may become more segregated and rigid, with the husband becoming more invested in his career and the wife more involved in child rearing. This would decrease their adaptability toward the "structured" or even "rigid" levels.

STAGE 3: FAMILIES WITH ADOLESCENTS

The "storm and stress" that families with adolescents experience has frequently been discussed in the literature. This stage is the most volatile and challenging compared to all other stages in the life cycle. In some respects, it represents the onset of a series of exits from the family, contrasted with earlier stages, which require adjusting to entrances.

Balanced family types are clearly the ones that function best at the Adolescent stage, with Extreme family types being most problematic (see Figure 11.4). Balanced types have the highest levels of marital and family strengths, the lowest levels of stress, and the highest levels of marital and family satisfaction. It appears that balanced levels of cohesion and adaptability are necessary for dealing with the endless demands and stresses of the Adolescent stage. It should be emphasized that overall stress levels are highest at this stage of the life cycle (see Chapters VII and XIII).

Families with adolescents also have the largest number of variables that discriminate Balanced from Extreme families (see Table 11.2). These families apparently need to use all available resources to deal with adolescents. Their family strengths include higher levels of family pride and family accord. An additional family resource that Balanced families at this stage had is good parent-adolescent communication. The parents' marital relationship was also very strong, and they liked the

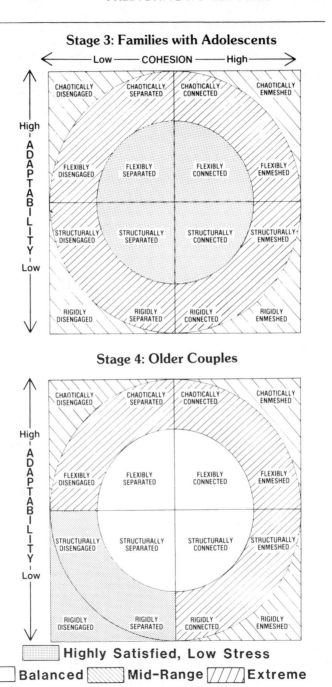

Stage 3: Families with Adolescents

Stage 4: Older Couples

Highly Satisfied, Low Stress

Balanced   Mid-Range   Extreme

Figure 11.4 Highly Satisfied and Low-Stress Families

way they communicated and resolved conflict. They reported enjoying the personality of their partner, having a good sexual relationship, appreciating their friends and relatives, and feeling confident about the way they jointly handled finances.

Balanced families at this stage are also more religious but do not participate in church activities (Congregational Activities Scale) as much as Extreme families do. More specifically, they agree on their religious values (Religious Orientation Scale) as a couple and solicit support from their church as a way of coping with their problems (Spiritual Support Scale). However, it appears that they are so involved in their own family life that they do not have time to participate as actively in church activities or accept as many positions or church duties as do Extreme families at this stage.

These Balanced families are lower in stress and use reframing as a coping strategy. In terms of satisfaction, these Balanced families are more satisfied with their marriages, families, and the quality of their lives. They are also higher in their levels of conventionality than Extreme families are.

STAGE 4: OLDER COUPLES

This last stage represents the longest stage of the life cycle, sometimes lasting more than twenty years. The family has shifted again to a smaller unit as the husband and wife now adjust to being a "couple" once again. In addition to losing their occupational roles through retirement, they often gain the role of grandparents. The couple must also adapt to the series of inevitable illnesses and losses. Typically, this stage has been described in a more pessimistic vein because Western culture glorifies youth. Those that can hold their own against these sociocultural forces are offered the opportunity to complete the last set of tasks that Erikson (1950) so eloquently identified as the achievement of "identify versus despair."

Although there were no specific variables that discriminated between the Balanced and Extreme couples at this stage, the prediction of which couples fall into these two types was still high (84 percent) based on the total set of variables. Balanced couples generally are less stressed and rely on spiritual support to cope with problems. Extreme couples are higher in stress but also somewhat happier as a couple and tend to fall into the *lower-left* quadrant. They are best described as having a more "structured" and "disengaged" relationship (see Figure 11.4). More specifically, these Extreme types could be described as "rigidly disengaged," but this group also includes "rigidly separated" and "structurally disengaged" Mid-Range types.

The results from this stage are more puzzling than are those for the other stages and suggest the need for further research. Part of the reason for the lack of clarity is that these couples represent a more heterogenous age group covering the span of 60 to 80 or more years. This group is described in greater detail when the focus shifts to high- and low-stress older couples (Chapter XII).

Summary

These analyses clearly demonstrate that the optimally functioning family systems are rather different at each stage of the family life cycle (see Figures 11.3 and 11.4). Different clusters of variables are important at the various stages (see Table 11.2). There was also considerable support for the general and specific hypotheses derived from the Circumplex Model regarding family types at the various stages of the family life cycle.

The accuracy of the predictions of Balanced and Extreme types was very high across specific stages using couple and family scores (see Table 11.1). Predictability was naturally lower when all stages were combined because of the differences across stages. The accuracy of prediction was the highest within stages, where it ranged between 80 and 100 percent. While these high levels of predictability do not imply a causal relationship between family resources and family types, they do indicate that these variables are significantly related.

chapter
XII
Predicting High- and Low-Stress
Families

ALTHOUGH THE PREVIOUS OVERVIEW (Chapter VIII) identified the major family stressors and strains across the family life cycle, we are left with several nagging questions. What are the roles of resources and coping in buffering or protecting families from the demands involved in establishing a marriage, bearing and rearing children, promoting independence in adolescents, launching young adults, and retiring and aging as a couple? Second, what specific strengths, coping strategies, and resources are critical in facilitating family adjustment and adaptation to family life changes?

We will address these questions in an effort to shed light on what families report to be important marital strengths, coping strategies, and resources for managing demands created by normal transitions across the life span. For the purpose of simplifying this presentation, we will refer to marital strengths, family strengths, coping strategies, and resources collectively as *family resources*. Using the concept of family resources to include strengths and coping is in keeping with family stress theory and research (Burr, 1973; McCubbin, 1979; McCubbin & Patterson, 1982).

The primary focus of this chapter is on important and critical family resources in the management of the pile-up of stressors and strains and their impact on the family. Figure 12.1 sets the stage for the analysis by outlining comparisons to be made. Specifically, having already identified the accumulation of stressors, prior strains, and hardships as family "pile-up" and "demands" (on the left side of the balance board), we will attempt to fill in the list of family resources (on the right side of the balance board) used to manage them. The balance board is presented to reflect the Double ABC-X theory of family stress and adjustment, which assumes that the process of managing stress and transitions involves balancing demands with family resources (McCubbin and Patterson, 1983).

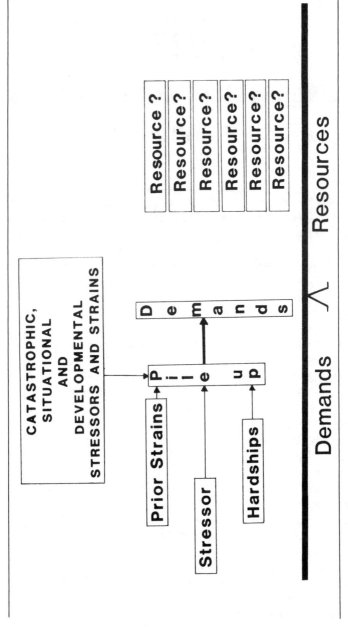

Figure 12.1 Balancing Family Demands with Family Resources

Method of Stress Analysis

To examine the association of family strengths, coping, and resources to high- and low-stress families, we first classified families into extreme groups (high- and low-stress groups) on the basis of couple scores on the Family Inventory of Life Events (FILE).

COMPUTING COUPLE SCORES

One premise in the family field assumes that within relationships, individuals will develop over time and maintain a shared perspective of the world (see Berger & Luckman, 1966). Differing perceptions of experiences will be negotiated by individual family members in an effort to cultivate a shared definition of the family and its relationship to the world (Reiss, 1981). Reiss (1981) has expanded this proposition and advanced the argument that families over time develop a "paradigm" or shared world view.

In the face of family stressors and transitions, which often force a structural change in the family unit and/or a major shift in family patterns of behavior, the family unit is called on to negotiate a new family "meaning" or "schema" that will serve to guide family functioning in the future (see McCubbin & Patterson, 1983).

In order to incorporate the concepts of family paradigms and shared meanings, a *couple stress score* was developed. This score represents the fact that if an event is stressful, it has an impact on the entire family system. The couple stress score was obtained by: (a) identifying those family life events, changes, and strains that one or both partners marked (checked "yes") as occurring within the family during the past year; (b) assigning family life change units (standard weights indicating the intensity of the demands placed on the family as a result of the event/change/strain occuring) to each of the demands; and (c) summing the family life change units for each family (see Appendix F on Couple and Family scores).

The rationale for using weights for each event is based on the realization that each event, change, or strain has a differential impact on family life. For example, the death of a child may be more stressful than a child making a transition to a new school. The general procedures for scoring and the development of weights are reported elsewhere (see McCubbin & Patterson, 1981b; Olson et al., 1982).

TABLE 12.1   High- and Low-Stress Groups at Four Combined Stages

| | Stress Score | | Sample Size | | Accuracy of |
	Low	High	Low	High	Prediction[a]
Stage 1: Young Couples	0-352	588- 1075	16	19	97
Stage 2: Couples with Children	0-396	609- 2617	51	64	81
Stage 3: Adolescent Stage	0-397	621- 1948	93	106	75
Stage 4: Older Couples	0-271	332- 2714	25	30	89
Totals			185	219	86[b]

a. In percentages.
b. Average stress of the four ages.
NOTE: High stress = upper one-third. Low stress = lower one-third.

CLASSIFICATION OF FAMILIES

For this analysis, families were grouped into four stages of the family cycle: *Young Families Without Children, Families with Young Children, Families with Adolescents,* and *Older Couples.* On the basis of the couple scores on FILE, families within each stage were classified into either the high-stress, moderate-stress, or low-stress group. The number of families in each group and the cutoff scores used in classifying families in each of the four family stages are presented in Table 12.1.

Given our natural tendency to view high-stress families and low-stress families to mean "problem" and "nonproblem" families, respectively, it is important to emphasize two points. First, families under stress should be viewed along a continuum ranging from "extremely high stress" to "high stress" to "low stress" and finally to "extremely low stress." Second, families in this study clustered in the central area of this "stress" continuum. In other words, 85 percent of the families were classified in the *mid-range* of family stress. As this study focused on normative and developmental processes in families, it is important to emphasize that this analysis does not focus on comparing problem and nonproblem families.

Once classified, the high-stress and the low-stress families were studied in greater depth. The goal was to discover whether low-stress families utilized different types and amounts of family resources (family strengths and coping strategies) than did high-stress families. Discrimi-

nant analysis was used to distinguish statistically between the two extreme groups of families. The logic behind this particular analysis is that
once a set of "discriminating" variables that distinguished between
high- and low-stress families was found, these variables could be used
to predict stress levels (high or low) in other families.

Because of the interest in identifying the most "critical" family
strengths, coping, and resources, a stepwise statistical procedure was
used. This procedure selects the variables best able to improve the
discrimination between high- and low-stress families. All variables are
considered in the analysis, but only the significant variables are used to
make the predictions.

The accuracy of predicting families high and low in stress was very
high. The accuracy levels in percentages correct are indicated in Table
12.1. The accuracy was highest with the Young Couples (Stage 1) at 97
percent, and lowest with the Families with Adolescents (Stage 3) at 75
percent.

CRITICAL FAMILY RESOURCES ACROSS THE LIFE CYCLE

Stage 1: Young Couples Without Children

Of the 22 family strengths, coping, and resources that were used to
discriminate between high- and low-stress Couples without Children,
eleven variables appear to be most important (see Table F.1).

Couples in the low-stress group appear to make an effort to develop
good health practices and have a positive appraisal of their marriage
and quality of life. Satisfaction with marital communication helps promote the couples' efforts to resolve personality issues, reduce conflict,
develop social support from family and friends, and share leisure activities.

If we examine the eleven important discriminating variables in
greater depth and evaluate the strength of their relationship to our
outcome criterion of high- and low-stress families, we can better determine which are "critical" variables. To conduct such an analysis, a
stepwise procedure examined the standardized discriminant function
coefficients to determine the relative contribution and value of each
variable.

In this analysis, six resources emerged from the eleven as being of
critical importance. The critical family resources are highlighted in Figure 12.2. Couples most capable of managing stressors and strains

appear to be characterized as more involved in promoting family accord and feeling satisfied with their family financial management, communication, personality of partner, and their leisure activities; they also tended to have better health practices.

In summary, it appears that couples experiencing low stress have certain resources that they use more frequently than high-stress couples do. Unfortunately, we cannot assess whether these resources serve to buffer the family from the impact of life stressor and strains or whether they are developed in response to the impact of stressors. However, the fact that these resources are linked with low-stress couples might make these resources important for more highly stressed families to develop. We can also begin to identify possible targets for education and prevention programs designed to support families at this stage of the family cycle.

Stage 2: Families with Young Children

As already noted, families face many demands in raising children. Children not only tax parental patience and esteem on a daily basis, but they also introduce additional demands (e.g., expenses, need for independence). How well families navigate their way through this transition period appears to be associated with several important family resources.

Nineteen family resources are important discriminators between high-stress and low-stress families at the childbearing and child-rearing stages of the family cycle. In general, this rather extensive list of family resources indicates the importance of marital strengths and family accord. Additionally, low-stress families have a more positive appraisal of marriage and family life, quality of life, and their sexual relationship. Predictably, these families are also characterized by positive communication, conflict resolution, agreement on religious orientation, and a positive orientation toward children. Low-stress families also have a positive assessment of their shared leisure activities, family and friends, financial management abilities, communication, and the resolution of personality issues. In contrast, high-stress families describe themselves as having more social support, being more involved in congregational activities, and relying more on passive appraisal (e.g., waiting for problems to solve themselves) to cope with their stress (see Table F.2).

Of the nineteen important family resources that discriminated between high- and low-stress families, *eight resources* appeared to be of

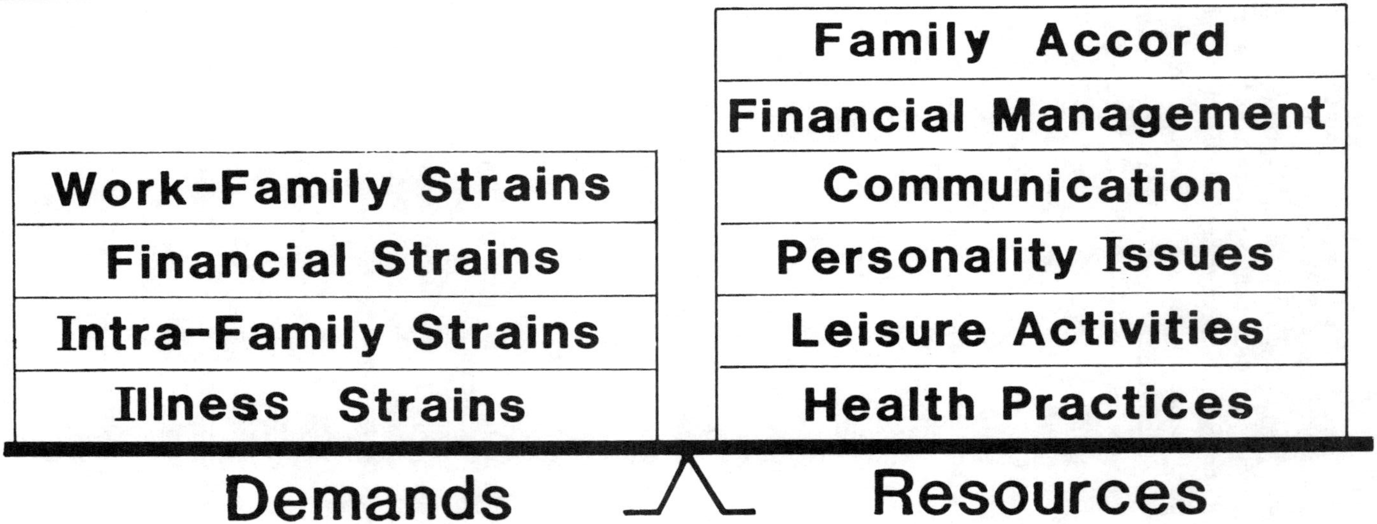

Figure 12.2 Stage 1: Couples Without Children

critical importance (see Figure 12.3). Interestingly, families at the preschool and school-age stages of the family cycle appear to buffer themselves against the demands of raising children by developing their marital and family strenghts. More specifically, low-stress families have high levels of family accord and feel good about their financial management, communication, relationships with family and friends, and their children. They also rely on their friends and relatives for social support. These low-stress families are generally satisfied with their family lives and the overall quality of their lives.

Our comparative analysis of the most frequently cited areas of family demands in relationship to critical family resources reveals the family's need for a broader set of family resources (compared with Stage 1 couples), particularly in the areas of support from family and friends.

Stage 3: Families with Adolescents

This study on families in the adolescent stages of the family life cycle indicated how stressful this stage is for families. As we reported in Chapter VIII, families not only struggle with the developmental changes of young adults and the movement of members outside of the family unit; they are also faced with fanancial strains that place heavy demands on everyone. While this stage is particularly stressful for most families, we did observe differences in the types of resources on which families will call to manage these demands.

Sixteen important family resources appear to contribute to a more positive family adjustment at this stage of the family cycle. As was true for the childbearing and child-rearing stage, the family's internal strengths emerge as being of vital importance in buffering itself against the rapid change in adolescent member(s) and the transition of these young adults from the home (see Table F. 3).

Specifically, low-stress families are buffered from the impact of stressors and strains by their positive appraisal of the quality of their lives, marital and family strengths, communication, supportive networks of valued relatives and friends, leisure activities, strong health practices, and satisfaction with children. It comes as no surprise to note the importance of their family problem-solving skills in terms of family strengths of conflict resolution, financial management, resolution of personality issues, and reframing (i.e., redefining the situation into a more constructive and manageable form). It is important to note, however, that high-stress families emphasize passive appraisal (i.e., a more

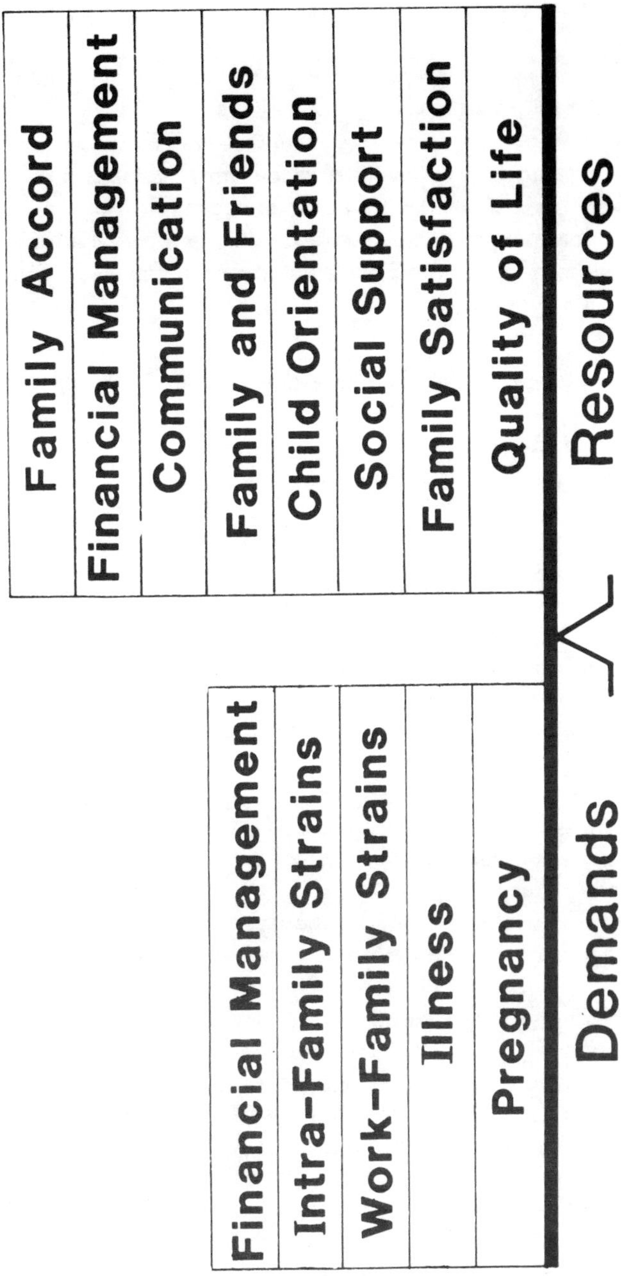

Figure 12.3 Stage 2: Childbearing/Child Rearing

fatalistic approach) as a major coping strategy for the management of stress (see Figure 12.4).

Of these sixteen resources, six resources seemed most critical in distinguishing between the high- and low-stress families. Low-stress families feel good about their financial management, like the personality of their partner, and enjoy their extended family and friends. The couple have a good sexual relationship and are happy with their marriage and the overall quality of their life.

Stage 4: Older Couples (Empty Nest and Retired)

As children and young adults move out of the family nest, the marital pair face a new set of demands in moving from full-time parents and employed individuals into the retirement and the associated "aging" status of the human cycle of development. The demands of family life are not necessarily minimized. Families at these stages face the hardships of loss, illness, and economic demands. In classifying these couples into high- and low-stress family units and examining the discriminating family strengths, coping, and resources, we identified eight important dimensions of family life.

Low-stress families moving into the latter stages of the family cycle call on family resources such as a positive assessment of the quality of their lives, the resolution of personality issues, and strong family bonds of cohesiveness as well as family adaptability. In comparison with results reported earlier (where family resources were associated with "low-stress" families), we now observe high-stress families scoring higher in the areas of positive health practices, marital satisfaction, family satisfaction, and positive communication to cope with these demands (see Table F.4).

Of the eight important resources that discriminated between high- and low-stress couples, three variables appeared most critical (see Figure 12.5). While low-stress families were very satisfied with the personality of their partner, high-stress families had higher levels of positive communication and better health practices. This shift in resources to the high-stress group can be explained in part by the heavy demands of the transition into the empty nest and retirement, including a predictable instability in health and the need to deal with marital strains. It seems reasonable that high-stress families need to emphasize or increase the use of family resources such as communication and health practices to cope with these demands.

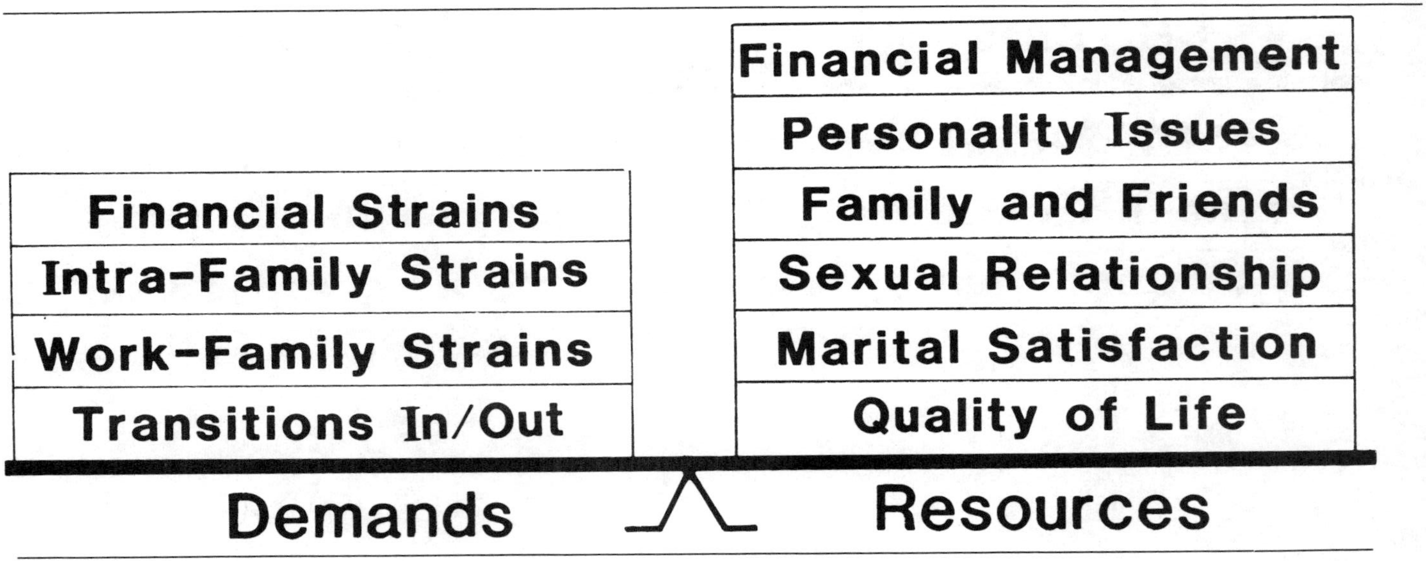

Resources

- Financial Management
- Personality Issues
- Family and Friends
- Sexual Relationship
- Marital Satisfaction
- Quality of Life

Demands

- Financial Strains
- Intra-Family Strains
- Work-Family Strains
- Transitions In/Out

Figure 12.4 Stage 3: Adolescent/Launching

213

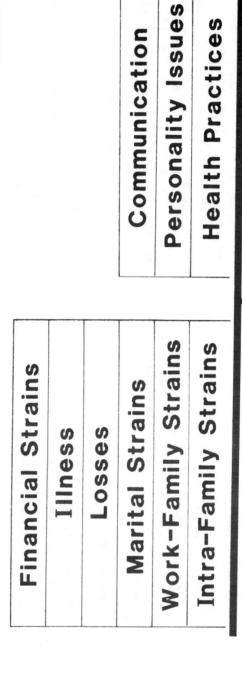

Demands

Financial Strains
Illness
Losses
Marital Strains
Work–Family Strains
Intra–Family Strains

Resources

Communication
Personality Issues
Health Practices

Figure 12.5 Stage 4: Empty Nest/Retirement

Summary of Critical Family Strengths, Coping, and Resources

Families face a host of stressors and strains throughout the life cycle. These demands change in terms of their frequency, type, and intensity, making family adjustment and coping seemingly impossible tasks. It is true that some families are unable to manage these demands and may experience rather severe consequences such as violence, extreme interpersonal conflicts, or ill health. However, many families are able to endure and cope and have demonstrated the capacity to make adjustments to challenges throughout the family life cycle. We have chosen deliberately to focus our attention on, and to learn from, those "surviving" or "coping" families.

In attempting to understand how and why these families appear relatively successful in their adjustments to demands, we can gain a deeper appreciation of what it takes to cope with the challenges of becoming a couple, raising children, and entering retirement. We have also can obtain a fuller understanding of what resources are necessary to increase the family's resistance to stressors.

A brief review of the critical family resources identified for each stage of the life cycle is presented in Table 12.2. Specifically, the results of this study lead us to the following conclusions and propositions about the relationship between family demands and family resources.

Family resistance to stress and recovery from distress may well be facilitated, in part, by family strengths, coping, and resources. The importance and critical nature of specific family and social resources vary according to the stage of the family life cycle and the demands unique to each stage of family development. A summary of the most important resources characteristic of *low-stress families* at each stage is given below.

(1) *Young Couples Without Children:* family accord, good financial management, satisfactory communication, resolved personality issues, shared leisure activities, and good health practices.

(2) *Families with Young Children:* accord, financial management, communication, satisfaction with family and friends, a supportive social network, satisfaction with child rearing, a positive appraisal of family life, and satisfaction with the overall quality of their life.

(3) *Families with Adolescents:* financial management, resolved personality issues, a supportive network of family and friends, and a positive appraisal of their marital relationship, sexual relationship, and quality of life.

TABLE 12.2   Critical Family Resources in High- and Low-Stress Families

Stage 1: Couples Without Children	Stage 2: Families with Young Children	Stage 3: Families with Adolescents	Stage 4: Older Couples
Family Strengths			
Family Accord	Family Accord		
Marital Strengths			
Financial Management	Financial Management	Financial Management	
Communication	Communication		Communication
Personality Issues		Personality Issues	Personality Issues
	Family and Friends	Family and Friends	
Leisure Activities			
	Children and Marriage		
		Sexual Relationship	
Family Coping Strategies			
Health Practices			Health Practices
Satisfaction Variables			
		Marital Satisfaction	
	Family Satisfaction		
	Quality of Life	Quality of Life	

NOTE: High stress = upper one-third. Low stress = lower one-third.

    (4) *Older Couples:* satisfaction with their quality of life, lack of person-
ality conflicts with spouse, and high cohesion and adaptability.

Summary and Conclusions

    The findings presented in this chapter offer researchers, clinicians,
educators, and policymakers some useful information to guide present

and future efforts in support of families throughout the life cycle. The family scholar should be encouraged to probe deeper into the dynamics of family adjustment and coping in relation to stress and change. This research has only begun to shed light on which family strengths, coping strategies, and resources are important.

We can build on this research and explore how families use these resources, and in what combination, as they attempt to navigate their way through normative transitions (Mederer & Hill, 1983). We could also advance our understanding of families if we were to explore the use of family resources in family problem solving and the resolution of specific family demands (Klein, 1983). We would all benefit from greater understanding of how families reorganize, restructure, consolidate, and achieve a satisfactory level of adjustment to crises (McCubbin & Patterson, 1983). In other words, the findings of this investigation should encourage future research into the processes of family adjustment and adaptation to stress.

Clinical work with families under stress has been guided by research on why families fail. We have assumed that families who have overcome individual and family crises will help us understand important skills and resources for families to succeed. This study of family resources attempts to bring a more positive balance to clinical work with families by exploring what families might use to manage stress. In other words, this emphasis on family strengths, coping, and resources can provide clinicians with additional ideas regarding resources that could be used in counseling and treatment of problem families.

The data indicate that families who work to develop strengths, coping strategies, and basic resources will in the long run be more resistant to stressors and more resilient in the face of distress. In many respects, the findings of this research support the value of a dual focus in the treatment of families under stress: Families benefit from an appraisal of their weaknesses and vulnerabilities as well as from an appraisal of their strengths. Certainly, in situations of short-term counseling and crisis intervention, it would be useful to focus on strengths and resources that can facilitate the family's resolution of its own problems.

Family life educators and policymakers have also been guided, in part, by research on family problems and crises. Many programs and policies are designed to focus on specific family problems such as drug abuse or child abuse. However, the findings of this study should encourage educators and policymakers to address what can be done to facilitate the development of family strengths, coping, and family resources. These resources would enable families to help themselves in a preventive way without extensive intervention of professionals or government and social agencies. These findings lend support to the value of marital and family enrichment programs and stress management education programs.

chapter
XIII
Families with Adolescents

FAMILIES WITH ADOLESCENT children face challenges and stresses unique to this stage of the family life cycle. It is a time when adolescents experience a rapid period of maturation and their focus of identity shifts away from their family and toward their peer group. Earlier we noted that parents' reports of family adaptability and cohesion reached their lowest points during these Adolescent and Launching stages and that adolescents reported even lower levels of cohesion and adaptability than their parents did.

What happens in families with adolescents and why are these years stressful? What is unique about these years when adolescents are growing toward adulthood and their parents are looking to the end of their years of most active parenting? These are some of the issues that will be addressed in this chapter. The focus of this chapter is on all the families in the study that had at least one adolescent at home. Families from the Adolescent (Stage 4) and the Launching (Stage 5) stages were combined for this family analysis.

One important aspect of this stage is that information was obtained on the family from the parents and from one adolescent in each family. This chapter highlights the perceptions of all three family members: husband-father, wife-mother, and adolescent. Our objectives include comparing the ways in which each member assessed certain dimensions of family life, such as the way members communicate, the degree of stress experienced, the way in which they cope with difficulties, and the kinds of resources they have available. Second, a variety of family scores were developed for use in this chapter. This chapter begins with an overview of the discrepant realities of the three family members.

Assessing Individual Perceptions

No phase of the family life cycle seems to be more stressful than the adolescent years. Part of this stress comes from the changing needs and

TABLE 13.1 Agreement Between Family Members (Correlations)

Scale	Husband-Wife	Husband-Adolescent	Wife-Adolescent
FACES II			
Family cohesion	.46	.46	.39
Family adaptability	.32	.31	.21
Family Strengths (Total)	.40	.39	.34
Family pride	.31	.37	.28
Family accord	.36	.25	.23
Parent-Adolescent Communication	.30	.32	.34
Congregational Activities	.62	.45	.39
Family Inventory of Life Events (Total)	.42	.29*	.35*
Family Coping (Total)	.20	.12	.14
Reframing	.16	.12	.16
Acquiring social support	.26	.15	.16
Seeking spiritual support	.31	.27	.27
Mobilizing to acquire/ accept help	.25	.05	.12
Passive appraisal	.26	.10	.14
Personal Health Behaviors	.34	.11	.20
Family Satisfaction	.35	.31	.29
Quality of Life	.35	.28*	.22*

*Analysis was done of comparable items from the Parent and Adolescent scales.

preferences of the adolescents as they increasingly seek independence from their family. However, a rarely considered factor is the lack of congruence between family members' perceptions of their relationships and interactions. The level of intrafamily stress may be elevated due to the discrepant perspectives of parents and their adolescents regarding family issues and dynamics.

Parents and their adolescents live in rather different worlds. This is demonstrated by a comparison on all the major variables in this study (see Table 13.1). More specifically, the degree of agreement between husbands and their adolescent children ranged from correlations as high as .46 on family cohesion to a low of .05 on the coping strategy labeled "mobilizing to accept help from others." The level of agreement between the adolescent and mother was equally poor, with a high correlation of .39 on family cohesion and a low correlation of .12 on "mobilizing to acquire help."

FAMILIES WITH ADOLESCENTS   221

As discussed earlier, the level of agreement between a husband and wife was also low, but it was generally higher between spouses than between the parent-child generations. Husband and wives were more likely to share similar perceptions of their world than was either parent and the adolescent.

PARENT-ADOLESCENT COMMUNICATION

Communication among family members is of major interest and concern in families with adolescents. At this stage of the family life cycle, one is likely to hear complaints about "poor communication." Parents frequently report not understanding their adolescents, while in turn, adolescents complain about the same problem with their parents. The generation gap characteristically widens. Because of its potential impact on family relationships, we will use communication to further illustrate the lack of agreement in perceptions between family members.

Communication is viewed as an underlying and facilitating dimension of the Circumplex Model. Communication facilitates the movement of families on each of the two major dimensions of family adaptability and family cohesion. This part of the study focuses on communication between adolescents and their parents, separately comparing the responses of adolescents with their mothers and with their fathers.

Parent-adolescent communication was assessed by responses to the Parent-Adolescent Communication Scale. This scale was developed to assess perceptions of intrafamily and intergenerational communication. This instrument contains two subscales: Open Family Communication, which assesses the degree of freedom with which information is exchanged between parents and children, and Problems in Family Communication, which measures difficulties or hindrances in the intergenerational exchange of information.

Each parent reported his or her perceptions of communication with their adolescent, and adolescents responded to the items twice, once as they viewed their interaction with their mother and a second time regarding their father. (For a complete discussion of the Parent-Adolescent Communication Scale see Olson et al., 1982.)

DISCREPANT REALITIES

How do various family members view their communication? The discrepancies between the generations are rather pronounced. Mothers perceived more satisfying communication with their children than did fathers. Adolescents expressed having a particularly difficult time communicating with both parents. The following discussion will compare these perceptions in greater detail.

The perceptions of parent-adolescent communication varied considerably between individual family members (see Figure 13.1). Based on the total scale, mothers reported significantly better communication with their teenagers than fathers did. This difference is primarily due to more openness of family communication reported by the mothers. A comparison of subscale scores indicates that mothers experience significantly more openness than fathers when communicating with their adolescents. By contrast, the two parents showed almost identical ratings on the problems in family communication aspect of communication.

Teenagers also expressed a greater degree of openness with their mothers than with their fathers, reporting significantly better communication with their mothers than with their fathers, based on total scale scores. As before, this was primarily due to a significantly greater degree of openness with their mothers that was lacking in their communication with their fathers. As with the parents' reports, there were almost no differences in the amount of problems they reported in relating to their mothers or fathers.

Whereas the previous analysis compared all the fathers, mothers, and adolescents as three separate groups, the following are the results from a *family analysis* in which the father, mother, and adolescent from the same family are compared. In the family analysis, the adolescents described their communication with each parent and each parent described how he or she perceived communication with the adolescent. It is here that we can compare the adolescent's description with each parent's description.

The results from the family analysis are similar to those reported when the groups of fathers, mothers, and adolescents are compared. Mothers consistently saw their communication with their teenagers as more positive than fathers did, and most of this difference was due to mother's emphasizing higher levels of openness in their parent-child exchanges. When adolescent responses were compared with their parents, adolescents also viewed communication with their mothers more positively than interactions with their fathers. Here again the difference is due to a greater level of openness with their mothers than with their fathers. Adolescents rate their parents fairly equally in terms of the problems they experience in trying to communicate with them.

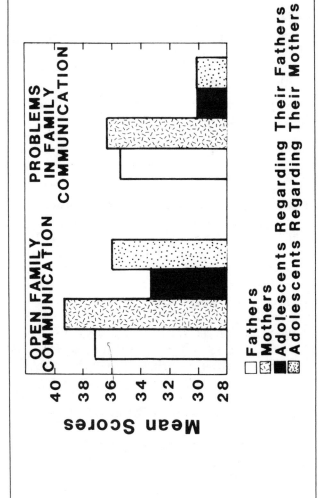

Figure 13.1 Parent-Adolescent Communication

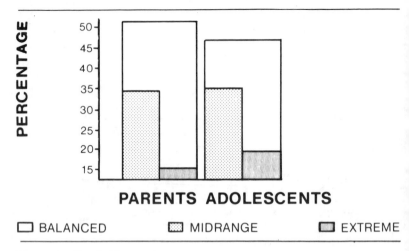

Figure 13.2 Family Type

Both parents rated these interactions as significantly more open and less problematical than was reported by their adolescents. Clearly, adolescents viewed their families with greater negativism. There are many hypotheses that might explain this phenomenon. One possibility is that the adolescent is struggling with issues of independence, and it is necessary for the adolescent to distance him- or herself from the family, minimizing aspects of family life, such as positive communication, that encourage dependency. The adolescent, by striving to move outside the family system, may "objectify" the group and adapt what he or she assumes would be an outsider's view. This hypothesis will, of course, need further empirical testing and will be explored in more detail at a future time.

Balanced Families versus Extreme Families

Throughout the text we have discussed three types of family systems: Balanced, Mid-Range, and Extreme. We have described differences in degrees of stress, coping strategies, kinds of resources, and strengths in these three systems. It is at the adolescent stage that the importance of family resources becomes the most apparent and where the Balanced families clearly seemed to function much better than Extreme families. But before focusing on these findings in more detail, it is important to describe how adults and adolescents see their families in terms of cohesion and adaptability.

Parents and their adolescents seem to agree more on the levels of cohesion ($r = .46$ with fathers, $r = .39$ with mothers) in their family than on any other characteristic. There is less agreement, however, on adaptability ($r = .31$ with fathers, $r = .21$ with mothers). However, when we group all parents and all adolescents together, we find that the two groups have considerably fewer overall differences. Figure 13.2 illustrates the percentages of Balanced, Mid-Range, and Extreme family types that are perceived by parents and adolescents. As expected, adolescents see their families as more Extreme than do parents, and, conversely, parents see their families as more Balanced than adolescents do. These are group differences, however, and do *not* necessarily reflect the reality within a family.

Predicting Balanced and Extreme Families

An important goal in this study was to discover what family resources were related to Balanced and Extreme family types. One analysis, therefore, focused on the marital and family resources, levels of stress, and degree of satisfaction that might help distinguish Balanced from Extreme families. A second analysis focused on what types of families and what kinds of resources differentiated low- from high-stress groups. The difference between these discriminant analyses and those reported in earlier chapters is that here a family score is used instead of individual or couple scores. The family score consisted of integrating the adolescent's and parents' reports into one score.

In the earlier analysis using couple scores, the relative advantages and limitations of the couple mean and couple discrepancy score were discussed. These two scores also complement each other, can provide a more comprehensive picture of a couple's relationship, and can be more empirically discriminating. For this analysis two new scores were created: the family mean z and family discrepancy score. The family mean is conceptually equivalent to the couple mean score. The Family discrepancy score is comparable to the couple discrepancy score, measuring the differences among fathers, mothers, and adolescents. Because using the couple mean and discrepancy scores in combination proved useful earlier, it seemed logical to try this same approach with family scores. (For a more complete explanation of the methodology employed to compute family scores, see Appendix F.)

Balanced families, in contrast to Extreme families, on the Circumplex Model clearly did better at the Adolescent stage. Balanced families at the Adolescent stages (Stages 4 and 5) scored higher on family pride, accord, and quality of life. These families reported *less* stress when faced with difficulties, and they reframed these situations in more positive terms. Balanced families also reported more family satisfaction than the Extreme group did.

As suggested earlier, this stage of the life cycle seems to require major shifts in the family system to accommodate the needs of adolescent members. Families with adolescents may need to become more flexible and open to adolescent input on decisions. In addition, these families may need to tolerate less emotional closeness from their adolescent and allow him or her to develop relationships with individuals outside their family. These findings suggest that the individuation process of adolescents triggers many other processes within the family. It may increase the degree of family discrepancy or the amount of difference in how members see their families.

An example of the benefits gained by using both the family mean z and family discrepancy scores for each variable is illustrated in the following discriminant analysis. The findings indicate that when one scoring method is significant for a variable, the second method is also significant. In other words, the family mean z score and the family discrepancy score for the same variable often complemented each other.

As might be expected, the family discrepancy scores are *higher* for the Extreme families. In other words, Extreme family types showed a *greater discrepancy* between members' perceptions of the level of stress in their family, their ability to reframe the situation positively, their level of family satisfaction, and the quality of life they experience than Balanced families did (see Table 13.2).

The notion of circular causality from systems theory aids in explaining the relationship between stress and discrepant family perceptions. As Hill (1958) discussed, the impact from stressors produces different effects on the various subsystems in the family and results in differing perceptions among members. This *perceptual factor* accounts for the unique interpretations that individual family members create to explain the stressor event.

Increased stress consumes the system's resources, decreasing the amount of time available for individual members to negotiate their realities. Thus, during times of stress, discrepancies in perceptions are more evident. To complete this circular process, discrepant perceptions increase the stress level. This is most evident by the clustering of strain items that most typically follow a stressor event. It may be argued that a

TABLE 13.2   Balanced versus Extreme Types: Discriminant Analysis at the Family Level (standard scores)[a]

Family Resources	Family Mean		F_b	Family Discrepancy		F_b
	Balanced	Extreme		Balanced	Extreme	
Family Resources						
Family Strengths	51.2	44.5	21.1	54.5	55.8	5.1[c]
• Family pride	51.4	44.5	18.3			
• Family accord	51.0	45.9	12.2			
Parent-Adolescent Communication	50.6	48.0	3.3	58.9	60.7	3.7[c]
Family Stress	51.1	45.7	16.6	53.9	55.2	6.5[c]
Family Coping						
• Reframing	50.5	47.6	4.2	55.4	56.8	5.0[c]
Satisfaction						
Family Satisfaction	49.0	43.9	12.6	55.1	56.3	4.2[c]
Quality of Life	50.3	47.2	4.4	55.0	57.0	11.7[c]

a. The family mean z scores and discrepancy scores were converted to standardized scores with a mean of 50 and SD of 10.

b. Significant univariate F-ratio $p > .01$.

c. Extreme families have higher scores on these variables, indicating that Extreme families have higher levels of discrepancy than Balanced families do.

by-product of the discrepant realities is increased stress. And with increasing stress, we come full circle to increases in the discrepancies of perceptions between family members.

Parent-Adolescent Stressors and Strains

Family stressors and strains have an impact on the development of adolescents. However, we have not previously had a clear picture of the nature of these demands or how the adolescent perceives them. As part of this study, we learned about the adolescent-family life stressors and strains directly from the adolescents. By examining the percentage of adolescents who recorded their family stressors and strains on A-FILE, we can begin to understand what demands are placed on these young individuals.

We find little similarity between adolescents' and parents' perceptions of stressors within the family. This is due in part to the fact that they were responding to slightly different questionnaires on specific stressors

TABLE 13.3   Parents' Profile of Family Stressors and Strains: Stage 4 (Families with Adolescents)

Stressor/Strain	Percentage Reporting Strain
Intrafamily Strains	
Increased difficulty in managing teenage children.	30
Increase in the amount of "outside activities" in which the children are involved.	68
Increase in the number of tasks or chores that do not get done.	48
Finance and Business Strains	
Took out a loan or refinanced a loan to cover increased expenses.	33
Change in conditions (economic, political, weather) that hurts family investments and/or income.	34
A member purchased a car or other major item.	43
Increased strain on family "money" for medical/dental expenses.	31
Increased strain on family "money" for food, clothing, energy, home care.	62
Increased strain on family "money" for children's education.	30
Work-Family Transitions and Strains	
A member was promoted at work or given more responsibilities.	30

and strains. While parents felt that most of the stress was related to finances (60 percent) and some to family strains (30 percent), adolescents felt that most of the stress was in dealing with their family (50 percent) and very little in the area of finance (10 percent). Not only is there little agreement on the general areas of stress for adolescents and parents, but there is considerable difference between the specific types of stressors (see Tables 13.3 and 13.4).

From the adolescents' perspective, the major family stressors were the day-to-day "hassles" with their parents. Specifically, adolescents point to parent-child conflicts revolving around use of the car, times to stay out or return home, choice of friends or social activities, and increasing arguments over getting jobs done. They also experience parental pressure to do well in school. These appear to be typical issues

TABLE 13.4   Adolescents' Profile of Family Stressors and Strains: Stage 4 (Families with Adolescents)

Stressor/Strain	Percentage Reporting Strain
Intrafamily Strains	
Increased arguments about getting jobs done at home.	41
Increased pressure for a member in school to get "good grades" or do well in sports or school activities.	36
Child or teenage member resists doing things with the family.	29
Parent(s) and teenager(s) have increased arguments (hassles over use of car or hours to stay out).	29
Parent(s) and teenager(s) have increased arguments (hassles) over choice of friends and/or social activities.	25
Illness and Family Care Strains	
Family member was hospitalized.	29
Grandparents became seriously ill.	24
Finance and Business Strains	
Increased family living expenses for medical care, food, clothing, energy costs (gasoline, heating).	63
Losses	
Close family relative died.	30
Transitions	
A member started junior high or high school.	53

occurring in the Adolescent stage suggesting, in part, that the strains reported by adolescents are basically normal. (For a detailed listing of the frequency of stressor events for adolescents, see Appendix E.)

Adolescents may also do things that increase the stress levels in their families. For example, the adolescents themselves reported that their alcohol, drug, or cigarette use increased problems in their family. A small percentage (12 percent) of adolescents reported involvement in sexual intercourse as another family stressor and source of strain.

Adolescents are also affected by the hardships and strains that their parents face. Parents appear to start new jobs or to change jobs more frequently at this point in their lives. Parents frequently are called on to take on more responsibility for aging parents. At some point during these years, they may also face strains from parental illnesses. Hospitalization of a family member is frequently mentioned as a stressor.

Parents and adolescents typically disagree over attendance at religious activities, personal appearance, and pressures to do well in sports or school activities. Predictably there are struggles in the family over control of the adolescent's behavior and parental anxieties over adolescent independence and the direction of his or her development.

However, there is another side to this developmental phase that incorporates many transitional concerns. Specifically, the data indicate that while the adolescents are changing, the parents are also changing. Parents are struggling with their own developmental needs and concerns as well as with financial strains. The transition of mothers into the work force is but one example of major personal transitions that occur for adults during this phase of family life.

Predicting Low- and High-Stress Families

Families at the adolescent stage call on a host of family resources to manage the high levels of stress and demands of raising and launching adolescents (see Table 13.5). Families that are low in stress tend to be Balanced rather than Extreme types.

Low-stress families tend to rely heavily on their marital strengths as identified by the instrument ENRICH used in the study. Parents reported feeling confident about themselves as a couple and were satisfied with their communication and conflict resolution skills, their partner's personality, their sexual relationship, how they manage their finances, and their relationship with their children, other friends, and family.

Good parent-adolescent communication is also a family strength characteristic of low-stress families. Rather than passively waiting for problems to improve with time, low-stress families actively reframed their problems and worked toward resolving the stress. The result is that families low in stress report feeling more satisfied with their marriage, family, and quality of life.

In general, the analysis identified salient differences between high- and low-stress families and did so with 84 percent accuracy. The specific variables that were the most "critical" in distinguishing between those high and low in stress were four marital strengths (family and friends, sexual, finances, and personality), satisfaction with the marriage relationship, and satisfaction with their quality of life (these critical items are marked with superscripts b's in Table 13.5).

TABLE 13.5   Characteristics Discriminating Families with Adolescents High and Low in Stress (ANOVA)[a]

	F	*Relationship to Low Stress*
Marital Strengths (ENRICH)		
Communication	32.5	+
Conflict resolution	34.5	+
Personality issues[b]	48.7	+
Sexual relationship[b]	19.9	+
Financial management[b]	63.0	+
Children and marriage	31.3	+
Friends and family[b]	15.9	+
Family Coping Strategies		
Reframing	16.4	+
Passive appraisal	15.6	(−)
Family Strengths		
Parent-adolescent communication	17.5	+
Satisfaction		
Marriage satisfaction[b]	60.0	+
Family satisfaction	31.1	+
Quality of life[b]	48.5	+

a. High stress = upper one-third. Low stress = lower one-third.

b. These items were the most discrimination in the two groups.

Summary

One principal finding that has emerged from this focus on the adolescent stage is the high level of stress and tension in these families. Balanced families most clearly emerge as those that are best prepared to deal with this difficult period of time; not only do they seem to have lower levels of stress and higher levels of satisfaction, but they also use more marital and family resources than they do at any other stage.

It is also clear that the high stress level and the discrepancies in how the parents and adolescent perceive the world are related. Not only are they related, but each of these factors also tends to escalate the other. This relationship, therefore, tends to exacerbate the tensions in the parent-adolescent relationship that seem to emerge at this stage.

chapter
XIV
Summary and Conclusions

THIS STUDY HAS ATTEMPTED to provide a panoramic perspective of normative family processes across the family life cycle. At times, we have captured some of the complexity of marriage and family life, and at other times we continue to be perplexed and amazed at the diversity in families. There are, however, commonalities that have emerged in these families in terms of their family types and dynamics, the stressors and strains they face, their methods of coping, and the levels of their marital and family satisfaction. This chapter will briefly review the entire study and highlight and integrate some of the findings.

This study was based on a national survey of 1140 married couples and families from 31 states. These couples and families were obtained from a stratified, randomly selected sample from seven stages of the family life cycle. To obtain this developmental perspective, data were obtained from couples who were newly married through those in their retirement years.

Because of the design and focus of the study, the sample consisted entirely of intact marriages and families. The families were predominately white, middle-income couples in their first marriages. While almost half (45 percent) of the sample lived in a community of 25,000 or more, about one-quarter (26 percent) lived on farms or in rural areas. They had an average of three children.

In spite of the homogeneity of the sample, the results from this national survey were very similar to two other large-scale studies completed at the same time this study was conducted. The results from a national Gallup poll focusing on "quality of life" and including several items identical to ours were nearly identical to the results of this study, indicating the comparability of these groups. In addition, a study of Harvard Medical School faculty found personal health behaviors similar to those of the families in this study. The similarity in findings between two other major studies and this sample of families increases our confidence in making generalizations from this research. However, caution must be exercised since future studies will need to compare these findings across a wider spectrum of families (e.g., other family structures, other socioeconomic and ethnic groups).

A limitation of past family research is that only one family member was included in the study. In an attempt to overcome this problem and, it was hoped, to capture more of the richness of the marriage and family systems, both husbands and wives were asked to describe their marriages and family lives. At the Adolescent and Launching stages, one adolescent was also asked to participate. All the data were collected in a group setting, with family members separated from each other while they independently completed the questionnaires.

The use of a variety of couple and family scores provided a more comprehensive and multifaceted perspective on these families, helping to combine marital and family system aspects into a single score that could be evaluated empirically. This task was made more necessary and challenging by the lack of agreement among family members. In fact, there was often a higher relationship among research scales than among family members on the same scale.

The research instruments used had high levels of reliability (alpha and test/retest) and validity. All of the major analyses were done at the individual, couple, and family levels. Most of the analyses were also replicated at least once, and multivariate techniques (factor analysis, multiple regression, and discriminant function analysis) were generally used.

In spite of the conceptual and methodological strengths of this study, it also had some limitations. Its focus was "normal" families who were willing and able to participate. While some of these families may have had high levels of stress and related symptoms, the range of the scores on some variables (e.g., cohesion, adaptability, communication, stress, coping) may have been restricted in this sample. More specifically, these families may be lower on family stress, less extreme on family cohesion (i.e., enmeshed), and less extreme on family adaptability (i.e., chaotic) than other families not sampled.

Family Systems Across the Life Cycle

Major differences were found across the stages of the family life cycle and among the various members in the family. Stage differences were consistently found for many of the family characteristics and can be accounted for in at least two ways. First, these differences reflect the unique developmental tasks and different family structures at each stage of the family life cycle. Second, the cohort differences between, for example, younger and older couples may be a result of historical contexts in which they live, of the cultural environment and life experiences they have had, and of the norms and values of their culture.

The significant differences among individual family members' descriptions of family dynamics are striking when you consider that these people live in the same household. Even more surprising is the fact that the relationships (correlations) among the major family variables are higher than the relationship between husbands and wives on the same variable. While there is little agreement between husbands and wives, there is even less agreement between adolescents and their parents in how they describe their own family. This leads to the conclusion that one should *assume disagreement* and a lack of congruence among family members rather than assume that one is dealing with an integrated and highly congruent group of individuals.

These data clearly demonstrate the importance of taking stage differences and individual differences into account when planning any type of research study, program, or service with families. Family researchers and program planners should, therefore, integrate individual and stage differences into their projects. Because of the potency of the stage breakdown used in this study, program planners might want to use the four stages for their work. The four stages are: Couples Without Children, Families with Children, Families with Adolescents, and Older Couples.

Stages and sex differences will now be briefly summarized for the five major family dimensions used in this study: *family types, family resources, family stress, family coping,* and *family satisfaction.* Separate chapters explored each of these variables in greater depth.

In regard to family types based on the Circumplex Model, few differences were observed across stages or between family members in the percentages of Balanced, Mid-Range, and Extreme types. However, when the dimensions of cohesion and adaptability were considered, significant differences across the stages and among family members on these two dimensions appeared. Generally, wives viewed their families as more cohesive and adaptable than their husbands did. Adolescents reported substantially lower levels of both family cohesion and adaptability than their parents. The general trend between stages indicated that levels of adaptability and cohesion dropped through the first four or five stages to a low point at the Adolescent and Launching stages and then recovered somewhat in the later two stages. These findings clearly indicate differing perceptions among family members and differences between stages.

Many family strengths showed significant differences across the family life cycle. Wives consistently perceived higher levels of family pride and were more satisfied with their leisure activities, friends, and relatives and were generally more religious. Husbands tended to feel more positive about their marital communication than wives did.

Family stressors and strains varied considerably at different stages of the life cycle. Parents and adolescents also reported different stressors at the Adolescent stage. While major social and family stressors (death of a family member, unemployment) were important, it was often the day-to-day hassles that appear to be of importance as these events have a cumulative impact. This supports the value of assessing the pile-up of stressors.

To cope with family stress, individuals in these families tended to rely primarily on internal resources rather than external supports offered by community agencies. The internal resource that was used most frequently was reframing difficulties in order to make them more manageable. More passive approaches were seldom used. Only if family members could not cope using their internal resorces would they turn to the more formalized community services for help. In general, they participated in few educational programs but enjoyed those that they experienced. They also expressed some interest in programs that were related to the development stages and stress they were encountering.

Family members' personal health behaviors were examined and compared, with particular focus on seven personal health behaviors considered in past national surveys. The results clearly indicated that family members in this study had reasonably good health behaviors. Comparing these results with a recent study of Harvard Medical School faculty revealed that the two groups were very comparable and both had generally good health practices.

Marital and family satisfaction was higher at early and later stages of the family life cycle when couples were living without children. Satisfaction was lowest at the Adolescent stage, when family stress was the highest. There was strong relationship between marital satisfaction, family satisfaction, and overall quality of life. Satisfaction increased with higher levels of cohesion and adaptability. As mentioned earlier, there was a strong association between these satisfaction measures and marital and family strengths. When family satisfaction was high, stress had minimal impact on the family. In other words, these families seem to have considerable resistance to stressful life events.

Circumplex Model, Family Strengths and Family Stress

The overall results from this study provide considerable support for hypotheses derived from the Circumplex Model. While there was support for the general hypothesis that Balanced family types seem to function more adequately across the family life cycle, the importance of stage differences emerged as critical.

As hypothesized by the Circumplex Model, different types seem to function better at the various stages of the family life cycle. Those that were considered to be functioning better had higher levels of marital and family strengths, lower levels of family stress, higher levels of family coping, and higher levels of marital and family satisfaction. The seven stages of the family life cycle used throughout the book were reduced to four in order to determine which family types functioned better.

The findings clearly indicate that different family types seem to function better at different various stages and that the number and types of marital and family strengths on which families rely also varied. Young Couples Without Children seemed to function best in the upper-right-hand quadrant of the Circumplex Model, and Families with Children seemed to function best in the upper-right- and lower-left-hand quadrants. Families with Adolescents clearly functioned best in the Balanced (central) area, and Older Couples did best in the lower-right quadrant.

In order to test the potency of the relationship between family types and the other variables, a series of predictive analyses were performed. The analysis used the multitude of family variables to predict Balanced and Extreme family types. The accuracy of predicting Balanced and Extreme types ranged from 80 to 100 percent. Accuracy was highest when the predictions were made separately by stage of the family life cycle rather than by using all stages combined. This finding demonstrates again the important differences between stages. Accuracy also increased when subscales rather than total scores were used. While these high levels of predictability do not imply a causal relationship between family types and other family variables, they do indicate that these variables are significantly related.

There was also considerable support for the Double ABC-X Model of Family Stress, which hypothesizes a relationship between family resources, family stress, and family coping. To investigate some of these ideas, an analysis was done to determine the characteristics that discriminated beween those families experiencing high levels of stress and those experiencing low levels of stress. The results indicated important differences in family resources for the two groups and demonstrated that specific resources used varied by stage of the family life cycle. When these family resources were used to predict high- and low-stress families, the level of predictability was high and accuracy ranged from 75 to 97 percent.

One important discovery from this study is that marital and family strengths are very significant, positive characteristics of families. Marital strengths included the eleven variables assessed in ENRICH: communication, conflict resolution, role relationship, sexual relationship, among others. Family strengths included family pride and accord and good parent-adolescent communication.

Couples and families possessing these strengths seemed to function more adequately across the life cycle. They also tended to be more satisfied with their marriages and family lives. These strengths seem to operate as major buffers or resistors to stressful life events. It could also be that having these strengths helped these families deal more effectively with the stress and changes that occur across the life cycle. In other words, high levels of marital and family strengths might serve a significant preventive function for families.

These findings regarding marital and family strengths have important implications for programs and services to families. First, it is important to note that certain specific marital and family strengths were important at the various stages. This suggests that separate programs could be developed around specific topics for various stages of the life cycle. The fact that these marital and family strengths seem to make couples and families less vulnerable to stress indicates the potential *preventive* role they might play in families. It also reinforces the value of developing and supporting programs that can help couples and families build these relationship strengths.

Because of the importance of the Adolescent stage, considerable attention was focused on these families. Families with Adolescents included those with at least one living in the home (Stage 4) and those launching adolescents from the home (Stage 5). Data were collected from both parents and from the adolescent, and a variety of family scores were created to describe these families.

As expected, there were considerable differences in the descriptions of the family as seen by the parents and the adolescent. Parents perceived more cohesion and adaptability, less stress, and better communication than their adolescents did. Another expected finding was the high levels of stress reported by both the parents and the adolescent.

While they all agreed that the levels of tension were high, they disagreed somewhat on the specific issues. Parents were more concerned with finances, and adolescents were more troubled by the day-to-day problems over responsibilities. The discrepancies in how the family members described their families also had a strong relationship to their levels of stress. Families with higher discrepancies had higher levels of family stress. These two factors seemed to escalate each other, thus increasing the tensions in the parent-adolescent relationship.

Balanced family types were clearly the ones that functioned most effectively at this stage. These families had lower levels of stress, higher levels of marital and family strengths, and higher levels of marital and family satisfaction than extreme family types did. This provides strong support for the main hypothesis derived from the Circumplex Model.

In conclusion, this study has made a major step toward providing a normative picture of family process over the life cycle. It demonstrated both the complexity of family systems and some of the predictable patterns. The importance of considering the stage of the family life cycle was consistently demonstrated. The potency of marital and family strengths was also important in helping families deal with the stress and changes that occur in their lives.

Theoretically and methodologically, we have also learned a great deal. Both the Circumplex Model (family types) and the Double ABC-X Model (family stress) received considerable support from this study. The usefulness of couple and family scores was also demonstrated, and advances in statistical programs helped move the analysis from the descriptive to the predictive level.

This study began with the goal that we would begin more clearly to comprehend the commonalities and complexities of "normal" families across the life cycle. While this first step is now completed, we are now aware of numerous questions that are even more intriguing and challenging. We now concur with Winston Churchill, who so poignantly stated: "This is not the end. It is not even the beginning of the end. Let us hope it is the end of the beginning."

APPENDIX A: BACKGROUND CHARACTERISTICS OF FAMILIES (ENRICH)

TABLE A.1   Marital Status

	Absolute Frequency	Relative Frequency
Married, first marriage	1018	90.6
Married, formerly divorced	46	4.1
Married, formerly widowed	10	.9
No Response	50	4.4
Total	1124	100.0

TABLE A.2   Years Married

Years	Absolute Frequency	Relative Frequency
0-5	156	13.9
6-10	147	13.1
11-15	127	11.3
16-20	191	17.0
21-25	139	12.3
26-30	74	6.6
31-35	89	7.9
36-40	69	6.1
41-45	63	5.6
46-50	33	3.0
51-55	8	.7
56-60	2	.2
61	1	.1
No Response	25	2.2
Total	1124	100.0

242   FAMILIES

TABLE A.3   Employment

| | Males | | Females | |
	Frequency	Percentage	Frequency	Percentage
Full-time job only	787	70.0	363	32.3
Full-time and part-time job	134	11.9	74	6.6
Part-time job only	45	4.0	268	23.9
None	86	7.7	350	31.1
No Response	72	6.4	69	6.1
Totals	1124	100.0	1124	100.0

TABLE A.4   Current Residence

| | Males | | Females | |
	Frequency	Percentage	Frequency	Percentage
Large city, over 100,000	266	23.7	238	21.2
Small city, 25-100,000	234	20.8	259	23.0
Town, 2500-25,000	227	20.2	233	20.7
Town, 2500 or less	71	6.3	88	7.8
Rural but not farm	152	13.5	146	13.0
Farm	139	12.4	135	12.0
No Response	35	3.1	25	2.3
Totals	1124	100.0	1124	100.0

TABLE A.5   Adolescent Information

	Frequency	Percentage
Sex of Adolescent		
Male	207	50.0
Female	207	50.0
Total	414	100.0
Birth Order (Position)		
1	247	60.1
2	53	12.9
3	52	12.7
4	37	9.0
5	14	3.4
6	3	.7
7	1	.2
8	1	.2
9	1	.2
Total	425	100.0
How Much Do You Like School?		
Very much like	74	18.0
Generally like	273	66.6
Somewhat dislike	50	12.2
Dislike	13	3.2
What Grade Do You Mostly Receive?		
As	139	33.6
Bs	184	44.4
Cs	89	21.5
Ds	2	.5
Total	414	100.0

APPENDIX B: RESEARCH SCALES AND RELIABILITY

FACES II: Family Adaptability and Cohesion Scales

Family Satisfaction

Parent-Adolescent Communication

ENRICH: Enriching and Nurturing Relationship Issues, Communication and Happiness

FILE: Family Inventory of Life Events and Changes

A-FILE: Adolescent-Family Inventory of Life Events and Changes

F-COPES: Family Coping Strategies

Family Strengths

Quality of Life.

Authors' Note: All these scales are copyrighted, and permission must be obtained from the copyright holders for their use. More detailed descriptions of the scales; their development, reliability, and validity; and scoring procedures and norms are presented in *Family Inventories,* which can be purchased by writing David H. Olson, Family Social Science, 290 McNeal Hall, University of Minnesota, St. Paul, MN 55108.

245

TABLE B.1   Research Methods and Reliabilities

Method	Alpha Reliability	Test/Retest Reliability
Faces II	.90	.90
Family adaptability	.78	.80
Family cohesion	.87	.83
Parent-Adolescent Communication	.88	.60
Open communication	.87	.78
Problems in communication	.78	.77
ENRICH Inventory		
Conventionality	.92	.92
Marital communication	.68	.90
Conflict resolution	.75	.90
Personality issues	.73	.81
Leisure activities	.76	.77
Sexual relationship	.48	.92
Children and marriage	.77	.89
Family and friends	.72	.82
Egalitarian roles	.71	.90
Financial management	.74	.88
Marital satisfaction	.81	.86
Family Satisfaction	.92	.75
Quality of Life	.92	.65
FILE (Stress)	.81	.80
Strains	.72	.73
Marital	.16	.68
Pregnancy	.24	.84
Finances	.60	.64
Work	.55	.80
Illness	.56	.66
Losses	.34	.71
Transitions	.52	.72
Legal	.66	.83
A-FILE (Stress)	.82	.84
Transitions	.52	.80
Sexuality	.43	.90
Losses	.45	.82
Responsibilities	.74	.69
Substance abuse	.66	.81
Legal conflict	.45	.82
F-COPES (Coping)	.86	.81
Spiritual support	.81	.95
Social support	.84	.78
Reframing	.82	.61
Mobilizing family	.71	.78
Passive appraisal	.64	.75
Personal Health Practices	.41	.67

FACES II

David H. Olson, Joyce Portner, & Richard Bell

(1) Family members are supportive of each other during difficult times.

(2) In our family, it is easy for everyone to express his/her opinion.

(3) It is easier to discuss problems with people outside the family than with other family members.

(4) Each family member has input in major family decisions.

(5) Our family gathers together in the same room.

(6) Children have a say in their discipline.

(7) Our family does things together.

(8) Family members discuss problems and feel good about the solutions.

(9) In our family everyone goes his/her own way.

(10) We shift household responsibilities from person to person.

(11) Family members know each other's close friends.

(12) It is hard to know what the rules are in our family.

(13) Family members consult other family members on their decisions.

(14) Family members say what they want.

(15) We have difficulty thinking of things to do as a family.

(16) In solving problems, the children's suggestions are followed.

(17) Family members feel very close to each other.

(18) Discipline is fair in our family.

(19) Family members feel closer to people outside the family than to other family members.

(20) Our family tries new ways of dealing with problems.

(21) Family members go along with what the family decides to do.

(22) In our family, everyone shares responsibilities.

(23) Family members like to spend their free time with each other.

(24) It is difficult to get a rule changed in our family.

(25) Family members avoid each other at home.

(26) When problems arise, we compromise.

(27) We approve of each other's friends.

(28) Family members are afraid to say what is on their minds.

(29) Family members pair up rather than do things as a total family.

(30) Family members share interests and hobbies with each other.

Family Satisfaction

David H. Olson & Marc Wilson

How satisfied are you . . .

(1) with how close you feel to the rest of your family?

(2) with your ability to say what you want in your family?

(3) with your family's ability to try new things?

(4) with how often parents make decisions in your family?

(5) with how much mother and father argue with each other?

(6) with how fair the criticism is in your family?

(7) with the amount of time you spend with your family?

(8) with the way you talk together to solve family problems?

(9) with your freedom to be alone when you want to?

(10) with how strictly you stay with who does what chores in your family?

(11) with your family's acceptance of your friends?

(12) with how clear it is what your family expects of you?

(13) with how often you make decisions as a family rather than individually?

(14) with the number of fun things your family does together?

Parent-Adolescent Communication: Adolescent Form

Howard L. Barnes & David H. Olson

Mother	Father	
(1) ____	(21) ____	I can discuss my beliefs with my mother/father without feeling restrained or embarrassed.
(2) ____	(22) ____	Sometimes I have trouble believing everything my mother/father tells me.
(3) ____	(23) ____	My mother/father is always a good listener.
(4) ____	(24) ____	I am sometimes afraid to ask my mother/father for what I want.
(5) ____	(25) ____	My mother/father has a tendency to say things to me that would be better left unsaid.
(6) ____	(26) ____	My mother/father can tell how I'm feeling without asking.
(7) ____	(27) ____	I am very satisfied with how my mother/father and I talk together.
(8) ____	(28) ____	If I were in trouble, I could tell my mother/father.
(9) ____	(29) ____	I openly show affection to my mother/father.
(10) ____	(30) ____	When we are having a problem, I often give my mother/father the silent treatment.
(11) ____	(31) ____	I am careful about what I say to my mother/father.
(12) ____	(32) ____	When talking to my mother/father, I have a tendency to say things that would be better left unsaid.
(13) ____	(33) ____	When I ask questions, I get honest answers from my mother/father.
(14) ____	(34) ____	My mother/father tries to understand my point of view.

(15) ___	(35) ___	There are topics I avoid discussing with my mother/father.
(16) ___	(36) ___	I find it easy to discuss problems with my mother/father.
(17) ___	(37) ___	It is very easy for me to express all my true feelings to my mother/father.
(18) ___	(38) ___	My mother/father nags/bothers me.
(19) ___	(39) ___	My mother/father insults me when s/he is angry with me.
(20) ___	(40) ___	I don't think I can tell my mother/father how I really feel about some things.

ENRICH: Enriching and Nurturing Relationship Issues, Communication and Happiness

David H. Olson, David G. Fournier, & Joan M. Druckman

I. IDEALISTIC DISTORTION

(1) My partner and I understand each other completely.

(2) My partner completely understands and sympathizes with my every mood.

(3) My relationship is not a perfect success.

(4) I have some needs that are not being met by my relationship.

(5) I have never regretted my relationship with my partner, not even for a moment.

II. MARITAL SATISFACTION

(1) I am not pleased with the personality characteristics and personal habits of my partner.

(2) I am very happy with how we handle role responsibilities in our marriage.

(3) I am not happy about our communication and feel my partner does not understand me.

(4) I am very happy about how we make decisions and resolve conflicts.

(5) I am unhappy about our financial position and the way we make financial decisions.

(6) I am very happy with how we manage our leisure activities and the time we spend together.

(7) I am very pleased about how we express affection and relate sexually.

(8) I am not satisfied with the way we each handle our responsibilities as parents.

(9) I am dissatisfied about our relationship with my parents, in-laws, and/or friends.

(10) I feel very good about how we each practice our religious beliefs and values.

III. PERSONALITY ISSUES

(1) My partner is too critical or often has a negative outlook.

(2) Sometimes I am concerned about my partner's temper.

(3) At times, I am concerned that my partner appears to be unhappy or withdrawn.

(4) My partner's smoking and/or drinking habits are a problem.

(5) At times, my partner is not dependable or does not always follow through on things.

(6) When we are with others, I am sometimes upset with my partner's behavior.

(7) Sometimes my partner is too stubborn.

(8) It bothers me that my partner is often late.

(9) Sometimes I have difficulty dealing with my partner's moodiness.

(10) At times, I think my partner is too domineering.

IV. COMMUNICATION

(1) It is very easy for me to express all my true feelings to my partner.

(2) When we are having a problem, my partner often gives me the silent treatment.

(3) My partner sometimes makes comments that put me down.

(4) I am sometimes afraid to ask my partner for what I want.

(5) I wish my partner was more willing to share his/her feelings with me.

(6) Sometimes I have trouble believing everything my partner tells me.

(7) I often do not tell my partner what I am feeling because he/she should already know.

(8) I am very satisfied with how my partner and I talk with each other.

(9) I do not always share negative feelings I have about my partner because I am afraid he/she will get angry.

(10) My partner is always a good listener.

V. CONFLICT RESOLUTION

(1) In order to end an argument, I usually give up too quickly.

(2) My partner and I have very different ideas about the best way to solve our disagreements.

(3) When discussing problems, I usually feel my partner understands me.

(4) When we are having a problem, I can always tell my partner what is bothering me.

(5) Sometimes we have serious disputes over unimportant issues.

(6) I would do anything to avoid conflict with my partner.

(7) I sometimes feel our arguments go on and on and never seem to get resolved.

(8) When we have a disagreement, we openly share our feelings and decide how to resolve our differences.

(9) I usually feel that my partner does not take our disagreements seriously.

(10) When we argue, I usually end up feeling the problem was all my fault.

VI. FINANCIAL MANAGEMENT

(1) Sometimes I wish my partner was more careful in spending money.

(2) We always agree on how to spend our money.

(3) We have difficulty deciding on how to handle our finances.

(4) I am satisfied with our decisions about how much we should save.

(5) We are both aware of our major debts, and they are not a problem for us.

(6) We keep records of our spending so we can budget our money.

(7) Use of credit cards and charge accounts has been a problem for us.

(8) Deciding what is most important to spend our money on is a concern for us.

(9) It bothers me that I cannot spend money without my partner's approval.

(10) I am concerned about who is responsible for the money.

VII. LEISURE ACTIVITIES

(1) My partner and I seem to enjoy the same type of parties and social activities.

(2) My partner does not seem to have enough time or energy for recreation with me.

(3) I'd rather do almost anything than spend an evening by myself.

(4) I am concerned that my partner does not have enough interests or hobbies.

(5) I seldom feel pressured to attend social functions with my partner.

(6) I always feel good about where and how we spend our holidays with our families.

(7) I feel good about the kinds of trips and vacations we take.

(8) I am concerned that my partner and I do not spend enough of our leisure time together.

(9) I seldom have fun unless I am with my partner.

(10) My partner and I have a good balance of leisure time together and separately.

VIII. SEXUAL RELATIONSHIP

(1) I am completely satisfied with the amount of affection my partner gives me.

(2) We try to find ways to keep our sexual relationship interesting and enjoyable.

(3) I am concerned that my partner may not be interested in me sexually.

(4) It is easy and comfortable for me to talk with my partner about sexual issues.

(5) I sometimes worry that my partner may have thought about having a sexual relationship outside of our marriage (affair).

(6) Our sexual relationship is satisfying and fulfilling to me.

(7) I am reluctant to be affectionate with my partner because it is often misinterpreted as a sexual advance.

(8) Sometimes I am concerned that my partner's interest in sex is not the same as mine.

(9) I am satisfied with our decisions regarding family planning or birth control.

(10) It bothers me that my partner uses or refuses sex in an unfair way.

IX. CHILDREN AND MARRIAGE

(1) In our family, the father does not spend enough time with our children.

(2) I am satisfied with how we share the responsibilities of raising our children.

(3) We agree on how to discipline our children.

(4) Children seem to be a major source of problems in our relationship.

(5) We agree on the number of children we would like to have.

(6) It bothers me that my partner seems to place more importance on the children than on our marriage.

(7) Having children has brought us closer together as a couple.

(8) My partner and I have different views on the religious education of our children.

(9) Since having our children, we seldom have time together as a couple.

(10) Conflicts about how much we should do for our children is a problem for us.

X. FAMILY AND FRIENDS

(1) Some friends or relatives do things that create tension in our marriage.

(2) We spend the right amount of time with our relatives and friends.

(3) I think my partner is too involved with or influenced by his/her family.

(4) I do not enjoy spending time with some of our relatives or in-laws.

(5) My partner likes all of my friends.

(6) Sometimes my partner spends too much time with friends.

(7) I feel that our parents expect too much attention or assistance from us.

  (8) I feel that our parents create problems in our marriage.

  (9) I really enjoy being with all my partner's friends.

(10) It does not bother me when my partner spends time with friends of the opposite sex.

XI. EGALITARIAN ROLES

  (1) I believe that the woman's place is basically in the home.

  (2) If both of us are working, the husband should do the same amount of household chores as the wife.

  (3) In our family, the wife should not work outside the home unless it is an absolute financial necessity.

  (4) In our marriage, the wife should be more willing to go along with the husband's wishes.

  (5) Even if the wife works outside the home, she should still be responsible for running the household.

  (6) In our marriage, the husband is the leader of our family.

  (7) For us, the husband's occupation is always regarded as more important than the wife's.

  (8) If there are (were) young children, the wife should not work outside the home.

  (9) The husband should have the final word in most of the important decisions in our family.

(10) The wife should trust and accept the husband's judgments on important decisions.

XII. RELIGIOUS ORIENTATATION

  (1) It is hard for me to have complete faith in some of the accepted teachings of my religion.

  (2) I believe that religion should have the same meaning for both of us.

  (3) Sharing religious values helps our relationship grow.

  (4) My religious beliefs are an important part of the commitment I have to my partner.

  (5) My partner and I disagree on how to practice our religious beliefs.

  (6) It is important for me to pray with my partner.

  (7) I believe that our marriage includes active religious involvement.

(8) In loving my partner, I feel that I am able to better understand the concept that God is love.

(9) My partner and I disagree about some of the teachings of my religion.

(10) My partner and I feel closer because of our religious beliefs.

FILE

Hamilton I. McCubbin, Joan M. Patterson, & Lance R. Wilson

I. INTRAFAMILY STRAINS

(1) Increase of husband/father's time away from family.

(2) Increase of wife/mother's time away from family.

(3) A member appears to have emotional problems.

(4) A member appears to depend on alcohol or drugs.

(5) Increase in conflict between husband and wife.

(6) Increase in arguments between parent(s) and child(ren).

(7) Increase in conflict among children in the family

(8) Increased difficulty in managing teenage child(ren).

(9) Increased difficulty in managing school-age child(ren) (6-12 yrs.).

(10) Increased difficulty in managing preschool-age child(ren) (2½-6 yrs.).

(11) Increased difficulty in managing toddler(s) (1-2½ yrs.).

(12) Increased difficulty in managing infant(s) (0-1 yrs.).

(13) Increase in the amount of "outside activities" in which the child(ren) are involved.

(14) Increased disagreement about a member's friends or activities.

(15) Increase in the number of problems or issues that do not get resolved.

(16) Increase in the number of tasks or chores that do not get done.

(17) Increased conflict with in-laws or relatives.

II. MARITAL STATUS

(18) Spouse/parent was separated or divorced.

(19) Spouse/parent has an "affair."

(20) Increased difficulty in resolving issues with a "former" or separated spouse.

(21) Increased difficulty with sexual relationship between husband and wife.

III. PREGNANCY AND CHILDBEARING STRAINS

(22) Family member experiencing menopause.

(23) Spouse had unwanted or difficult pregnancy.

(24) An unmarried member became pregnant.

(25) A member had an abortion.

(26) A member gave birth to or adopted a child.

IV. FINANCE AND BUSINESS STRAINS

(27) Took out a loan or refinanced a loan to cover increased expenses.

(28) Went on welfare.

(29) Change in conditions (economic, political, weather) that hurts family investments and/or income.

(30) Change in agriculture market, stock market, or land values that hurts family investments and/or income.

(31) A member started a new business.

(32) Purchased or built a home.

(33) A member purchased a car or other major item.

(34) Increasing financial debts due to overuse of credit cards.

(35) Increased strain on family "money" for medical/dental expenses.

A-FILE

Hamilton I. McCubbin, Joan M. Patterson,
Edward Bauman, & Linda H. Harris

I. FAMILY TRANSITIONS

(1) Family member started new business (farm, store, etc.).

(2) Parent quit or lost a job.

(3) Parents separated or divorced.

(4) Parent remarried.

(5) Family member was found to have a learning disorder.

(6) Family member was married.

(7) Parents adopted a child.

(8) A member started junior high or high school.

(9) Child or teenager transferred to a new school.

(10) Parent started school.

(11) Brother or sister moved away from home.

(12) Young adult member entered college, vocational training, or armed forces.

(13) Parent(s) started or changed to a new job.

(14) Family moved to a new home.

II. FAMILY SEXUALITY

(15) Unmarried family member became pregnant.

(16) Family member had an abortion.

(17) Birth of a brother or sister.

(18) Teenager began having sexual intercourse.

III. FAMILY LOSSES

(19) Family went on welfare.

(20) Damage to or loss of family property due to fire, burglary, or other disaster.

(21) Brother or sister died.

(22) Parent died.

(23) Close family relative died.

(24) Death of a close friend or family member.

(25) Family member or close family friend attempted or committed suicide.

IV. FAMILY RESPONSIBILITIES AND STRAINS

(26) Family member became seriously ill or injured (*not* hospitalized).

(27) Family member was hospitalized.

(28) Family member became physically disabled or was found to have a long-term health problem (allergies, asthma, diabetes, etc.).

(29) Family member has emotional problems.

(30) Grandparent(s) became seriously ill.

(31) Parent(s) have more responsibility to take care of grandparent(s).

(32) Family member ran away.

(33) More financial debts due to credit cards or charges.

(34) Increased family living expenses for medical care, food, clothing, energy costs (gasoline, heating).

(35) Increase of parent's time away from family.

(36) Child or teenager resists doing things with family.

(37) Increase in arguments between parents.

(38) Children or teenagers have more arguments with one another.

(39) Parent(s) and teenager(s) have increased arguments (hassles) over: use of car or hours to stay out.

(40) Parent(s) and teenager(s) have increased arguments (hassles) over: choice of friends and/or social activities.

(41) Parent(s) and teenager(s) have increased arguments (hassles) over: attendance at religious activities.

(42) Parents(s) and teenager(s) have increased arguments (hassles) over: personal appearance (clothes, hair, etc.).

(43) Increased arguments about getting the jobs done at home.

(44) Increased pressure for a member in school to get "good" grades or do well in sports or school activities.

V. SCHOOL STRAINS AND SUBSTANCE ABUSE

    (45) Family member uses drugs (not given by doctor).

    (46) Family member drinks too much alcohol.

    (47) Child or teenage member was suspended from or dropped out of school.

    (48) Parent(s) and teenager(s) have increased arguments (hassles) over: use of cigarettes, alcohol, or drugs.

VI. FAMILY LEGAL CONFLICTS

    (49) Family member went to jail, juvenile detention, or was placed on court probation.

    (50) Family member was robbed or attacked (physically or sexually).

F-COPES

Hamilton I. McCubbin, Andrea S. Larsen, & David H. Olson

When we face problems or difficulties in our family, we respond by . . .

    (1) sharing our difficulties with relatives.

    (2) seeking encouragement and support from friends.

    (3) knowing we have the power to solve major problems.

    (4) seeking information and advice from persons in other families who have faced the same or similar problems.

    (5) seeking advice from relatives (grandparents, etc.).

    (6) asking neighbors for favors and assistance.

    (7) seeking assistance from community agencies and programs designed to help families in our situation.

    (8) accepting that we have the strength within our own famiy to solve our problems.

    (9) accepting gifts and favors from neighbors (food, taking in mail, etc.).

    (10) seeking information and advice from the family doctor.

    (11) facing problems "head-on" and trying to get solutions right away.

(12) watching television.

(13) showing that we are strong.

(14) attending church services.

(15) accepting stressful events as a fact of life.

(16) sharing concerns with close friends.

(17) knowing luck plays a big part in how well we are able to solve family problems.

(18) accepting that difficulties occur unexpectedly.

(19) doing things with relatives (get-togethers, dinners, etc.).

(20) seeking professional counseling and help for family difficulties.

(21) believing we can handle our own problems.

(22) participating in church activities.

(23) defining the family problem in a more positive way so that we do not become too discouraged.

(24) asking relatives how they feel about problems we face.

(25) feeling that no matter what we do to prepare, we will have difficulty handling problems.

(26) seeking advice from a minister.

(27) believing if we wait long enough, the problem will go away.

(28) sharing problems with neighbors.

(29) having faith in God.

Family Strengths

David H. Olson, Andrea S. Larsen, & Hamilton I. McCubbin

Please rate the following items as they apply to your family:

(1) We can express our feelings.

(2) We tend to worry about many things.

(3) We really do trust and confide in each other.

(4) We have the same problems over and over.

(5) Family members feel loyal to the family.

(6) Accomplishing what we want to do seems difficult for us.

(7) We are critical of each other.

(8) We share similar values and beliefs as a family.

(9) Things work out well for us as a family.

(10) Family members respect one another.

(11) There are many conflicts in our family.

(12) We are proud of our family.

Quality of Life
(Parent Form)

David H. Olson & Howard L. Barnes

How satisfied are you with . . .

Marriage and family life

(1) your family.

(2) your marriage.

(3) your children.

(4) number of children in your family.

Friends

(5) your friends.

(6) your relationship with relatives (aunts, uncles, grandparents, etc.).

Health

(7) your own health.

(8) health of other family members.

Home

(9) your current housing arrangement.

(10) your household responsibilities.

(11) other family members' household responsibilities.

(12) space for your own needs.

(13) space for your family needs.

Education

    (14) the amount of education you have.

    (15) the educational programs designed to improve marriage and family life.

Time

    (16) amount of free time.

    (17) time for self.

    (18) time for family.

    (19) time for housework.

    (20) time for earning money.

Religion

    (21) the religious life of your family.

    (22) the religious life in your community.

Employment

    (23) your principal occupation (job).

    (24) your job security.

Mass media

    (25) the amount of time family members watch TV.

    (26) the quality of TV programs.

    (27) the quality of movies.

    (28) the quality of newspapers and magazines.

Financial well-being

    (29) your level of income.

    (30) money for family necessities.

    (31) your ability to handle financial emergencies.

    (32) amount of money you owe (mortgage, loans, credit cards).

    (33) level of saving.

    (34) money for future needs of family.

Neighborhood and community

    (35) the schools in your community

    (36) the shopping in your community.

(37) the safety in your community.

(38) the neighborhood you live in.

(39) the recreational facilities (parks, play grounds, programs, etc.).

(40) the health care services.

© 1982 by David Olson, Family Social Science, University of Minnesota. Reprinted by permission.

Quality of Life
(Adolescent Form)

David H. Olson & Howard L. Barnes

How satisfied are you with . . .

Your family life

(1) your family.

(2) your brothers and sisters.

(3) number of children in your family.

Friends

(4) your friends.

Extended family

(5) your relationship with relatives (aunts, uncles, grandparents, etc.).

Health

(6) your own health.

(7) health of other family members.

Home

(8) your current housing arrangements (the place you live).

(9) your responsibilities around the house.

Education

(10) your current school situation.

Leisure

(11) amount of free time you have.

(12) the way you use your free time.

Religion

    (13) the religious life of your family.

    (14) the religious life in your community.

Mass media

    (15) the amount of time family members watch TV.

    (16) the quality of TV programs.

    (17) the quality of movies.

    (18) the quality of newspapers and magazines.

Financial well-being

    (19) your family's ability to buy necessities.

    (20) your family's ability to buy luxuries.

    (21) the amount of money you have to spend.

Neighborhood and community

    (22) the availability of shopping in your community.

    (23) the safety in your community.

    (24) the neighborhood you live in.

    (25) the recreational facilities (parks, playgrounds, programs, etc.).

APPENDIX C: CORRELATIONS OF RESEARCH SCALES

TABLE C.1 Overall Correlations Between Major Variables[a]

	Coh	Adapt	Strn	Conv	Pers	Comm	ConR	Mgt	Leis	Sex	Chil	Frnds	Relig	PACom	Stress	FSat	MSat
FACES II																	
Cohesion																	
Adaptability	.66																
Family Strengths	.55	.54															
ENRICH																	
Conventionality	.39	.36	.50														
Personality	.36	.36	.51	.58													
Communication	.44	.46	.56	.66	.67												
Conflict resolution	.45	.46	.57	.62	.62	.78											
Financial management	.31	.31	.43	.43	.45	.47	.44										
Leisure	.32	.31	.39	.39	.39	.39	.41	.35									
Sexuality	.38	.36	.47	.61	.52	.62	.62	.40	.36								
Children	.39	.36	.46	.45	.47	.44	.45	.37	.38	.45							
Family and friends	.38	.36	.47	.43	.57	.51	.51	.43	.47	.45	.50						
Egalitarian roles																	
Religious orientation			.33	.33	.38	.38	.31	.33	.32	.34	.43	.43	.43				
Congregational Activities													.51				
Parent-Adolescent Communication	.50	.48	.54	.28	.38	.46	.60	.39	.33	.33	.48	.41	.41				
Family Stress (FILE)			-.34	-.35	-.32			-.31									
Family Coping (F-COPES)														.33			
Family Satisfaction	.61	.56	.62	.58	.63	.46	.60	.41	.42	.49	.45	.46	.49				
Marital Satisfaction (Enrich)	.50	.49	.73	.73	.63	.70	.70	.56	.50	.68	.57	.59	.44	.39	-.37	.64	
Quality of Life	.36	.36	.48	.49	.38	.41	.41	.40	.32	.37	.39	.40	.40	.40	-.40	.68	.51

Please Note: Certain variables were left off the horizontal axis of this table because they did not significantly correlate with other variables greater than .30 (p < .001). These include congregational activities, egalitarian roles, coping, and health practices

a. Only correlations above .30 are listed here.

APPENDIX D: DATA COLLECTION PROCEDURES

One basic goal in data collection was to obtain at least 1000 couples and families from across the family life cycle. To acquire a stratified random sample of couples and families, initial lists were compiled by the research department of a large fraternal organization with a well-developed system of branch offices serving families around the country. From the initial list, people were grouped together in families according to name, address, and age. Families were tentatively placed at specific life-cycle stages on the basis of husband/wife ages and/or the age of the oldest child.

After being grouped by the stage, the final group of participants was randomly selected from each category. Also, for each stage, back-up families were provided in case the families initially identified did not choose to participate. Some stages of the life cycle were intentionally oversampled in proportion to other stages in order to assure sufficient representation in the final data pool.

Data were collected in two phases around the United States. Phase I data collection began in June 1981 and ended in November 1981. Phase II began in November 1981, and all of the data were collected by February 1982.

The procedure used for collecting the data was to have families come to a group meeting, at which time they were given the questionnaire survey. This design was used to maximize the independence and honesty in the responses from family members. In order to accomplish this, family members were physically separated when completing the questionnaires. Another reason for the group meeting was to provide an orientation to the importance and value of this study. Lastly, group meetings were used to encourage both the husband and wife to attend, and adolescents were required to attend when the families had adolescents living at home.

Group leaders were recruited from around the United States, and they organized group meetings where the data were collected. Two types of group leaders were used in this study. In both phases of data collection, volunteer leaders from a large fraternal organization with branches throughout the country were used. Leaders were asked to verify the placement of fifteen families within seven stages of the family life cycle.

Once the group leaders had volunteered to collect the data, they were sent a packet of materials that explained how to work with the families, organize the group meetings, administer the questionnaires, and return the completed materials. Each group leader was asked to collect data from fifteen families from across the seven stages of the family life cycle.

269

During Phase I, packets of materials for 15 couples and families were sent to 125 group leaders throughout the nation. Packets were returned from 99 group leaders (79 percent). Those 26 leaders who did not return any packets gave the following reasons: "task bigger than led to believe," 13; "proscrastination," 5; "scheduling problems (too busy)," 3; "poor response from families," 3; and "illness," 2. Of the 15 possible couples who could participate, complete data were obtained from 5.2 couples (35 percent) and partial data from another 2.4 couples (16 percent), making a combined data set from 7.6 couples (51 percent). In other words, almost half of the contacted families (49 percent) did not participate (see Table D.1).

TABLE D.1   Data Collection Number of Completed Families

Average Number of Families	Phase I		Phase II	
	Number	Percentage	Number	Percentage
All Forms Completed	5.2	35	5.7	38
Partial Forms Completed	2.4	16	3.1	21
Complete and Partial Combined	7.6	51	8.8	59
No Forms Returned	7.5	49	6.2	41

During Phase II, there were 55 group leaders; 51 returned packets (93 percent). Not only did more of them collect data, but they also obtained a somewhat higher average rate of participation from couples and families. Of the 15 couples and families, they obtained complete data from 5.7 couples (38 percent) and partial data from 3.1 couples (21 percent), making a total of 8.8 packets (59 percent). In their group, a smaller number of couples and families (41 percent) declined to participate in the study.

The response rate of families varied somewhat by stage of the family life cycle. Families with School-Age Children (Stage 3) had the highest response rate, with almost two-thirds (63 percent) participating, followed by Families with Pre-School Children (Stage 2), where about half (55 percent) participated. The participation rate for most stages was in the 40 percent range and dropped to the lowest (37 percent) for Young Couples Without Children (Stage 1). The actual participation rate for the other stages was: Families with Adolescents (Stage 4) = 42%; Launching Families (Stage 5) = 45%; Empty Nest (Stage 6) = 45%; and Retired Couples (Stage 7) = 40%.

In summary, it appears that it is very difficult to get both the husband and wife to volunteer to participate in this type of study. It was made more difficult in this study because they were required to come together as a couple on one or two possible nights. Also, it became increasingly difficult when an adolescent was also required to attend with the parents (Stages 4 and 5). It is interesting to note that the lowest rate of participation was from Young Couples Without Children. Why some couples and families were willing to volunteer and actually participate and others were unable to participate is still an open question.

APPENDIX E: COUPLE AND FAMILY SCORES

Developing couple and family scores is like dealing with a double-edged sword. You want to obtain concise measures that will cut through the complexity of marital and family systems without destroying the individual components that make up the family system. For example, a couple or family mean summarizes family characteristics but does serious injustice to extreme individual differences.

A variety of couple and family scores were developed to describe more adequately the marriage and family as a unit. The following couple scores were developed for the various instruments used in this survey: *couple mean scores, maximized couple scores, couple discrepancy scores, positive couple agreement scores,* and *couple distance scores.* The procedures for computing these scores will be described and the relative agreement among them compared.

Family scores were also developed for families at the Adolescent stage. At this stage, data were obtained from the fathers, mothers, and one adolescent in each family. Family scores are primarily used in Chapter XII (Families with Adolescents).

Couple Mean Scores

Conceptually and empirically, mean scores can ideally represent the couple as a unit. If husband and wife scores are similar, the mean score will give a reasonably accurate picture of the couple's position on that scale. However, if the couple's scores on a scale are very different, a couple mean score eliminates those differences and gives a distorted picture of husband and wife differences. So while couple mean scores are relatively easy to compute, they can be misleading if the husband's and wife's scores are very discrepant.

One method for assessing the degree of agreement between husband score and wife score is through their correlation with each other. At this time, we have not empirically determined any specific levels for deciding if correlations are sufficiently high or too low for using couple mean scores. However, it can be possible to have at least a correlation of .50, because even at that level $(r = .50; r^2 = .25)$, one can accurately know a person's score based on their partner's score only 25 percent of the time.

In cases where there is considerable discrepancy in husband and wife scores, it might be desirable to keep individual scores for each spouse. Some attributes of a couple may be more accurately assessed by highlighting what each partner brings to the relationship rather than averaging them. For instance, a husband may be more skilled at reframing a problematic situation into a more positive perspective. The wife may be more adept at handling financial problems than the husband. In this case, an average score would tend to minimize a couple's strengths. Instead, these strengths may complement each other and not be dependent on the other partner being equally competent.

A more radical position is that a couple mean score may be an important measure *even when* it washes out the individual differences of the couple. This "average" may reflect the unit in a way that other scores cannot. Because the couple mean score falls between the individual scores of the spouses, it may more accurately reflect the behavior of the couple as a unit. When there is a sizable discrepancy between spouses' perceptions, the collective assessment of the couple would be expected to show a *compromise* somewhere between the individual positions. Such compromise might be more accurately assessed by the couple mean score. Mean scores may be particularly important for certain variables and not for others. Teasing out the empirical utility of specific scores and then making conceptual sense out of them was an important task of this project.

Couple Discrepancy Score

To assess the degree of difference between a husband's and wife's perception, a discrepancy score can be computed. This can be done by subtracting the wife's score from the husband's (or vice versa) and changing this to an absolute value.

The couple mean and the couple discrepancy scores each have advantages that overcome the limitations of the other. Whereas a mean score has the disadvantage of concealing individual differences between a husband and wife, the discrepancy score highlights these differences. While the couple mean provides a location for the couple on a scale, the couple discrepancy score does not. Because of the complementary nature of these two scores, they are both used in some of the analysis.

Maximized Couple Score

A maximized couple score is used whenever it is important to record an event as occuring in the relationship, even if it only occurred to one person. This score is based on the assumption from systems theory that if an event affects one person, it affects the entire system, i.e., couple or family. One situation in which this score is used in this study is in regard to stress. If *either* the husband or the wife indicates a stressful event, it is scored as a stressful event for the couple. If *both* checked the event as stressful, it is still counted as one event.

Couple Ratio Scores

Couple ratio scores are computed by dividing the score for each spouse by the sum of the scores of both [husband or wife score/(husband + wife score)]. It provides a measure of the difference between the spouses and an indication of the *relative balance* in the relationship on a particular dimension. However, a ratio score, like the discrepancy score, does *not* provide an index of location on the variable.

Percentage Couple Agreement

This score assesses the percentage agreement between the husband and wife on a given set of items. The main disadvantage with this score is that the percentage score has restricted use for most statistical analysis. However, it is possible to develop norms on these percentage scores if the sample is sufficiently large.

Couple Distance Score

The couple distance score is used with the two-dimensional Circumplex Model. Conceptually, it is simply the distance from the center of the Circumplex Model to the point that is halfway between the husband's and wife's location on the Circumplex. This is a continuous score that can be trichotomized into couple/family types: Balanced, Mid-Range, and Extreme. Computation of the couple distance score and the cutting points for the three major types are presented in Tables E.1 and E.2.

Comparison of Five Couple Scores on the ENRICH Scales

Since it was possible to compute several different types of couple scores on the ENRICH Inventory, an analysis was done to compare the amount of congruence between these various measures. The five types of couple's scores developed were the following: *couple mean* (raw score), *couple mean* (percentile), *positive couple agreement, couple discrepancy* (raw), and *couple*

TABLE E.1   Couple Distance and Couple Discrepancy Scores on FACES II

Couple Distance Score from Center (CDFC) or Circumplex Model

$$CDFC = \sqrt{\left(\frac{(HA - \overline{A}) + (WA - \overline{A})}{2}\right)^2 + \left(\frac{(HC - \overline{C}) + (WC - \overline{C})}{2}\right)^2}$$

$$= \sqrt{\frac{(HA + WA - 2\overline{A})^2 + (HC + WC - 2\overline{C})^2}{4}}$$

where: HA = husband's adaptability score
WA = wife's adaptability score
$\overline{A}$ = grand mean on adaptability
HC = husband's cohesion score
WC = wife's cohesion score
$\overline{C}$ = grand mean on cohesion

TABLE E.2   Norms for Couple Distance Scores

Family Type	Distance Cut-Off Point	Adjusted Frequencies (percentage)
Balanced	CDFC ≤ 7	53.9
Mid-Range	7 CDFC ≤ 11.8	31.5
Extreme	11.8 < CDFC	14.6

A couple discrepancy score (CDS) can also be computed that provides an agreement/disagreement measure for the couple. The formula for this score is given below.

$$CDS = \sqrt{(HA - WA)^2 + (HC - WC)^2}$$

discrepancy (percentile). The operational definitions of each of these couple scores will now be described.

First of all, a brief review of ENRICH might clarify the process of computing the couple scores. ENRICH has twelve subscales and each subscale contains ten items. The response scale uses a range of from 1 to 5, and so the range scores for each subscale is from 10 to 50. The ten subscales included the following categories: communication, conflict resolution, financial management, sexual relationship, marital satisfaction, role relationship, and others. (A more complete description of the ENRICH inventory is contained in the *Family Inventories* monograph; Olson et al., 1982.)

The *couple mean* (raw score) is the average of the husband and wife scores on a particular scale. The *couple mean* (percentile) is computed by first converting the individual scores to percentiles and then averaging the husband and wife percentiles.

The *couple discrepancy* (raw) is simply the absolute difference between the husband and wife raw scores on a particular scale. The *couple discrepancy* (percentile) is the absolute value of the difference between the husband and wife percentile scores.

The *positive couple agreement score* is determined by first selecting all the agreement items for the couple. These are the items for which the husband and wife responses on a five-point scale are within one point of each other. From that number, the items that are positive attributes are counted and those relating to negative attributes are not. The resulting score provides a rough idea of how much the couple agree with each other on positive aspects of their relationship. This score can either be computed as a sum score or as a percentage score. In the ENRICH scales, these scores are percentages and indicate the number of positive agreements out of the ten items in each category (see Table E.3).

As expected, the results of the analysis across all the ENRICH subscales clearly indicate that the couple mean based on the raw score and the percentile highly correlate ($r = .91$). What is more surprising is that they both correlate very highly with positive couple agreement, which is a very direct assessment of couple agreement. This high correlation is particularly surprising because the correlation between the husband and wife was .43 on the various ENRICH subscales. These data, therefore, support the idea that the mean score is robust and a reasonably accurate summary of the positive couple agreement between the spouses.

Another consistent finding is the lack of correlation ($r = .05$) between the couple mean scores (both raw and percentile) and the couple discrepancy scores (both raw and percentile). These data indicate that the two are measuring different and relatively independent aspects of a couple's relationship. As expected, the raw and percentile measures of couple discrepancy correlated rather highly ($r = .74$). Another expected finding was that there was a negative correlation ($r = -.21$ and $-.24$) between positive couple agreement and the two methods of computing the discrepancy score.

In summary, this analysis clearly indicates that the couple mean is a robust measure that correlates rather highly with positive couple agreement ($r = .85$). It also appears that the couple mean and couple discrepancy scores are uncorrelated and are measuring two different aspects of a couple's relationship. This indicates that it might be useful to use both couple means and couple discrepancy scores in the same analysis.

Comparison of Unweighted and Weighted Couple Stress Scores

In order to compare the empirical similarity of weighted and unweighted stress scores, the data from the stress scale used in this study were computed using these two scoring methods.

TABLE E.3 Correlation of Various Types of Couple Scores on ENRICH

	Couple Mean (Raw)	Couple Mean (Percentile)	Positive Couple Agreement	Couple Discrepancy (Raw)	Couple Discrepancy (Percentile)
Couple Mean (Raw)	—				
Couple Mean (percentile)	.91	—			
Positive Couple Agreement	.85	.80	—		
Couple Discrepancy (Raw)	.07	−.02	−.21	—	
Couple Discrepancy (Percentile)	−.06	.05	−.24	.74	—

The unweighted couple stress score was computed by summing items checked YES by *either* the husband or wife (maximized couple score). The rationale for using this approach is based on the property of circular causality from family systems theory (Bertalanffy, 1968; Buckley, 1967). Circular causality can be thought of as the "ripple effect"; change to one part of the system affects all other parts in the system. Therefore, if even one person experiences stress in a family, it will inevitably have an impact on the system as a whole.

The weighted couple stress score was computed by summing items that *either* the husband or the wife identified as a stress or strain. These items were then multiplied by weights ranging from 20 to 100 points.

The rationale for employing specific weights for different events goes back to the argument that conceptually some stressors and strains have more of an impact on families than others do. For example, the death of a family member would be more stressful for most families than a child making a transition to a new school. The weighting of life events represents a classic debate in the field.

Using Pearson's product-moment correlations to compare weighted and unweighted scores for husbands, wives, and adolescents, the correlation was consistently greater than .98. The data suggest that the weighted scores are virtually identical to the unweighted scores. Because of the similarities, the decision was made to honor the conceptual argument and use the weighted couple stress scores. Therefore, weighted scores were used for the remaining analysis.

Weighted couple stress scores were also compared to the individual weighted stress scores. The husband's weighted stress score correlated .82 and the wife's weighted score correlated .75 with the couple's weighted stress score.

The utility of their weighted couple score was shown in several analyses. One analysis compared the ability of couple versus individual scores to discriminate between high and low stress. Three sets of discriminant analyses were done with weighted husband's, wive's, and couple's stress scores to determine the accuracy of predicting family stress.

Husband's stress score	72%
Wive's stress score	73%
Couple's stress score	77%

The percentage of correctly classified cases on high and low stress was highest using the weighted couple stress score rather than either the husband's or the wife's stress score. (Further results on family stress are described in Chapter VII.)

Faces II: Couple Scores

Moving from individual to couple scores offers the possibility of combining individual perceptions to form a measure of the couple as a unit. Several options are available for deriving couple scores on the Circumplex Model. Each presents its own advantages and disadvantages. Using each dimension (cohesion and adaptability) separately, couple mean scores, couple discrepancy scores, or couple ratio scores can be computed based on the individual scores of the spouses.

Using a *couple mean score* allows one to assess the location of a couple on each dimension of the Circumplex Model, but it eliminates possible differences between the spouses. A *couple discrepancy score* (absolute value of husband score minus wife score) provides a measure of the spousal differences, but it does *not* indicate a location for the couple on the major dimensions.

Using any of these methods to combine the individuals' separate scores on each dimension into a couple score results in the blurring or loss of some potentially useful information about the individuals. At this point, this appears to be a necessary cost involved in deriving a score for the couple as a single unit.

Mean scores and discrepancy scores have been found to be empirically orthogonal (not correlated) in this study (all analysis on ENRICH). There was no correlation between mean scores and discrepancy scores, whether raw or percentile.

The *couple distance score* provides an advantageous alternative to the methods previously described when dealing with two dimensions simultaneously, as in the Circumplex Model. The two dimensions of the Circumplex Model intersect at the means for each dimension (exact center of the model). As mentioned earlier, one of the major family typologies derived from the Circumplex Model distinguished three family types: Balanced, Mid-Range, and Extreme.

Computing a couple distance score from the center of the Circumplex Model to a particular couple's mean score offers several advantages. A distance score simultaneously accounts for both dimensions of the Circumplex Model. It also provides a direct measure of Balanced, Mid-Range, or Extreme family types. Using this single distance measure overcomes the difficulties involved in using two separate variables (cohesion and adaptability) and provides a *single measure* of family type.

The formula for computing a couple distance score from the center of the Circumplex Model is given in Table E.1. The norms for each family type are also provided. The formula for computing a *couple discrepancy score* on the two dimensions combined is also presented in Table E.1.

FACES II: Family Scores

There are two different family scores that have been developed and used with FACES II. The first is a *Family Distance from Center* (FDFC) score, which indicates the distance from the center of the Circumplex Model to the family centroid, which is the point in the model at which the family mean adaptability and family mean cohesion scores meet. This score is used to classify the family as Balanced, Mid-Range, or Extreme on the Circumplex Model.

The advantage of this score is that it provides a single linear measure that simultaneously accounts for three or more family members' scores on the two circumplex dimensions. This score thereby opens up the possibility of doing correlational analysis with other variables. While this score indicates the distance of the family mean from the center of the Circumplex Model and the three major types (Balanced, Mid-Range, and Extreme), it does *not* indicate the specific location in terms of the sixteen family types.

The second score is the *Family Discrepancy Score* (FDS), which indicates the degree of agreement among family members on how tightly family members' scores are dispersed about the family centroid. The Family Discrepancy Score is an indication of the relative levels of agreement among family members as to their perceptions of the dynamics in their family.

Because the norms for the parents and adolescents on FACES II are different, the scores for each individual on cohesion and adaptability are converted to z scores. Parent norms are used for calculating the z score for the husband and wife, and adolescent norms are used for calculating the adolescent's z scores. The z scores are then used for the calculation of the Family Distance from Center and the Family Discrepancy Score. The formulas for these two scores are shown in Table E.4.

TABLE E.4   Family Distance and Family Discrepancy Scores on FACES II

Family Distance From Center (FDFC)

$$FC = \frac{HC + WC + AC}{3}$$

FC = Family mean cohesion z score
HC = Husband's cohesion z score
WC = Wife's cohesion z score
AC = Adolescent's cohesion z score

$$FA = \frac{HA + WA + AA}{3}$$

FA = Family mean adaptability z score
HA = Husband's adaptability z score
WA = Wife's adaptability z score
AA = Adolescent's adaptability z score

$$FDFC = \sqrt{FC^2 + FA^2}$$

(continued)

TABLE E.4   Continued

Family Type	*Norms for Family Distance Scores*	
	Distance Cutoff Point	*Adjusted Percentage*
Balanced	FDFC .89 or less	52.4
Mid-Range	FDFC .90 to 1.52	32.1
Extreme	FDFC 1.53 or more	15.5
		100.0

Family Discrepancy Score (FDS)

$$HDS = \sqrt{(HC - FC)^2 + (HA - FA)^2}$$
$$WDS = \sqrt{(WC - FC)^2 + (WA - FA)^2}$$
$$ADS = \sqrt{(AC - FC)^2 + (AA - FA)^2}$$
$$FDS = HDS + WDS + ADS$$

HDS: Husband's distance scores from the family centroid.
WDS: Wife's distance score from the family centroid.
ADS: Adolescent's distance score from the family centroid.
FDS = Family Discrepancy Score is a sum of the discrepancies for each family member. A mean FDS can also be used by dividing the total by the number of family members.

APPENDIX F: COMPARISON OF HIGH- AND LOW-STRESS FAMILIES

TABLE F.1 Stage 1 (Young Couples): Important Family Resources in Discriminating High- and Low-Stress Families*

Family Resources	F	P	Relationship to Low-Stress Families
Health practices	19.99	.0001	+
Quality of life	4.28	.0465	+
Family satisfaction	4.69	.0376	+
Marital satisfaction	6.24	.0176	+
Personality issues	13.34	.0009	+
Communication	5.11	.0304	+
Conflict resolution	13.38	.0009	+
Financial management	12.00	.0015	+
Family and friends	8.32	.0068	+
Leisure activities	5.20	.0291	+
Accord	14.83	.0005	+

*97.30 percent of grouped families correctly classified.

TABLE F.2   Stage 2 (Childbearing/Child Rearing): Important Family Resources in Discriminating High- and Low-Stress Families*

Family Resources	F	P	Relationship to Low-Stress Families
Health practices	3.77	.0546	+
Social support	4.44	.0372	−
Fatalism	10.95	.0013	−
Quality of life	21.82	.0000	+
Family satisfaction	12.19	.0007	+
Congregational activities	4.74	.0316	−
Marital satisfaction	26.93	.0000	+
Personality issues	18.69	.0000	+
Communication	18.69	.0000	+
Conflict resolution	13.75	.0003	+
Financial management	18.17	.0000	+
Sexual relationship	10.96	.0012	+
Religious orientation	6.40	.0128	+
Child orientation	4.73	.0318	+
Family and friends	18.39	.0000	+
Leisure activities	12.75	.0005	+
Accord	20.30	.0000	+
Cohesiveness	5.22	.0242	+
Adaptability	6.25	.0139	+

*76.72 percent of grouped families correctly classified.

TABLE F.3   Stage 3 (Adolescents/Launching): Important Family Resources in Discriminating High- and Low-Stress Families*

Family Resources	F	P	Relationship to Low-Stress Families
Health practices	3.85	.0510	+
Reframing	16.39	.0001	+
Fatalism	15.62	.0001	−
Quality of life	48.50	.0000	+
Family satisfaction	31.12	.0000	+
Marital satisfaction	59.99	.0000	+
Personality issues	48.71	.0000	+
Communication	32.54	.0000	+
Conflict resolution	34.48	.0000	+
Financial management	63.01	.0000	+
Sexual relationship	19.93	.0000	+
Religious orientation	6.61	.0109	+
Child and marriage	31.31	.0000	+
Family and friends	15.90	.0001	+
Leisure activities	19.83	.0000	+
Accord	56.40	.0000	+

*75 percent of group families correctly classified.

**TABLE F.4 Stage 4 (Older Couples): Important Family Resources in Discrimi-
nating High- and Low-Stress Families***

Family Resources	F	P	Relationship to Low-Stress Families
Health practices	17.61	.0080	−
Quality of life	6.78	.0119	+
Family satisfaction	4.99	.0297	−
Marital satisfaction	4.79	.0329	−
Personality issues	9.09	.0039	+
Communication	6.09	.0169	−
Cohesiveness	16.12	.0001	+
Adaptability	14.75	.0002	+

*89.09 percent of group families correctly classified.

TABLE G.1 Family Life Changes and Events Cited by Couples During the Past Year (in percentages)

	Stage 1 Couples N = (207)	Stage 2 Childbearing (269)	Stage 3 School-Age (232)	Stage 4 Adolescents (494)	Stage 5 Launching (352)	Stage 6 Empty Nest (230)	Stage 7 Retirement (234)
(1) Intrafamily strains							
Increase of husband/father's time away from family	32	32	30	23	16	11	
Increase of wife/mother's time away from family	19	28	27	26	22		
A member appears to have emotional problems	15	10	16	19	28	16	10
Increase conflict between husband and wife	16	18	14	14	16		
Increase in arguments between parent(s) and child(ren)		24	23	25	21		
Increase in conflict among children in the family		24	34	24	13		
Increase difficulty in managing teenage child(ren)				30	27		
Increase difficulty in managing school-age child(ren) (6-12 yrs.)			32	11			
Increase difficulty in managing preschool-age child (ren 2½-6 yrs.)		27	22				
Increase difficulty in managing toddler(s) (0-1 yrs.)		25					
Increase difficulty in managing infant(s) (0-1 yrs.)		19					

(continued)

TABLE G.1 Continued

	Stage 1 Couples N = (207)	Stage 2 Childbearing (269)	Stage 3 School-Age (232)	Stage 4 Adolescents (494)	Stage 5 Launching (352)	Stage 6 Empty Nest (230)	Stage 7 Retirement (234)
Increase in the amount of "outside activities" which the child(ren) are involved		40	70	68	49		
Increased disagreement about a member's friends or activities	17	15	14	18	24		
Increase in the number of problems or issues that do not get resolved	21	19	15	22	21	11	
Increase in the number of tasks or chores that do not get done	36	42	50	48	45	36	
Increase conflict with in-laws or relatives	16	21	11	15	14	11	23
(2) Marital Status							
Increase difficulty with sexual relationship between husband and wife	21	22	15	20	20	19	11
(3) Pregnancy and Childbearing Strains							
Family member experiencing menopause				12	29	31	11
Spouse had unwanted or difficult pregnancy		11					
A member gave birth to or adopted a child		34	11			16	
(4) Finance and Business Strains							
Took out a loan or refinanced a loan to cover increased expenses	38	33	29	33	35	17	
Change in conditions (economic, political, weather) that hurts family investments and/or income	24	32	26	34	24	27	13

Change in agriculture market, stock market, or land values that hurts family investments and/or income	12	18	12	18	18	18	14
A member started a new business	10	21	11			10	
Purchased or built a home	24	49	10			11	
A member purchased a car or other major item	50	49	49	43	51	32	23
Increasing financial debts due to overuse of credit cards	17	11	15	16	14		
Increased strain on family "money" for medical/dental expenses	20	31	29	31	23	13	17
Increased strain on family "money" for food, clothing, energy, home care	50	57	46	62	54	30	15
Increase strain on family "money" for child(ren)'s education		13	21	30	51		
Delay in receiving child support or alimony payments							
(5) Work-Family Transitions and Strains							
A member changed to a new job/career	46	29	29	24	34	16	10
A member lost or quit a job	26	16	14	12	24	12	23
A member retired from work	17	17	18	22	29	12	
A member started or returned to work						12	
A member stopped working for extended period (e.g., laid off, leave of absence, strike)	18	20	10	25	14	13	
Decrease in satisfaction with job/career	44	41	29		30	27	
A member had increased difficulty with people at work	40	28	27	15	24	22	
A member was promoted at work or given more responsibilities	54	31	35	30	34	22	
Family moved to a new home/apartment	26	19	12				

(continued)

TABLE G.1 Continued

	Stage 1 Couples N = (207)	Stage 2 Childbearing (269)	Stage 3 School-Age (232)	Stage 4 Adolescents (494)	Stage 5 Launching (352)	Stage 6 Empty Nest (230)	Stage 7 Retirement (234)
A child/adolescent member changed to a new school			33	36	33		
(6) Illness and Family Care Strains							
Parent/spouse became seriously ill or injured	11		11	10	10	16	14
Close relative or friend of the family became seriously ill	30	30	30	32	36	34	22
A member became physically disabled or chronically ill						11	
Increased difficulty in managing a chronically ill or disabled member						11	
Member of close relative was committed to an institution or nursing home	15		14		10	14	12
Increased responsibility to provide direct care or financial help to husband's and/or wife's parents(s)						13	
Experienced difficulty in arranging for satisfactory child care		14			12		

(7) Losses							
Death of husband's or wife's parents or close relative	19	19	23	21	23	22	21
Close friend of the family died	13	16	15	20	17	22	28
A member "broke up" a relationship with a close friend					17		
(8) Transitions "in and out"							
A member was married	10				15	14	12
Young adult member left home					38	13	
A young adult member began college (or post high school training)					45		
A member moved back home or a new person moved into the household				10	25		
(9) Family Legal Violations							
A member was picked up by police or arrested					10		

TABLE G.2 Family Life Changes for Adolescents (A-FILE)*

	Stage 4		Stage 5	
	M (175)	F (165)	M (26)	F (34)
N =				
(1) Transitions				
(1) Family member started new business (farm, store, etc.)	13	15	8	6
(2) Parent quit or lost a job	12	11	19	6
(3) Parents separated or divorced	2		4	
(4) Parent remarried	3	1	4	
(5) Family member was found to have a learning disorder	2	4	12	15
(6) Family member was married	10	7		0
(7) Parents adopted a child	5	1		29
(8) A member started junior high or high school	52	55	19	24
(9) Child or teenage member transferred to a new school	22	18	8	
(10) Parent started school	9	4	4	
(11) Brother or sister moved away from home	17	17	42	35
(12) Young adult member entered college, vocational training, or armed forces	15	19	73	56
(13) Parent(s) started or changed to a new job	17	19	19	18
(14) Family moved to a new home	10	6		3
(2) Sexuality				
(15) Unmarried family member became pregnant	3	1		6
(16) Family member had an abortion	2	1		
(17) Birth of a brother or sister	7	4	4	3
(18) Teenager began having sexual intercourse	13	8	12	18

290

(3) Losses

(19) Family went on welfare	2	1	8	9
(20) Damage to or loss of family property due to fire, burglary, or other disaster	9	6	4	
(21) Brother or sister died	2	1		
(22) Parent died	2	26	27	21
(23) Close family relative died	31	26	15	27
(24) Death of a close friend or family member	27	4	12	3
(25) Family member or close family friend attempted or committed suicide	6			

(4) Responsibilities and Strains

(26) Family member became seriously ill or injured (not hospitalized)	19	18	4	12
(27) Family member was hospitalized	31	26	31	18
(28) Family member became physically disabled or was found to have a long-term health problem (allergies, asthma, diabetes, etc.)	10	14	12	3
(29) Family member has emotional problems	11	7	15	9
(30) Grandparent(s) became seriously ill	27	20	31	24
(31) Parent(s) have more responsibility to take care of grandparent(s)	24	11	19	15
(32) Family member ran away	6	2	4	3
(33) More financial debts due to use of credit cards or charges	13	16	12	3
(34) Increased family living expenses for medical care, food, clothing, energy costs (gasoline, heating)	62	65	81	47
(35) Increase of parent's time away from family	22	22	23	24
(36) Child or teenage member resists doing things with family	27	32	19	27
(37) Increase in arguments between parents	15	20		15
(38) Children or teenagers have more arguments with one another	26	28		15
(39) Parent(s) and teenager(s) have increased arguments (hassles) over use of car or hours to stay out	27	33	19	44
(40) Parent(s) and teenager(s) have increased arguments (hassles) over choice of friends and/or social activities	21	29	15	32

(continued)

TABLE G.2 Continued

	Stage 4 M (175)	Stage 4 F (165)	Stage 5 M (26)	Stage 5 F (34)
N =				
(41) Parent(s) and teenager(s) have increased arguments (hassles) over attendance at religious activities	14	12	19	44
(42) Parent(s) and teenager(s) have increased arguments (hassles) over personal appearance (clothes, hair, etc.)	19	24	12	41
(43) Increased arguments about getting the jobs done at home	40	43	12	41
(44) Increased pressure for a member in school to get "good grades" or do well in sports or school activities	38	34	23	18
(5) Substance Use				
(45) Family member uses drugs (not given by doctor)	6	5	8	9
(46) Family member drinks too much alcohol	11	6	15	9
(47) Child or teenage member was suspended from school or dropped out of school	3	2	12	6
(48) Parent(s) and teenager(s) have increased arguments (hassles) over use of cigarettes, alcohol or drugs	10	10	24	18
(6) Legal Conflict				
(49) Family member went to jail, juvenile detention, or was placed on court probation	8	3		6
(50) Family member was robbed or attacked (physically or sexually)	4	2	4	3

*In percentages.

292

REFERENCES

Alexander, J. F., & Barton, C. Behavioral systems therapy for families. In D. H. Olson (Ed.), *Treating relationships*. Lake Mills, IA: Graphic, 1976.

Aldous, J., Condon, T., Hill, R., Straus, M., & Tallman, I. *Family problem solving*. Hinsdale, IL: Dryden, 1971.

Andrews, F. M., & Withey, S. B. Developing measures of perceived life quality: Results from several national averages. *Journal of Social Indicators Research*, 1974, *1*.

Angell, R. C. *The family encounters the depression*. New York: Charles Scribner & Sons, 1936.

Antonovsky, A. *Health, stress and coping*. San Francisco: Jossey-Bass, 1979.

Ashby, W. *Design for a brain*. London: Chapman & Hall, 1960.

Bader, E., Microys, G., Sinclair, L., Willett, E., & Conway, B. Do premarital programs really work: a Canadian experiment. *Journal of Marital and Family Therapy*, 1980, *6*, 171-179.

Bahr, S. J., & Rollins, B. C. Crises and conjugal power. Journal of Marriage and the Family, 1971, *33*, 360-367.

Balswick, J. O., & Macrides, C. Parental stimulus for adolescent rebellion. *Adolescence*, 1975, *10*, 253-266.

Barrett-Lennard, G. T. Dimensions of therapist response as causal factors in therapeutic change. *Psychological Monographs: General and Applied*, 1962, *76* (43, Whole No. 562).

Bateson, G. *Mind and nature*. New York: E. P. Dulton, 1979.

Beam, W. W. College students' perception of family strengths. In N. Stinnett, B. Chesser, & J. De Frain (Eds.), *Building family strengths: Blueprints for action*. Lincoln: University of Nebraska Press, 1979.

Beavers, W. *Psychotherapy and growth: A family systems perspective*. New York: Brunner/Mazel, 1977.

Beavers, W. & Voeller, M. N. Family models: Comparing and contrasting the Olson circumplex model with the Beaver's system model. *Family Process*, 1982, *21*, 250-260.

Becker, J., & Iwakami, E. Conflict and cominance within families of disturbed children. *Journal of Abnormal Psychology*, 1969, *74* 330-335.

Becker W., & Krug, R. A circumplex model for social behavior in children. *Child Development*, 1964, *35*, 371-396.

Bell, J. C. Recent advances in family group therapy. *Journal of Child Psychology and Psychiatry*, 1962, *2*, 1-15.

Bell, L. G., & Bell, D. C. Family climate and the role of the family adolescent: Determinants of adolescent functioning. *Family Relations*, 1982, *31*, 519-527.

Bell, N. W., & Vogel, E. F. *The family*. Glencoe, IL: Free Press, 1960.

Bell, R. Parent-adolescent interaction in runaway families. Unpublished doctoral dissertation, University of Minnesota, St. Paul, 1982.

Belloc, N., & Breslow, L. Relationship of physical health status and health practices. *Preventative Medicine*, 1972, *4*, 409-421.

Belloc, N., Breslow, L., & Hochstim, J. Measurement of physical health in a general population survey. *American Journal of Epidemiology*, 1971, *93*, 5, 328-336.

Benjamin, L. Structural analysis of social behavior. *Psychological Review*, 1974, *81*, 392-425.

Benjamin, L. Structural analysis of a family in therapy. *Journal of Counseling and Clinical Psychology*, 1977, *45*, 391-406.

Berger, P. L., & Luckmann, T. *The social construction of reality*. New York: Doubleday, 1966.

Bergtson, V., & Black, K. *Solidarity between parents and children: Four perspectives on theory development*. Paper presented at the annual meeting of the National Council of Family Relations, 1973.

Berkman, P. & Syme, L. Social networks, host resistance, and mortality: A nine-year follow-up study on Alameda County residents. *American Journal of Epidemiology*, 1979, *109*, 2.

Berkman, P. Measurement of mental health in a general population survey. *American Journal of Epidemiology*, 1971, *2*, 405-411.

Bertalanffy, L. von *General systems theory*. New York: Braziller, 1968.

Bienvenu, M. J. Sr. Measurement of marital communication. *Family Coordinator*, 1970, *19*, 26-31.

Birchler, B., Weiss, R., & Vincent, J. Multimethod analysis of social reinforcement exchange between maritally distressed and non-distressed spouse and stranger dyads. *Journal of Personality and Social Psychology*, 1975, *31*, 349-360.

Booth, A. Sex and social participation. *American Sociological Review*, 1972, *32*, 183-192.

Boss, P. G. The relationship of psychological father absence, wife's personal qualities and wife/family dysfunction in families of missing fathers. *Journal of Marriage and the Family*, 1980, *45*, 541-549.

Boss, P., McCubbin, H., & Lester, G. The corporate executive wife's coping patterns in response to routine husband-father absence: Implications for family stress theory. *Family Process*, 1979, *18*, 79-86.

Bott, E. G. *Family and social network*. London: Tavistock, 1957.

Bowen, M. The family as the unit of study and treatment. *American Journal of Orthopsychiatry*, 1960, *31*, 40-60.

Breslow, L. Prospects for improving health through reducing risk factors. *Preventative Medicine*, 1978, *7*, 449-458.

Breslow, L. Benefits and limitations of health monitoring. *American Journal of Medicine*, 1980, *77*, 919-920.

Breslow, L., & Engstrom, E. Persistence of health habits and their relationship to mortality. *Preventative Medicine*, 1980, *9*, 469-483.

Breslow, L., & Somers, A. The lifetime health monitoring program: A realistic approach to preventative medicine. *New England Journal of Medicine*, 1977, *296* (11), 601-608.

Broderick, C. B. In D. H. Olson (Ed.), *Treating relationships*. Lake Mills, IA: Graphic, 1976.

Broderick, C. B., Williams, P., & Krager, H. Family process and child outcomes. In W. Burr, R. Hill, I. Nye, & I. L. Reiss (Eds.), *Contemporary theories about the family.* New York: Free Press, 1979.

Bronfenbrenner, U. Toward a theoretical model for the analysis of parent-child relationships in a social context. In J. D. Clidewell (Ed.), *Parental attitudes and child behavior.* Springfield, IL: Charles C Thomas, 1961.

Bross, I. How to use ridit analysis. *Biometrics,* 1958, *14,* 18-38.

Buckley, Walter. *Sociology and modern systems theory.* Englewood Cliffs, NJ: Prentice-Hall, 1967.

Burgess, E. W., & Locke, H. J. *The family: From institution to companionship.* New York: American Books, 1945.

Burke, R. J., & Weir, T. Marital helping relationships: The moderator between stress and well-being. *Journal of Psychology,* 1977, *95,* 121-130.

Burr, W. R. *Theory construction and the sociology of the family.* New York: John Wiley, 1973.

Burr, W. R., Leigh, G. K., Day, R. D., & Constantine, J. Symbolic interaction and the family. In W. R. Burr et al. (Eds.), *Contemporary theories about the family.* New York: Free Press, 1979.

Cafferata, G. L. Taking responsibility for health. *Journal of American College Health Association,* 1980, *4,* 196-200.

Campbell, A., Converse, P. E. & Rodgers, W. L. *The quality of life: Perceptions, evaluations and satisfactions.* New York: Russell Sage Foundation, 1976.

Campbell, E. E. The effects of couple communication training on married couples in the child-rearing years: A field experiment (Doctoral dissertation, Arizona State University, 1974). *Dissertation Abstracts International,* 1974, *35/04,* 1942-A. (University Microfilm No. 74-23, 420)

Canadian Task Force. Periodic health examination. *CMA Journal,* 1980, *121,* 1193-1254.

Cannon, W. B. *Bodily changes in pain, hunger, fear and rage.* New York: D. Appleton, 1929.

Caplan, G. *Support systems of community mental health.* New York: Behavioral, 1974.

Caplan, G. The family as a support system. In G. Caplan and M. Killilea (Eds.), *Support systems and mutual help.* New York: Grune & Stratton, 1976.

Caplan, G., & Killilea, M. *Support systems and mutual help.* New York: Grune & Stratton, 1976.

Carisse, C. Family leisure: A set of contradictions. *Family Coordinator,* 1975, *24,* 191-197.

Carnes, P. J., & Laube, H. Becoming us: An experiment in family learning and teaching. *Small Group Behavior,* 1975, *6* (1), 106-120.

Carter, E., & McGoldrick, M. *The family life cycle: A framework for family therapy.* New York: Gardner, 1980.

Cartwright, D., & Zander, A. (Eds.). *Group dynamics: Research and theory.* Evanston, IL: Row, Peterson, 1962.

Cassel, J. The contribution of the social environment resistence. *American Journal of Epidemiology,* 1976, *102,* 2, 107-123.

Cavan R., & Ranck, K. R. *The family and the depression.* Chicago: University of Chicago Press, 1938.

Cobb, S. Social support as a moderator of life stress. *Psychosomatic Medicine,* 1976, *38,* 300-314.

Cobb, S. Social support and health through the life course. In M. W. Riley (Ed.), *Aging from birth to death: Interdisciplinary perspectives*. Washington, DC: American Association for the Advancement of Science, 1979.

Coddington, R. D. The significance of life events as an etiologic factor in the diseases of children II: A study of a normal population. *Journal of Psychosomatic Research*, 1972, *16*, 205-213.

Coles, R., & Coles, J. *Women of crisis, lives of struggle and hope*. New York: Dell, 1978.

Comeau, J. *FIRM-Family inventory of resources for management: An assessment of resources in families of chronically ill children (myelomeningocele and cerebral palsy)*. Unpublished paper. University of Minnesota, 1981.

Constantine, L. *A verified system theory of human process*. Paper presented at University of Minnesota, Family Social Science, October, 1977.

Corrales, R. The influence of family cycle categories, marital power, spousal agreement and communication styles upon marital satisfaction in the first six years of marriage (Doctoral dissertation, University of Minnesota, 1974). *Dissertation Abstracts International*, 1974, *35(5-A.)*, 3141-A. (University Microfilms No. 72-26, 179)

Craddock, A. E. *Marital problem solving as a function of a couple's marital power expectations and marital value system*. Unpublished manuscript, 1978.

Craddock, A. E. Relationship between authoritarianism, marital power expectations, and marital value systems. *Australian Journal of Psychology*, 1977, *29*(3), 211-221.

Cromwell, R. E., & Olson, D. H. (Eds.). *Power in families*. New York: John Wiley, 1975.

Cromwell, R. E., Olson, D. H., & Fournier, D. G. Diagnosis and evaluation in marital and family counseling. In D. H. Olson (ed.), *Treating relationships*. Lake Mills, IA: Graphic, 1976.

Croog, S. H., Lipson, A. A., & Levine, S. Help patterns in severe illness: The rules of kin networks, non-family resources, and institutions. *Journal of Marriage and the Family*, 1972, *34*, 32-41.

Cuber, J. F., & Haroff, P. B. *The significant Americans: A study of sexual behavior among the affluent*. New York: Appleton-Century, 1955.

Cutley, B. R., & Dyer, W. Initial adjustment processes in young married couples. *Social Forces*, 1965, *44*, 195-201.

Davis, E. S. *The assessment of family pride*. Unpublished dissertation, University of Wisconsin-Madison, 1980.

D'Augelli, A. R., Deyss, D. S., Guerney, B. G., Jr., Hershenberg, B., & Sborolsky, S. L. Interpersonal skill training for dating couples: An evaluation of an educational mental health service. *Journal of Counseling Psychology*, 1974, *21*, 385-389.

Deacon, R. E., & Firebaugh, R. M. *Home management: Context and concepts*. Boston: Houghton Mifflin, 1975.

Dell, P. Researching the family theories of schizophrenia: An exercise in epistomological confusion. *Family Process*, 1980, *19*, 321-335.

Devereux, E. Socialization in cross-cultural perspective: Comparative study of England, Germany and the United States. In R. Hill (Ed.), *Families in east and west*. Paris: Mouton, 1970.

Dohrenwend, B. S., Krasnoff, L., Askenasy, A. R., & Dohrenwend, B. P. Exemplification of a method for scaling life events: The PERI life event scale. *Journal of Health and Social Behavior*, 1978, 19(2), 205-229.

Druckman, J. A. Family oriented policy and treatment program for juvenile status offenders. *Journal of Marriage and the Family*, 1979, *41*, 627-636.

Duvall, E. *Family Development* (4th ed.). Philadelphia: J. B. Lippincott, 1970.

Duvall, E. *Marriage and family development.* Philadelphia: J. B. Lippincott, 1977.

Edmonds, V. H. Marital conventionalization: Definition and measurement. *Journal of Marriage and the Family,* 1967, *29,* 681-688.

Edmonds, V. H., Withers, G., & Dibatista, B. Adjustment, conservation and marital conventionalization. *Journal of Marriage and the Family,* 1972, *34,* 96-103.

Eggersten, S., Schneeweiss, R., & Bergman, J. An updated practoral for pediatric health screening. *Journal of Family Practice,* 1980, *10,* 1, 25-37.

Epstein, N. B., Bishop, D. S., & Levin, S. The McMaster model of family functioning. *Journal of Marriage and Family Counseling,* 1978, *40,* 19-31.

Epstein, N. B., & Jackson, E. An outcome study of short-term communication training with married couples. *Journal of Consulting and Clinical Psychology,* 1978, *46*(2), 207-212.

Epstein, N. B., & Santa-Barbara, J. Interpersonal perceptions and stable outcomes of conflict behavior in clinical couples. *Family Process,* 1975, *14,* 51-66.

Erikson, E. H. *Childhood and society.* New York: W. W. Norton, 1950.

Erikson, E. *Identity and the life cycle: Psychological issues.* New York: International Universities, 1959.

Erikson, E. *Adulthood.* New York: W.W. Norton, 1976.

Farina, A., & Dunham, R. M. Measurement of family relationships and their effects. *Archives of General Psychiatry,* 1963, *9,* 64-73.

Feldman, L. B. Goals of family therapy. *Journal of Marriage and Family Counseling,* 1976, *2,* 103-113.

Ferreira, A. Decision-making in normal and pathological families. *Archives of General Psychiatry,* 1963, *8,* 63-73.

Ferreira, A., & Winter, W. Family interaction and decision-making. *Archives of General Psychiatry,* 1965, *13,* 214-223.

Ferreira, A., & Winter, W. Stability in interaction variables in family decision-making. *Archives of General Psychiatry,* 1966, *14,* 352-355.

Festinger, L., Schachter, S., & Back, K. *Social pressures in informal groups.* New York: Harper, 1950.

Fiedler, F., & Neuwese, W. Leader's contribution to task performance in cohesive and non-cohesive groups. In I. Steiner & M. Fishbein (Eds.), *Current studies in social psychology.* New York: Holt, Rinehart & Winston, 1965.

Fisher, B. L., Gibbin, P. R., & Hoopes, M. H. *Journal of Marital and Family Therapy,* 1982, *8,* 273-282.

Fisher, B. L., & Sprenkle, D. H. *Assessment of healthy family functioning and its relation to goals of family therapy.* Unpublished manuscript, Purdue University, 1977.

Fisher, B. L., & Sprenkle, D. H. Therapists' perceptions of healthy family functioning. *International Journal of Family counseling,* 1978, *6,* 1-10.

Fletcher, S., & Spitzer, W. The periodic health examination: 1980. *Annals of Internal Medicine,* 1980, *92*(2), 252-253.

Foa, U. Convergences in the analysis of the structure of interpersonal behavior. *Psychological Review,* 1961, *68,* 341-353.

Fournier, D. G. *Validation of PREPARE: A pre-marital counseling inventory.* Unpublished doctoral dissertation, University of Minnesota, 1979.

Fournier, D. G., Springer, J. S., & Olson, D. H. *The inventory of pre-marital conflict: Clinical and educational applications.* Paper presented at the annual meeting of the National Council on Family Relations, San Diego, October 1978.

Frame, P., & Carlson, S. A critical review of period health screening using specific screening criteria. *Journal of Family Practice,* 1975, *2*(1), 29-36.

Framo, J. L. (Ed.). *Family interaction: A dialogue between family researchers and family therapists.* New York: Springer, 1972.

French, A. P., & Guidera, B. J. *The family as a system in four dimensions: A theoretical model.* Paper presented at American Academy of Child Psychiatry, San Francisco, 1974.

French, J. R. P., Jr., Rodgers, W. L., & Cobb, S. Adjustment as a person-environment fit. In B. V. Coelho, D. Hamburg, & J. Adams (Eds.), *Coping and adaptation.* New York: Basic Books, 1974.

Fuhr, R., Moos, R., & Dishotsky, N. The use of family assessment and feed-back in on-going family therapy. *American Journal of Family Therapy,* 1981, *9,* 24-36.

General Mills. *American family report 1978-1979: Family health in an era of stress.* Minneapolis: General Mills, 1979.

George, L. *Role transitions in later life.* Belmont, CA: Brooks/Cole, 1980.

Gerhardt, V. Coping and social action: Theoretical of the life event approach. *Sociology of Health and Illness,* 1979, *1,* 195-225.

Gersten, J. C., Langner, T. S., Eisenberg, J. G., & Orzech, J. Child behavior and life events. In B. Dohrenwend & B. Dohrenwend (Eds.), *Stressful life events and changes.* New York: John Wiley, 1974.

Gewirtz, J. L. Mechanisms of social learning. In D. A. Goslin (Ed.), *Handbook of socialization theory and research.* Chicago: Rand McNally, 1969.

Geyman, J. Systematic evaluation of medical technology: An urgent need. *The Journal of Family Practice,* 1980, *10*(3), 403-404.

Gibran, K. *The prophet.* New York: Alfred A. Knopf, 1968.

Gilles, J. *My needs, your needs, our needs.* Bergenfield, NJ: New American Library, 1974.

Glazer, B., & Straus, A. *The discovery of grounded theory: Strategies for qualitative research.* Chicago: Aldine, 1967.

Glenn, N. D., & McLanahan, S. Children and marital happiness: A further specification of the relationship. *Journal of Marriage and the Family,* 1982, *1,* 63-72.

Glenn, N. D., & Weaver, C. N. The contribution of marital happiness to global happiness. *Journal of Marriage and the Family,* 1981, *43,* 161-168.

Glueck, S., & Glueck, E. *Unraveling juvenile delinquency.* Cambridge, MA: Harvard University Press, 1950.

Goetzel, V. Mental illness and cultural beliefs in a southern Italian immigrant family. *Canadian Psychiatric Association Journal,* 1973, *18,* 219-222.

Goffman, Erving. *The presentation of self in everyday life.* Garden City, NY: Doubleday, 1959.

Golan, N. *Passing through transitions.* New York: Free Press, 1981.

Goldstein, H. K., & Kling, F. *The measurement of family solidarity.* Unpublished manuscript, Florida State University, 1975.

Goodrich, D., Ryder, R., & Rausch, H. Patterns of newlywed marriage. *Journal of Marriage and the Family,* 1963, *30,* 383-389.

Group for the Advancement of Psychiatry (GAP). *Treatment of families in conflict.* New York: Science House, 1970.

Guerney, L. F. Filial therapy program. In D. H. Olson (Ed.), *Treating relationships.* Lake Mills, IA: Graphic, 1976.

Gurin, G., Veroff, J., & Feld, S. *Americans view their mental health*. New York: Basic Books, 1960.

Gurman, A. S., & Kniskern, D. P. Research in marital and family therapy: Empirical, clinical and conceptual issues. In S. L. Garfield & A. E. Bergin (Eds.), *Handbook of psychotherapy and behavior change* (rev. ed.). New York: John Wiley, 1978.

Guttman, L. A new approach to factor analysis: The radex. In P. F. Lazarsfeld (Ed.), *Mathematical thinking in the social sciences*. Glencoe, IL: Free Press, 1954.

Haan, N. *Coping and defending*. New York: Academic, 1977.

Haley, J. The family of the schizophrenic: A model system. *Journal of Nervous and Mental Disorders*, 1959, *129*, 357-374.

Haley, J. Family experiments: A new type of experimentation. *Family Process*, 1962, *1*, 265-293.

Haley, J. *Strategies of psychotherapy*. New York: Grune & Stratton, 1963.

Haley, J. Research on family patterns: An instrument measurement. *Family Process*, 1964, *3*, 41-65.

Haley, J. Experiment with abnormal families: Testing done in a restricted communication setting. *Archives of General Psychiatry*, 1967, *17*, 53-63.

Haley, J. *Leaving home*. New York: McGraw-Hill, 1980.

Hall, J. The case for health hazard appraisals: Which health-screening techniques are cost-effective? *Diagnosis*, February 1980, 60-82.

Hamburg, D., & Adams, J. A perspective on coping behavior: Seeking and utilizing information in major transitions. *Archives of General Psychiatry*, 1967, *17*, 277-284.

Hansen, D., & Hill, R. Families under stress. In H. Christensen (Ed.), *Handbook of marriage and the family*. Chicago: Rand McNally, 1964.

Hansen, D. & Johnson V. Rethinking family stress theory: Definitional aspects. In W. Burr, R. Hill, I. Reiss, & R. Nye (Eds.), *Contemporary theories about the family*. New York: Free Press, 1979.

Hansen, G. L. Marital adjustment and conventionalization: A re-examination. *Journal of Marriage and the Family*, 1981, *43*, 855-864.

Harvard Study, Harvard Medical School, Health Letter, 79 Garden Street, Cambridge, MA, June 1982.

Hawkins, J. L. *A measure of marital cohesion*. Unpublished manuscript. University of Minnesota, 1968. (a)

Hawkins, J. L. Association between companship, hostility and marital satisfaction. *Journal of Marriage and the Family*, 1968, *30*, 647-650. (b)

Hawkins, J. L., Weisberg, C., & Ray, D. Spouse differences in communication style: preference, perception, behavior. *Journal of Marriage and the Family*, 1980, *42*, 585-593.

Hawkins, N. G., Davies, R., & Holmes, T. H. Evidence of psychosocial factors in the development of pulmonary tuberculosis. *American Review of Tubercular and Pulmonary Disease*, 1957, *75*(5), 768-780.

Hess, R., & Handel, G. *Family worlds: A psychological approach to family life*. Chicago: University of Chicago Press, 1959.

Hicks, M., & Platt, M. Marital happiness and stability: A review of the research in the sixties. *Journal of Marriage and the Family*, 1970, *32*, 553-574.

Hill, R. *Families under stress*. New York: Harper, 1949.

Hill, R. Generic features of families under stress. *Social Casework*, 1958, *49*, 139-150.

Hill, R. Methodological problems with the development approach to family study. *Family Process,* 1964, *3*(1), 5-22.

Hill, R. *Family development in three generations.* Cambridge, MA: Schenkman, 1970.

Hill, R. Modern systems theory and the family: A confrontation. *Social Science Information,* 1971, *10,* 7-26.

Hill, R., Moss, J., & Wirths, C. G. *Eddyville's families.* Chapel Hill: University of North Carolina, 1953.

Hill, R., & Rodgers, R. The developmental approach. In H. T. Christensen (Ed.), *Handbook of marriage and the family.* Chicago: Rand McNally, 1964.

Hill, R., & Hansen, D. A. The identification of conceptual frameworks utilized in family study. *Marriage and Family Living,* 1960, *22,* 299-311.

Hinkle, J. E., & Moore, M. A student couples program. *Family Coordinator,* 1971, *2*(20), 153-158.

Hobart, C. W. Disillusionment in marriage and romanticism. *Marriage and Family Living,* 1958, *20,* 156-162.

Hobart, W., & Klausner, W. L. Interactional correlates of marital agreement and marital adjustment. *Marriage and Family Living,* 1959, *21,* 256-263.

Hoffman, L. "Enmeshment" and the too richly cross-joined system. *Family Process,* 1975, *14,* 457-468.

Hoffman, L. *Foundations of family therapy.* New York: Basic Books, 1981.

Holmes, T. H., & Masuda, M. Life change and illness susceptibility. In B. S. Dohrenwend & B. P. Dohrenwend (Eds.), *Stressful life events: Their nature and effects.* New York: John Wiley, 1974.

Holmes, T. H., & Rahe, R. The social readjustment rating scale. *Journal of Psychosomatic Research,* 1967, *11,* 213-218.

House, J. *Work stress and social support.* Reading, MA.: Addison-Wesley, 1981.

Hunt, D. G. Parental permissiveness as perceived by the offspring and the degree of marijuana usage among offspring. *Human Relations,* 1974, *27,* 267-285.

Hunt, M., & Hunt, B. *The divorce experience.* New York: McGraw-Hill.

Jackson, D. The question of family homeostasis. *Psychiatry Quarterly,* 1957, *31,* 79-90.

Jackson, D. Family rules. *Archives of General Psychiatry,* 1965, *12,* 589-594.

Jackson, D., & Weakland, J. H. Conjoint family therapy: Some considerations on theory, technique and results. *Psychiatry,* 1961, *24,* 30-45.

Jacob, T. Family interaction in disturbed and normal families: A methodological and substantive review. *Psychological Bulletin,* 1975, *82,* 33-65.

Jorgensen, S. R. & Gaudy, J. C. Self-disclosure and satisfaction in marriage: The relation examined. *Family Relations,* 1980, *29,* 281-287.

Jourard, S. M. *Self-disclosure: An experimental analysis of the transparent self.* New York: John Wiley, 1971.

Jurich, A., Bollman, S., Bunge, J., Kennedy, G., & Schumm, W. *Place of residence and quality of life: Conceptual idea paper.* Unpublished manuscript, Kansas State University, 1975.

Kantor, D., & Lehr, W. *Inside the family.* San Francisco: Jossey-Bass, 1975.

Kantor, S., Winkelstein, W., & Ibrahim, M. A note on the interpretation of the ridit as a quantile rank. *American Journal of Epidemiology,* 1968, *87*(3), 609-615.

Kaplan, B. H., O. C. Cassel, & S. Gore. Social support and health. *Medical Care,* 1977, *25,* 47-58.

Karpel, M. Individuation: From fusion to dialogue. *Family Process,* 1976, *15,* 65-82.

Kelsey-Smith, M., & Beavers, W. Family assessment: Centripetal and centrifugal family systems. *American Journal of Family Therapy, 1981, 9,* 3-12.

Kerckhoff, A., & Bean F. *Exploration of a circumplex model of interpersonal relations.* Paper presented at the American Sociological Association, 1969.

Kieren, D. and Tallman, I. *Adaptability: A measure of spousal problem-solving* (Tech. Rep. 1). Minneapolis: Family Study Center, April, 1971.

Kieren, D., & Tallman, I. Spousal adaptability: An assessment of marriage competence. *Journal of Marriage and the Family, 1972, 34,* 247-256.

Killorin, E., & Olson, D. H. *Clinical application of the circumplex model to chemically dependent families.* Unpublished manuscript, 1980.

Kitson, G. C., & Sussman, M. B. *Marital complaints, demographic characteristics, and symptoms of mental distress among the divorcing.* Paper presented at the meeting of the Midwest Sociological Society, Minneapolis, April 1977.

Klein, D. Family problem solving and family stress. In H. I. McCubbin, M. B. Sussman, & J. M. Patterson (Eds.), *Social stress and the family: Advances and developments in family stress theory and research.* Marriage and Family Review, Vol. 6, Numbers 1/2. New York: Haworth, 1983.

Klein, D., & Hill, R. Determinants of family problem solving effectiveness. In W. Burr, R. Hill, I. Reiss, & F. Nye (Eds.), *Contemporary theories about the family.* New York: Free Press, 1979.

Klugman, J. Enmeshment and fusion. *Family Process, 1976, 15,* 321-323.

Kohn, M. *Class and conformity.* Homewood, IL: Dorsey, 1969.

Koos, E. L. *Families in trouble.* New York: King's Crown, 1946.

L'Abate, L. *Understanding and helping the individual in the family.* New York: Grune & Stratton, 1980.

Lazarus, R. *Psychological stress and the coping process.* New York: McGraw-Hill, 1966.

Lazarus, R. Cognitive and coping processes in emotion. In A. Monet and R. Lazarus (Eds.), *Stress and coping.* New York: Columbia University Press, 1977.

Leary, T. *Interpersonal diagnosis or personality.* New York: Ronald, 1957.

Lederer, W., & Jackson, D. *Mirages of marriage.* New York: W. W. Norton, 1968.

Leif, A. (Ed.). *The commonsense psychiatry of Dr. Adolf Meyer.* New York: McGraw-Hill, 1948.

Le Masters, E. E. Parenthood as crises. *Marriage and Family Living, 1957, 19,* 352-355.

Lennard, H., Beaulieu, M., & Embrey, N. Interaction in families with a schizophrenic child. *Archives of General Psychiatry, 1965, 12,* 166,183.

Lennard, H., & Bernstein, A. *Patterns in human interaction.* San Francisco, Ca; Jossey-Bass, 1969.

Levinger, G. Marital cohesiveness and dissolution: An integrative review. *Journal of Marriage and the Family, 1965, 27,* 1928.

Levinger, G., & Senn, D. J. Disclosure of feelings in marriage. *Merrill-Palmer Quarterly, 1967, 13,* 237-249.

Levinson, D. *The seasons of a man's life.* New York: Alfred A. Knopf, 1978.

Lewis, J. M., Beavers, W. R., Gosssert, J. T., & Philips, V. A. *No single thread: Psychological health in family systems.* New York: Brunner/Mazel, 1976.

Lewis, R. A., & Spanier, G. B. Theorizing about the quality and stabilty of marriage. In W. R. Burr, R. Hill, R. I. Nye, & I. L. Reiss (Eds.), *Contemporary theories about the family* (Vol. 1). New York: Free Press, 1979.

Lidz, T., Cornelison, A. R., Fleck, S., & Terry, D. The interfamilial environment of schizophrenic patients. *American Journal of Psychiatry, 1957, 114,* 241-248.

Lindsay, J. S. B. Balance theory: Possible consequences of number of family members. *Family Process,* 1976, *15,* 245-249.

Litwak, F., & Szelenyi, I. Primary group structure and their functions: Kin networks, and friends. *American Sociological Review,* 1969, *34,* 465-481.

Lively, E. Toward a conceptual clarification: The case of marital interaction. *Journal of Marriage and the Family,* 1969, *31,* 108-114.

Locke, H. J., & Wallace, K. M. Short marital adjustment tests: Their reliability and validity. *Marriage and Family Living,* 1959, *21,* 251-255.

McCubbin, H. I. Integrating copying behavior in family stress theory. *Journal of Marriage and the Family,* 1979, *41,* 237-244.

McCubbin, H. I., Boss, P., Wilson, L., & Lester, G. Developing family invulnerability to stress: Coping strategies wives employ in managing separation. In Jan Trost (Ed.), *Proceedings: World congress of sociology.* Beverly Hills, CA: Sage, 1979.

McCubbin, H. I., Dahl, B., Lester, G., Benson, D., & Robertson, M. Coping repertoires of wives adapting to prolonged war-induced separations. *Journal of Marriage and the Family,* 1976, *38,* 461-471.

McCubbin, H. I., Dahl, B., Lester, G., & Ross, B. The returned prisoner of war: Factors in family reintegration. *Journal of Marriage and the Family,* 1975, *37,* 471-478.

McCubbin, H. I., Joy, C., Cauble, A., Comeau, J., Patterson, J., & Needle, R. Family stress and coping: A decade review. *Journal of Marriage and the Family,* 1980, *42,* 855-871.

McCubbin, H. I., & Lester, G. *Coping behaviors in the management of the dual stressors of family separation and reunion.* Paper presented at the Military Family Research Conference, San Diego, September 1977.

McCubbin, H. I., & Olson, D. H. Beyond family crisis: Family adaptation. In O. Hultaker and J. Trost (Eds.), *Families in disaster.* Uppsala, Sweden: International University Library Press, 1982.

McCubbin, H. I., & Patterson, J. M. Broadening the scope of family strengths: An emphasis on family coping and social support. In N. Stinnett, J. DeFrain, K. King, P. Knaub, & G. Rowe (Eds.), *Family strengths 3: Roots of well-being.* Lincoln: University of Nebraska Press, 1981 (a)

McCubbin, H. I., & Patterson, J. M. *Systematic assessment of family stress resources and coping: Tools for research, education, and clinical intervention.* St. Paul: University of Minnesota, Family Social Science, 1981. (b)

McCubbin, H. I., & Patterson, J. M. Family adaptation to crises. In H. McCubbin, A. Cauble, & J. Patterson (Eds.), *Family stress, coping and social support.* Springfield, IL: Charles C Thomas, 1982.

McCubbin, H. I., & Patterson, J. The family stress process: The double ABCX model of adjustment and adaptation. In H. I. McCubbin, M. B. Sussman, & J. M. Patterson (Eds.), *Social stress and the family: Advances and developments in family stress theory and research.* Marriage and Family Review, Vol. 6, Numbers ½. New York: Haworth, 1983.

McCubbin, H. I., Patterson, J., Bauman, E., & Harris L. *AFILE-Adolescent-Family Inventory of Life Events and Changes.* St. Paul: University of Minnesota, Family Social Science, 1981.

McCubbin, H. I., Patterson, J., & Wilson, L. *Family inventory of life events and changes (FILE) Form A.* St. Paul: University of Minnesota, Family Social Science, 1980.

Mace, D. R. *Geting ready for marriage.* Nashville: Abingdon, 1972.

Mace, D. R. Marriage enrichment: The new frontier. *Personnel and Guidance Journal,* 1977, *55*(9) 520-522.

Maruyama, M. The second cybernetics: Deviation-amplifying, mutual causal processes. *American Scientist,* 1963, *51*.

Mechanic, D. Social structure and personal adaptation: Some neglected dimensions. In G. Coelho, D. Hamburg, & J. Adams (Eds.), *Coping and adaptation.* New York: Basic Books, 1974.

Mechanic, D. The stability of health and illness behavior: Results from a 16 year follow-up. *American Journal of Public Health,* 1979, *69*(11), 1142-1145.

Mederer, H., & Hill, R. Critical transitions over the life span: Theory and research. *Marriage and Family Review,* 1983.

Meneghan, E. Assessing the impact of family transitions on marital experience. In H. McCubbin, E. Cauble, & J. Patterson (Eds.). *Family stress, coping and social support.* Springfield, IL: Charles C Thomas, 1982.

Meneghan, E. Individual coping efforts and family studies. In H. I. McCubbin, M. B. Sussman, & J. M. Patterson (Eds.), *Social stress and the family: Advances and developments in family stress theory and research.* Marriage and Family Review, Vol. 6, Numbers ½. New York: Haworth, 1983.

Miller, D., & Westman, J. Family teamwork and psychotherapy. *Family Process,* 1966, *5,* 49-59.

Miller, S. L. The effects of communication training in small groups upon self-disclosure and openness in engaged couples' systems of interaction: A field experiment. (Doctoral dissertation, University of Minnesota, 1971). *Dissertation Abstracts International,* 1971-1972, *32/5,* 2819-A. (University Microfilms No. 71-28, 263)

Miller, S. L. Couple communication patterns and marital satisfaction. *Visiting Scholars Seminars,* 1974, 13-34. Home Economics Centers for Research, University of North Carolina.

Miller, S. *Family crisis, intervention and growth.* Unpublished manuscript, University of Minnesota, 1969.

Miller, S., Corrales, R., & Wackman, D. B. Recent progress in understanding and facilitating marital communication. *Family Coordinator,* 1975, *24*(2), 143-152.

Miller, S., Nunnally, E. W., & Wackman, D. Minnesota couples communication program: Premarital and marital groups. In D. H. Olson (Ed.), *Treating relationships.* Lake Mills, IA: Graphic, 1976.

Minuchin, S. *Families and family therapy.* Cambridge, MA: Harvard Univeristy Press, 1974.

Minuchin, S., Montalvo, B., Guerney, B. G., Rossman, B. L., & Schumer, R. *Families of the slums.* New York: Basic Books, 1967.

Minuchin, S., Rossman, B. L., & Baker, L. *Psychosomatic families.* Cambridge, MA: Harvard University Press, 1978.

Mishler, E., & Waxler, N. *Interaction in families.* New York: John Wiley, 1968.

Moos, R. H. *Family environment scale.* Palo Alto: Consulting Psychologists, 1974.

Moos, R. H. & Moos, B. A typology of family social environments. *Family Process,* 1976, *15,* 357-371.

Murphy, L. Coping, vulnerability, and resilience in childhood. In G. Coelho, D. Hamburg & J. Adams (Eds.), *Coping and adaptation.* New York: Basic Books, 1974.

Napier, A. Y. The rejection-instrusion pattern: A central family dynamic. *Journal of Marriage and Family Counseling,* 1978, *4,* 5-12.

Navran, L. Communication and adjustment in marriage. *Family Process,* 1967, *6,* 173-184.

Nelson, P. T., & Banonis, B. Family concerns and strengths identified in Delaware's White House Conference on families. In N. Stinnett, B. Chesser, & J. DeFrain (Eds.), *Family strengths 3: Roots of wellbeing.* Lincoln: University of Nebraska, 1981.

Newman, L., & Craddock, A. E. *Relationships between family structure, ego-defensiveness and attitudes toward feminism.* Unpublished manuscript, Department of Psychology, University of Sydney, N.S.W. Australia, 1982.

Novak, A. L., & Van der Veen, F. Family concepts and emotional disturbance in the families of disturbed adolescents with normal siblings. *Family Process,* 1970, *9,* 157-171.

Nunnally, Elam W. Effects of communication training upon interaction awareness and empathic accuracy of engaged couples: A field experiment (Doctoral dissertation, University of Minnesota, 1971). Dissertation Abstracts International, 1971-1972, *32/8,* 4736-A. (University Microfilm No. 72-5561)

Nye, F. I. *Role structure and analysis of the family.* Beverly Hills, CA: Sage, 1976.

Nye, F. I. & Rushing, W. Toward family measurement research. In J. Hadden and E. Borgatta (Eds.), *Marriage and family.* Itasca, IL: Peacock, 1969.

O'Connor, W., & Stachowiak, J. Patterns of interaction in families with high adjusted, low adjusted and mentally retarded members. *Family Process,* 1971, *10,* 229-241.

Olson, D. H. Marital and family therapy: Integrative review and critique. *Journal of Marriage and the Family,* 1970, *32,* 501-538.

Olson, D. H. Empirically unbinding the double bind: Review of research and conceptual reformulations. *Family Process,* 1972, *11,* 69-94.

Olson, D. H. Bridging research, theory and application: The triple threat in science. In D. H. Olson (Ed.), *Treating relationships.* Lake Mills, IA: Graphic, 1976.

Olson, D. H. Insiders' and outsiders' view of relationships: Research strategies. In G. Levinger & H. Raush (Eds.), *Close relationships.* Amherst: University of Massachusetts Press, 1977.

Olson, D. H. Family typologies: Bridging family research and family therapy. In E. Filsinger & R. A. Lewis (Eds.), *Assessing Marriages.* Beverly Hills, CA: Sage, 1981.

Olson, D. H., & Craddock, A. E. Circumplex model of marital and family systems: Application to Australian families. *Australian Journal of Sex, Marriage and Family,* 1980, *1,* 53-69.

Olson, D. H., & Cromwell, R. E. Methodological issues in family power. In R. E. Cromwell & D. H. Olson (Eds.), *Power in families.* Beverly Hills, CA: Sage, 1975.

Olson, D. H., Fournier, D. G., & Druckman, J. M. *ENRICH.* Minneapolis: PREPARE-ENRICH, 1982.

Olson, D. H., & Gravatt, A. E. Attitude change in a functional marriage course. *Family Coordinator,* 1968, *17,* 99-104.

Olson, D. H., & McCubbin, H. I. Circumplex model of marital and family systems V: Application to family stress and crises intervention. In H. I. McCubbin (Ed.), *Family stress, coping and social support.* Springfield, IL: Charles C Thomas, 1982.

Olson, D. H., Russell, C. S., & Sprenkle, D. H. Circumplex model of marital and family systems II: Empirical studies and clinical intervention. In J. Vincent (Ed.), *Advances in family intervention, assessment and theory.* Greenwich, CT: JAI, 1979, 128-176.

Olson, D. H., Russell, C. S., & Sprenkle, D. H. Marital and family therapy: A decade review. *Journal of Marriage and Family,* 1980, *42,* 973-993.

Olson, D. H., Russell, L. S., & Sprenkle, D. H. Circumplex model VI: Theoretical update. *Family Process,* 1983, *22,* 69-83.

Olson, D. H., & Ryder, R. Inventory of marital conflicts (IMC): An experimental interaction procedure. *Journal of Marriage and the Family,* 1970, *32,* 443-448.

Olson, D. H. Sprenkle, D., & Russell, C. Circumplex model of marital and family systems I: Cohesion and adaptability dimensions, family types and clinical application. *Family Process,* 1979, *18,* 3-28.

Otto, H. A. The personal and family resource development programs — a preliminary report. *International Journal of Social Psychiatry,* 1962, *8,* 185-195.

Otto, H. A. Criteria for assessing family strength. *Family Process,* 1963, *2* (2), 329-337.

Otto, H. A. The personal and family strength research projects — some implications for the therapist. *Mental Hygiene,* 1964, *48,* 439-450.

Otto, H. A. *The family cluster: A multi-base alternative.* Los Angeles: Holistic, 1971. (a)

Otto, H. A. *Group methods to actualize human potential — a handbook.* Los Angeles: Holistic, 1971. (b)

Otto, H. A. The human potentialities movement — an overview. *Journal of Creative Behavior,* 1975, 258-265.

Otto, H. A. Developing human family potential. In N. Stinnett, B. Chesser, & J. DeFrain (Eds.), *Building family strengths: Blueprints for action.* Lincoln: University of Nebraska Press, 1979.

Otto, H. A., & Griffiths, A. C. Personality strengths concepts in the helping professions. *Psychiatric Quarterly,* 1965, *39,* 632-645.

Oxford, J., Oppenheimer, E., Egert, S., Hensman, C., & Guthrie, S. The cohesiveness of alcoholism-complicated marriages and its influence on treatment outcome. *British Journal of Psychiatry,* 1976, *128,* 318-339.

Ouellet, B. L., Romeder, J. J., & Lance, J. M. *Premature mortality attributable to smoking and hazardous drinking in Canada.* Ottawa: Department of Health and Welfare, 1977.

Palmore, E. Health practices and illness among the aged. *The Gerontologist,* 1970, *4,* 313-316.

Paolino, T. J., Jr., & McCrady, B. S. *Marriage and marital therapy: psychoanalytic, behavioral and systems theory perspectives.* New York: Brunner/Mazel, 1978.

Paolucci, B., Hall, O. H. & Axinn, N. W. *Family decision-making: An ecosystem approach.* New York: John Wiley, 1977.

Parsons, T., & Bales, R. F. *Family socialization and interaction process.* Glencoe, IL: Free Press, 1955.

Patterson, J., & McCubbin, H. I. The impact of family life events and changes on the health of a chronically ill child. *Family Relations,* 1983, *32,* 255-264.

Patterson, G. R. Interpersonal skills training for couples in the early stages of conflict, *Journal of Marriage and the Family,* 1975, *37,* 295-302.

Patterson, G. R. Parents and teachers as change agents: A social learning approach. In D. H. Olson (Ed.), *Treating relationships.* Lake Mills, IA: Graphic, 1976.

Pearlin, L., & Schooler, C. The structure of coping. *Journal of Health and Social Behavior,* 1978, *19,* 2-21.

Pollak, O. Design of a model of healthy family relationships as a basis for evaluative research. *Social Services Review,* 1953, *31,* 369-376.

Poloma, M. M. Role conflict and the married professional woman. In C. Saflios-Rothchild (Ed.), *Towards a sociology of women.* Lexington, MA: D. C. Heath, 1972.

Portner, J. *Parent-adolescent interaction of families in treatment.* Unpublished doctoral dissertation, University of Minnesota, St. Paul, 1980.

Powers, W. G., & Hutchinson, K. The measurement of communication apprehension in the marriage relationship. *Journal of Marriage and the Family,* 1979, *41,* 89-95.

Pratt, L. The relationship of socioeconomic status to health. *American Journal of Public Health,* 1971, *61,* 281-291.

Pratt, L. *Family structure and effective health behavior: The energized family.* Boston: Houghton Mifflin, 1976.

Rainwater, L. *Family design: Marital sexuality, family size, and contraception.* Chicago: Aldine, 1965.

Rappoport, R. Normal crises, family structure and mental health. *Family Process,* 1963, *2,* 68-79.

Rausch, H. L., Barry, W. A., Hertel, R. K., & Swain, M. A. *Communication, conflict, and marriage.* San Francisco: Jossey-Bass, 1974.

Ravich, R., & Wyden, B. *Predictable pairing.* New York: Peter H. Wyden, 1974.

Regula, Ronald R. Marriage encounter: What makes it work? *Family Coordinator,* 1975, *24*(2), 153-159.

Reiss, D. Varieties of consensual experience I: A theory for relating family interaction to individual thinking. *Family Process,* 1971, *10,* 1-27. (a)

Reiss, D. Varieties of consensual experience II: Dimensions of a family's experience of its environment. *Family Process,* 1971, *10,* 28-35. (b)

Reiss, D. Varieties of consensual experience III: Contrast between families of normals, delinquents and schizophrenics. *Journal of Nervous and Mental Diseases,* 1971, *152,* 73-95. (c)

Reiss, D. *The family's construction of reality.* Cambridge, MA: Harvard University Press, 1981.

Reiss, D., & Oliveri, M. E. Family paradigm and family coping: A proposal for linking the family's intrinsic adaptive capacities to its response to stress. *Family Relations,* 1980, *29,* 431-444.

Renne, K. Health and marital experience in an urban population. *Journal of Marriage and the Family,* 1971, *33,* 338-350.

Riegel, K. F. Adult life crises: A dialectic interpretation of development. In N. Datan & L. H. Ginsberg (Eds.), *Life-span developmental psychology.* New York: Academic, 1975.

Riskin, J. Methodology for studying family interaction. *Archives of General Psychiatry,* 1963, *8,* 343-348.

Riskin, J., & Faunce, E. E. Family interaction scales III: Discussion of methodology and substantive findings. *Archives of General Psychiatry,* 1970, *22,* 527-537.

Rollins, B. C., & Galligan, R. The developing child and marital satisfaction of parents. In R. M. Lerner & G. B. Spanier (Eds.), *Child influences on marital and family interaction: A life-span perspective.* New York: Academic, 1978.

Rollins, B. C., & Thomas, D. L. A theory of parental power and child compliance. In R. C. Cromwell & D. H. Olson (Eds.), *Power in families.* New York: John Wiley, 1975.

Rosenblatt, P. C., & Budd, L. Territoriality and privacy in married and unmarried cohabiting couples. *Journal of Social Psychology,* 1975, *97,* 67-76.

Rosenblatt, P. C., & Cunningham, M. R. Television watching and family tensions. *Journal of Marriage and the Family*, 1976, *38*, 105-111.

Rosenblatt, P. C., Nevaldine, A., & Titus, S. L. Farm families: Relation of significant attributes of farming to family interaction. *International Journal of Sociology of the Family*, 1972, *8*, 89-99.

Rosenblatt, P. C., & Russell, M. The social psychology of potential problems in family vacation travel. *Family Coordinator*, 1975, *24*, 209-215.

Rosenblatt, P. C., & Titus, S. L. Together and apart in the family. *Humanities*, 1976, *12*, 367-379.

Rosenblatt, P. C., Titus, S. L., & Cunningham, M. R. Disrespect, tension, and togetherness-apartness in marriage. *Journal of Marriage and Family Counseling*, 1979.

Rosenblatt, P. C., Titus, S. L., Nevaldine, A., & Cunningham, M. R. Togetherness-apartness and tensions in marriages of elementary and high school teachers with summer-long vacation. *International Journal of Family Counseling*, 1979. (a)

Rosenblatt, P. C., Titus, S. L., Nevaldine, A., Cunningham, M. R. Marital system differences and summer-long vacations: Togetherness-apartness and tension. *American Journal of Family Therapy*, 1979, *7*, 77-84.

Rubin, Z., & Shrenkers, S. Friendship, proximity and self-disclosure, *Journal of Personality*, 1978, *46*(1), 1-22.

Russell, C. S. Transition to parenthood: Problems and gratifications. *Journal of Marriage and the Family*, 1974, *36*, 294-302.

Russell, C. S. *A factor analysis of family cohesion and adaptability scales.* Unpublished manuscript, 1978.

Russell, C. S. Circumplex model of marital and family systems III: Empirical evaluation of families. *Family Process*, 1979, *18*, 29-45.

Russell, C. S. A methodological study of family cohesion and adaptability. *Journal of Marriage and Family Counseling*, 1980, *6*(4), 459-470.

Russell, C. S., & Olson, D. H. Circumplex model of marital and family systems: Review of empirical support and elaboration of therapeutic process. In D. A. Bagorozzi, A. Jurich, & R. Jackson (Eds.), *New perspectives in marriage and family therapy.* New York: Human Sciences, 1982.

Russell, C. S., Olson, D., Sprenkle, D., & Atilano, R. B. *From family symptom to family systems: Review of family therapy research.* Unpublished manuscript, 1982.

Ryder, R. Dimensions of early marriage. *Family Process*, 1970, *9*, 51-68.

Ryder, R. Profile factor analysis and variable factor analysis. *Psychological Reports*, 1964, *15*, 119-127.

Safilios-Rothchild, C. Family sociology or wives' family sociology? A cross-cultural examination of decision-making. *Journal of Marriage and the Family*, 1969, *31*, 290-301.

Sandberg, N., Sharma, V., Wodtli, T., & Rohila, P. Family cohesiveness and autonomy of adolescents in India and the United States. *Journal of Marriage and the Family*, 1969, *31*, 403-407.

Satir, V. *Conjoint family thereapy.* Palo Alto, CA: Science and Behavior Books, 1964.

Satir, V. *Peoplemaking.* Palo Alto, CA: Science and Behavior Books, 1972.

Schaefer, E. Converging conceptual models for maternal behavior and for child behavior. In J. Clidewell (Ed.), *Parent attitudes and child behavior.* Springfield, IL: Charles C Thomas, 1961.

Schaefer, E. A circumplex model for maternal behavior. *Journal of Abnormal and Social Psychology*, 1959, *59*, 226-235.

Schaffer, H. R. The too cohesive family: A form of group pathology. *International Journal of Social Psychology*, 1964, *10*, 266-275.

Schlein, S. P. Training dating couples in empathic and open communication: An experimental evaluation of a potential preventive mental health program (Doctoral dissertation, Pennsylvania State University, 1971). *Dissertation Abstracts International*, 1972, *32/11*, 6487-B. (University Microfilm No. 72-13929)

Schram, R. W. Marital satisfaction over the life cycle: A critique and proposal. *Journal of Marriage and the Family*, 1979, *40*, 7-12.

Schreiber, L. E. Evaluation of family group treatment in a family agency. *Family Process*, 1966, *5*, 21-29.

Schumm, W. R. The measurement of marital communication: A comparison of the construct validities of a self-report and an empathic accuracy instrument in relationship analysis (Doctoral dissertation, Purdue University, 1979). *Dissertation Abstracts International*, 1980, *40/09*, 5206-A. (University Microfilm No. 8995939)

Schvaneveldt, J. D. Mormon adolescents: Likes and dislikes toward parents and home. *Adolescents*, 1973, *8*, 171-178.

Scott, R. D., & Askworth, P. L. Closure at the first schizophrenic breakdown: A family study. *British Journal of Medical Psychology*, 1967, *40*, 109-145.

Sheehy, G. *Passages: Predictable crises of adult life.* New York: Dulton, 1976.

Sherwood, J. J., & Scherer, J. J. A model for couples: How two can grow together. *Small Group Behavior*, 1975, *6*(1), 11-29.

Shostrum, E., & Kavanaugh, J. *Between man and woman.* Los Angeles: Nash, 1971.

Skinner, D. Dual-career family stress and coping: A literature review. *Family Relations*, 1980, *29*, 473-481.

Spanier, G. B., & Cole, C. L. Toward a clarification and investigation of marital adjustment. *International Journal of the Sociology of the Family*, 1976, *6*, 121-146.

Spanier, G. B., & Lewis, R. A. Marital quality: A review of the seventies, *Journal of Marriage and the Family*, 1980, *42*, 96-110.

Spanier, G. B., Lewis, R. A., & Cole, C. L. Marital adjustment over the family life cycle: The issue of curvilinearity. *Journal of Marriage and the Family*, 1975, *36*, 263-275.

Speck, R., & Alteneave, C. Social network intervention. In J. Haley (Ed.), *Changing families.* New York: Grune & Stratton, 1971.

Speer, D. Family systems: Morphostasis and morphogenesis, or is homeostasis enough? *Family Process*, 1970, *9*, 259-278.

Sprenkle, D. The need for integration among theory, research and practice in the family field. *Family Coordinator*, 1976, *25*, 261-263.

Sprenkle, D., & Olson, D. H. Circumplex model of marital systems IV: Empirical study of clinic and non-clinic couples. *Journal of Marriage and Family Therapy*, 1978, *4*, 59-74.

Stahmann, R. F., & Hiebert, W. J. Premarital counseling: Process and content. In R. F. Stahmann and W. J. Hiebert (Eds.), *Klemer's counseling in marital and sexual problems: A clinician's handbook* (2nd ed.). Baltimore: Williams & Wilkins, 1977.

Stanton, M. D., & Todd, C. T. *The family therapy of drug abuse and addiction.* New York: Guilford, 1982.

Stein, H. F. The Slovak-American "swaddling ethos": Homeostat for family dynamics and cultural continuity. *Family Process*, 1978, *17*, 31-45.

Stephens, W. *The family in cross-cultural perspective.* New York: Holt, Rinehart & Winston, 1963.

Stierlin, H. *Separating parents and adolescents.* New York: Quadrangle, 1974.

Stinnett, N. In search of strong families. In N. Stinnett, B. Chesser, & J. DeFrain (Eds.), *Building family strengths: Blueprints for action.* Lincoln: University of Nebraska Press, 1981.

Stinnett, N., Chesser, B., DeFrain, J., & Knaub, P. *Family strengths: Positive models for family life.* Lincoln: University of Nebraska Press, 1980.

Stinnett, N., & Saur, K. H. Relationship characteristics of strong families. *Family Perspective,* 1977, *11,* (4), 3-11.

Stoeckler, H. S., & Gage, M. G. *Quality of life.* Agricultural Experiment Station, Miscellaneous Report 154, University of Minnesota, 1978.

Straus, M. Power and support structure of the family in relation to socialization. *Journal of Marriage and the Family,* 1964, *26,* 318-326.

Straus, M. Communication, creativity, and problem solving ability of middle-and working-class families in three societies. Reprinted in M. Sussman (Ed.), *Sourcebook in marriage and the family* (3rd ed.). Boston: Houghton Mifflin, 1968.

Strodtbeck, F. Family interaction, values, and achievement. In D. McClelland et al. (Eds.), *Talent and society.* Princeton, NJ: D. Van Nostrand, 1958.

Strommen, M. P., Brekke, M. L., Underwager, R. C., & Johnson A. L. *A study of generations.* Minneapolis: Augsburg, 192.

Stuart, R. B. An operant interpersonal program for couples. In D. H. Olson (Ed.), *Treating relationships.* Lake Mills, IA: Graphic, 1976.

Tallman, I. The family as a small problem solving group. *Journal of Marriage and the Family,* 1970, *32,* 94-104.

Tallman, I., & Miller, G. Class differences in family problem solving: The effects of verbal ability, hierarchical structure, and role expectations. *Sociometry,* 1974, *37,* 13-37.

Tanner-Nelson, P., & B. Banonis. Family consensus and stress identified in Delaware's White House Conference on the Family. In N. Stinnett, J. DeFrain, K. King, P. Knaub, and G. Rowe (Eds.), *Family strengths III: roots of well being.* Lincoln: University of Nebraska Press, 1981, 43-60.

Thibault, J., & Kelley, H. *The social psychology of groups.* New York: John Wiley, 1967.

Travis, R. P., & Travis, P. Y. Marital health and marriage enrichment. *Alabama Journal of Medical Science,* 1975, *12* (2), 172-176.

Tryon, R., & Baliley, D. *Cluster analysis.* New York: McGraw-Hil, 1970.

Unger, D. G., & Powell, D. R. Supporting families under stress: The role of social networks. *Family Relations,* 1980, *29* (4), 566-574.

U.S. Department of Health and Human Services. *Healthy people.* Washington, DC: U.S. Department of Health and Human Sevices, Office of the Surgeon General, 1979.

Van der Veen, F. The parent's concept of the family unit and child adjustment. *Journal of Counseling Psychology,* 1965, *12,* 196-200.

Van der Veen, F. *Content dimensions of the family concept test and their relation to childhood disturbance.* Unpublished manuscript, Institute for Juvenile Research, Chicago, 1976.

Van Zoost, B. Premarital communication skills education with university couples. *Family Coordinator,* 1973, *22,* 187-191.

Vincent, C. Familia spongia: The adaptive function. *Journal of Marriage and the Family,* 1966, *28,* 29-36.

Vincent, J. P., Weiss, R. L., & Brichler, G. R. A behavioral analysis of problem solving in distressed and nondistressed married and stranger dyads. *Behavior therapy,* 1975, *6,* 475-487.

Vogel, E. F., & Bell, N. W. The emotionally disturbed child as a family scapegoat. In N. W. Bell and E. F. Vogel (Eds.), *The family.* Glencoe, IL: Free Press, 1960.

Waldron, H., & Routh, D. K. The effect of the first child on the marital relationship. *Journal of Marriage and the Family,* 1981, *4,* 785-788.

Walsh, R. *Normal family processes.* New York: Guilford, 1982.

Watzlawick, P., Beavin, J. H., & Jackson, D. D. *Pragmatics of human communication: A study of interaction patterns, pathologies and paradoxes.* New York: W. W. Norton, 1967.

Watzlawick, P., Weakland, J., & Fisch, R. *Change: Principles of problem formation and problem resolution.* New York: W.W. Norton, 1974.

Weiss, R. L. The conceptualization of marriage from a behavioral perspective. In T. J. Paolino & B. S. McCardy (Eds.), *Marriage and marital therapy.* New York: Brunner/Mazel, 1978.

Weiss, R. L., Birchler, G., & Vincent, J. Contractual models for negotiation training in marital dyads. *Journal of Marriage and the Family,* 1974, *36,* 321-330.

Wertheim, E. Family unit therapy and the science and typology of family systems. *Family Process,* 1973, *12,* 361-376.

Wertheim, E. The science and typology of family systems II: Further theoretical and practical considerations. *Family Process,* 1975, *14,* 285-308.

Westley, W. A., & Epstein, N. B. *Silent minority: Families of emotionally healthy college students.* San Francisco: Jossey-Bass, 1969.

Wheaton, B. Interpersonal conflict and cohesiveness in dyadic relationships. *Sociometry,* 1974, *37,* 328-348.

Wheeler, L., & Nezlek, J. Sex differences in social participation. *Journal of Personality and Social Psychology,* 1977, *35,* 742-754.

White, R. W. Strategies of adaptation: An attempt at systematic description. In G. Coelho, D. Hamburg & J. Adams (Eds.), *Coping and adaptation.* New York: Basic Books, 1974.

Williams, A. *Behavioral interaction in married couples.* Unpublished doctoral dissertation, University of Florida, Gainesville, 1977.

Winter, W. D., & Ferreira, A. J. Interaction process analysis of family decision making. *Family Process,* 1967, *6,* 155-165.

Wittmer, J. Amish homogeneity of parental behavior characteristics. *Human Relations,* 1973, *26,* 143-154.

Wynne, L., Ryckoff, I. M., Day, J. & Hirsch, S. I. Pseudo-mutuality in the family relations of schizophrenics. *Psychiatry,* 1958, *21,* 205-222.

Yalom, I. *The theory and practice of group psychotherapy.* New York: Basic Books, 1970.

Young, K. *Family life in our society: The social welfare forum.* New York: Columbia University Press, 1953.

ABOUT THE AUTHORS

David H. Olson, Ph.D., is Professor of Family Social Science at the University of Minnesota, St. Paul. He is a Fellow in the American Association for Marriage and Family Therapy (AAMFT) and the American Psychological Association (APA). He is a recent past president of the National Council on Family Relations (NCFR) and is also on the editorial board of several family journals. He is author of more than 80 articles and 20 books, including *Treating Relationships, Power and Families, Family Studies Review Yearbook* (3 volume series), *Inventory of Marriage and Family Literature* (10 volumes), and *Circumplex Model: Systemic Assessment and Treatment of Families.*

Hamilton I. McCubbin, Ph.D., is Dean and Professor, School of Family Resources and Consumer Sciences, University of Wisconsin, Madison, Wisconsin. He is a past president of the National Council on Family Relations (NCFR) and is currently on the editorial board of 10 family and behavioral science journals. In addition to being a major contributor to professionals journals, he has already completed three books: *Family Assessment Inventories for Research and Practice, Family Types and Strengths: A Life Cycle and Ecological Perspective,* and *Balancing Work and Family Life on Wall Street: Stockbrokers and Families Coping with Economic Instability.*

Howard Barnes, Ph.D., is Assistant Professor, Family and Child Development, Kansas State University, Manhattan, Kansas.

Andrea Larsen, Ph.D., is a marriage and family therapist in private practice in Minneapolis, Minnesota.

Marla Muxen, M.A., is a marriage and family therapist in private practice in St. Paul, Minnesota, and also a doctoral student in Family Social Science at the University of Minnesota.

Marc Wilson, M.A., is a marriage and family therapist at Group Health, Inc., St. Paul, Minnesota, and is also a doctoral student in Family Social Science at the University of Minnesota.

311